SIGNING
Illustrated

Also by Mickey Flodin

Signing for Kids
Signing Is Fun
Signing Everyday Phrases

Coauthored by Mickey Flodin

The Perigee Visual Dictionary of Signing
The Pocket Dictionary of Signing
Signing Made Easy

SIGNING
Illustrated
The Complete Learning Guide

by Mickey Flodin

A Perigee Book

A PERIGEE BOOK
Published by the Penguin Group
Penguin Group (USA) Inc.
375 Hudson Street, New York, New York 10014, USA
Penguin Group (Canada), 90 Eglinton Avenue East, Suite 700, Toronto, Ontario M4P 2Y3, Canada
(a division of Pearson Penguin Canada Inc.)
Penguin Books Ltd., 80 Strand, London WC2R 0RL, England
Penguin Group Ireland, 25 St. Stephen's Green, Dublin 2, Ireland (a division of Penguin Books Ltd.)
Penguin Group (Australia), 250 Camberwell Road, Camberwell, Victoria 3124, Australia
(a division of Pearson Australia Group Pty. Ltd.)
Penguin Books India Pvt. Ltd., 11 Community Centre, Panchsheel Park, New Delhi—110 017, India
Penguin Group (NZ), 67 Apollo Drive, Rosedale, North Shore 0745, Auckland, New Zealand
(a division of Pearson New Zealand Ltd.)
Penguin Books (South Africa) (Pty.) Ltd., 24 Sturdee Avenue, Rosebank, Johannesburg 2196,
South Africa

Penguin Books Ltd., Registered Offices: 80 Strand, London WC2R 0RL, England

While the author has made every effort to provide accurate telephone numbers and Internet addresses
at the time of publication, neither the publisher nor the author assumes any responsibility for errors,
or for changes that occur after publication. Further, the publisher does not have any control over and
does not assume any responsibility for author or third-party websites or their content.

PRINTING HISTORY
First Perigee trade paperback edition / 1994
Revised Perigee trade paperback edition / 2004

Revised Perigee edition ISBN: 978-0-399-53041-8

The Library of Congress has catalogued the first Perigee edition as follows:

Flodin, Mickey.
Signing illustrated : the complete learning guide / Mickey Flodin.
     — 1st Perigee ed.
     p.   cm.
"A Perigee book."
Includes index.
ISBN 0-399-52134-8 (acid-free paper)
1. American Sign Language—Handbooks, manuals, etc.   I. Title.
     HV2474.F56   2004   94-14027
          416—dc20   CIP

PRINTED IN THE UNITED STATES OF AMERICA

10   9   8

Most Perigee Books are available at special quantity discounts for bulk purchases for sales promo-
tions, premiums, fund-raising, or educational use. Special books, or book excerpts, can also be created to fit specific needs. For details, write: Special Markets, Penguin Group (USA) Inc., 375 Hudson
Street, New York, New York 10014.

ACKNOWLEDGMENTS

My deepest gratitude to several key people for their kind assistance in the preparation of this book.

Karen Twigg, for taking the time to review the text, book chapter divisions, new signs, and for her invaluable suggestions. Karen brings a wide range of experience in her twenty-five years of teaching and interpreting sign language to this book. Her special abilities have earned her notable recognition as a leader in the deaf community. She has studied interpreting skills at Akron University, Akron, Ohio; has taught sign language at Baptist Bible College, Springfield, Missouri; and earned her B.A. and M.S. in education at Southwest Missouri State University, Springfield, Missouri. In addition, she has taught interpreters' classes and has been able to apply interpreting skills in schools, courtrooms, hospitals, and churches.

John Duff, publisher, Perigee Books, for his enthusiasm for this project.

Carol Flodin, who generously gave of her time by offering invaluable suggestions on the text, organizing the illustrations, compiling and checking the index, and for her tasty snacks that kept me fueled for the task.

Daniel Flodin, for his computer work on the practice pages and the chapter opener pages.

Rod Butterworth, for allowing me to use written descriptions from our three sign language books.

To my dear friend, Karen Twigg,
who knows heartache and triumph, and whose
signing and interpreting skills
are admired by many.

CONTENTS _____

INTRODUCTION

Each day the popularity of sign language becomes more evident. Signing has found its way, not only into the classroom, where it has been for many years, but into drama, singing presentations, movies, TV, and even into water sports. And now, with technology playing a major role in our everyday lives, over 200 technology and computer signs have been added to this revised edition to help the signer communicate more effectively. Many thousands of people are discovering the satisfaction, excitement, and communicative qualities of this expressive, visually rich language, and so can you. Whether you have a casual interest in signing, or a sincere desire to communicate with deaf people, Signing Illustrated provides all the basic vocabulary and instructions you need to learn how to sign. Even though it takes considerable time to become a proficient signer, you will soon be signing basic concepts after studying only a chapter or two. Persons who are deaf are pleased when others learn their language, and they are patient and understanding with the beginning signer.

American Sign Language (known also as ASL or Ameslan) is a visual-gesture language developed over many years by deaf people to communicate with each other. It is used by approximately 500,000 deaf people in the United States and Canada. It is not English of any kind—good, bad or broken. It is a unique language with its own syntax and grammatical rules, yet is as precise and multifaceted as English or any foreign language. As a visual language, it is acquired through the eyes. One must learn to "hear" with the eyes, in order to communicate.

You are embarking on a fascinating, challenging and rewarding journey. As your signing abilities increase, you will gain an even greater appreciation of the uniqueness of this eloquent language—the language of deaf people. Welcome to the wonderful and expressive world of signing.

A BRIEF HISTORY OF SIGN LANGUAGE

Today, American Sign Language is one of the most complete and expressive of all the sign languages in the world. As interest in signing continues to grow, many sign language classes are being offered in churches, colleges, libraries, and community centers. It is now the fourth most used language in the United States.

It is estimated that more than thirty million people in the United States have some degree of hearing loss. Of these, two million are considered deaf (though some consider this figure high). Some people were born deaf (congenitally deaf); others acquired deafness later in life, either through accident, illness, or aging (adventitiously deaf).

During the sixteenth century Geronimo Cardano, a physician in Padua, Italy, was the first to realize that deaf people did not need to hear speech to be educated. He proclaimed that, with writing or with pictures, deaf people could be taught.

Pedro de Ponce, a Spanish monk, was the first to succeed in educating deaf children of nobel families in 1555. Though it wasn't until 1620 that Juan Pablo de Bonet, another Spanish monk, published the first book on teaching sign language to deaf people, which contained the manual alphabet.

Two of the most prominent early educators of deaf people were Abbé Charles Michel de L'Épée, a French priest, and Samuel Heinicke of Germany. L'Épée, while visiting a poor section of Paris, met two deaf sisters and was asked by their mother to give them religious instruction. This meeting ignited L'Épée's desire to educate deaf children. Observing that deaf people already communicated without speech, he began to study and learn the signs that were already being used by a group of deaf people in Paris. To this knowledge he added his own creativeness which resulted in a signed version of spoken French. As he learned sign language from his deaf pupils, he used it to teach them the French language. The performance of his deaf students amazed his countrymen. With this success, he promoted the use of sign language as a way to educate deaf children.

Considered by many to be the father of deaf education, L'Épée founded the first free school for deaf people in Paris in 1755, attracting students from all over France. He trained teachers in his methods as well, and as other schools opened in the surrounding provinces a standard French Sign Language emerged.

Samuel Heinicke, an army officer, from Leipzig, Germany, another prominent deaf educator of the same period, did not use the manual method of communication but taught speech and speechreading. (Known as the oral method which attempts to educate a deaf person through speech and speechreading without the use of sign language or fingerspelling.) Heinicke established the first public school for deaf students that achieved government recognition.

The methods of teaching developed by L'Épée and Heinicke were the forerunners of today's concept of total communication that espouses the use of all means of available communication including sign language, fingerspelling, gesturing, pantomime, speechreading, speech, use of hearing aids, reading, writing, and pictures to educate deaf people.

Little has been recorded about the deaf community and the development of sign language in America prior to 1815. During the early 1800s, it is estimated that there were approximately 2,000 deaf people in America. Just as in L'Épée's France, it is likely that the small communities of deaf people in America developed their own signs for communicating. These early signs, many of which are related to present day ASL, are referred to as Old American Sign Language.

In 1815, a Congregational minister and Yale graduate, Thomas Hopkins Gallaudet, became interested in helping his neighbor's young deaf daughter, Alice Cogswell. At the age of twenty-seven, he traveled to Europe to study methods of communicating with deaf people. While in England he met Abbé Roche Ambroise Sicard, L'Épée's successor, and two of his most prominent students. Excited by what he saw, Gallaudet accepted Sicard's invitation to study at his Paris school for deaf students. Several months later he returned to the United States with Laurent Clerc, a deaf sign language instructor from the Paris school—one of Sicard's best teachers.

Thomas Gallaudet, with a public grant of five thousand dollars and private donations, founded the first school in America for deaf people in Hartford, Connecticut, in 1817, known today as the American School for the Deaf. Clerc became the first United States deaf sign language teacher. It was the merging of the Old American Sign Language and the French signs that became American Sign Language. Clerc worked for over forty years teaching deaf people and hearing people alike. For the first time in America, the Hartford school brought together a large number of deaf people, which nurtured the development of a deaf community. Many of the hearing people Clerc trained later became directors of schools for deaf people. Soon schools for deaf people opened in several states. By 1863 twenty-two schools had been established throughout the United States.

Gallaudet College, in Washington, D.C., was founded in 1864, and is the only liberal arts college for deaf students in the world. Edward Miner Gallaudet, the son of Thomas Hopkins Gallaudet became the first president of the new college. In 1891, Gallaudet College established the first training center for teachers of deaf people associated with a United States college.

The Horace Mann School of Boston, founded in 1869, was the first nonresidential school for students who are deaf . Today, there are more than 16,000 local public school districts serving student who are deaf or hard of hearing. Also, there are over sixty public residential schools for children who are deaf.

ABOUT THIS BOOK

Signing Illustrated contains over 1,550 of the basic signs in use today throughout the United States and Canada, though some local and regional variations may occur. This book does not contain all the signs of American Sign Language, however, it provides a wide range of vocabulary to express a vast array of concepts and ideas. It contains all the essential elements necessary for the sign language student to understand, learn, and communicate in this beautiful and expressive language. Not every word in the English language has a corresponding sign, so it is up to the signer to choose the sign that best conveys an idea or thought. The number of signs in a person's vocabulary is not as important as how the signs are used. If a sign or a combination of signs can't be found to express an exact thought, fingerspell it. This is common practice among all signers—deaf people and hearing people alike.

This book is divided into sixteen categorized chapters, each containing a concise number of signs that may be learned in only a few sessions. Each chapter covers a particular subject area, such as: Family, People, and Pronouns; or Food and Eating. You will notice that some signs within a certain category have similar shapes and movements. This facilitates learning, and aids in recalling the signs. If a particular sign cannot be found, look in the index at the back of the book. The index features many synonyms which may lead you to the desired word, or a word closest in meaning.

The chapters in this book have been arranged in the order they would be taught in a classroom setting, but there is no particular order that must be followed when learning sign language. It is recommended you learn the manual alphabet first for it will expand your ability to communicate with others. If you prefer, you can skip from chapter to chapter picking out the signs you wish or need to learn, or simply start at the beginning of the book and follow through to the end. A good place to begin is with the food, sport, and animal signs because their movements have an apparent relationship to their meaning, making them easier to recall.

As you begin, look at the illustration(s) and arrow(s) for the correct handshape and movement of the sign. Then read the description for additional instructions. Sometimes the sign is repeated, or the hands may "alternate," or they may "move simultaneously." Then read the memory aid. It will point out specific characteristics of a sign to help you to retain and recall the sign.

Full

The Dominant Hand

There are some signs that are performed using two different hand shapes. The dominant hand provides the movement while the other hand is motionless. Two examples of signs using one dominant hand and a motionless hand are full (at left), and about (page 131).

All the signs are illustrated for a right-handed person. Some left handed people find it impossible to use the right hand as the dominant hand, in this case you can make the signs with your left hand, which reverses the signs to the receiver. If you can use both hands equally well, it is recommended that you use the right hand.

Sign Directions

Virtually all of the illustrations in this book show the sign as you would see someone signing to you. However, a number of signs are shown from an angle or profile perspective for clarity. Some signs have been shown in close up to make the signs prominent and easier to follow. Remember, you always face the person to whom you are signing.

Look closely at the arrow(s) to determine the exact movement and direction of a sign. When a movement is described as clockwise or counterclockwise, it is from the viewpoint of the signer and not from the viewpoint of the observer.

Memory Aids

Memory aids have been added for each sign in this book. They are designed to help you to retain and recall a sign by calling attention to certain aspects of the sign, such as its shape or movement, but are not necessarily related to what may be considered as the origin of a sign.

Practice Pages

Included at the end of each chapter are practice pages for vocabulary review, such as: Name the Sign, Matching, Multiple Choice, Find the Food Signs, and Connect the Opposites (the end of the Technology chapter contains many acronymns, etc.). Each practice page is based on that chapter's vocabulary. These exercises will reinforce what you have studied and learned. The answers are listed in the back of the book on page 318.

Signing in English Word Order or ASL Word Order?

The signs in this book can be used in the word order of the English language or they may be used in a non-English word order, such as used in American Sign Language, which has its own unique syntax and grammar—the language used by the deaf community. The decision rests with the signer as to which method to use. Certainly, the deaf people with whom you associate, or your instructor, will influence whether you sign in the word order of English or ASL.

English Word Order

English Word Order takes the signs of ASL and places them in the grammatical order of the English language. There are many manually coded English Systems in use. Two well–known systems are Signing Exact English and Signed English, which use ASL signs, initialization of signs (the use of the manual alphabet handshape that begins with the first letter of the English word that expresses a similar concept), markers or inflections, and signs for definite and indefinite articles and infinitives to represent all features of the English language (see page 38).

In Signing Exact English, all words are signed. Markers (inflections) are used to change the form of a word—its tense, plural form, prefix or suffix. Not all words are signed in ASL. Conversely, one sign in ASL can represent several English words or a complete thought. Facial expressions, along with body language and speech are also used in the English systems.

These manually coded systems have been criticized, for they force a sign to represent an English word. However, they are useful in teaching deaf children exact English and, therefore, have found their way into the public educational system. (If you are interested in signing in English sentence format, you may want to consider two books, *Signing Everyday Phrases* and *Signing Made Easy*.)

The middle ground of the spectrum between ASL and English word order is occupied by a manual communication which combines the signs of ASL, and its body language and facial expressions, with the word order of the English language. What is created by mixing English and American Sign Language is a Pidgin Sign English (PSE) or "pidgin language." Hearing people, typically, want to attach a sign to an English word. It is easier for hearing people to learn the signs of American Sign Language but not its grammar or syntax, and to use

GLOSSARY

Adventitious Deafness Deafness in a hearing person, due to illness or accident.

American Sign Language Also known as ASL or Ameslan; it is the visual language used by deaf people in the United States and Canada.

Congenital Deafness Deafness at birth.

Dactylology Using the fingers and hands to fingerspell and communicate. (Some use this term for signing, also.)

Deaf Person A person who cannot hear speech or everyday sounds.

Deaf Community A group of people who share the same language (American Sign Language), similar experiences, attitudes, goals, and values and are deaf or hard-of-hearing.

Expressive Skill Using the language of signs and fingerspelling to express oneself.

Fingerspelling The use of the manual alphabet to spell words and sentences with the fingers one letter at a time.

Gesture The movement of the body or limbs to help express or emphasize a thought or idea.

Hard-of-hearing A hearing loss of some degree from mild to severe.

Iconicity The characteristic of a sign resembling what it represents. Example: The sign for *elephant* moves the hand, from the mouth, in the shape of a elephant's trunk.

Initialized Sign To form a sign using the manual alphabet hand shape that begins with the first letter of the English word that expresses a similar concept.

Interpreting To convey someone's spoken message by using sign language and fingerspelling to express thoughts and ideas.

Language Any means of communicating through the system of sounds, symbols, signs or gestures.

Lipreading, Speechreading A method used to understand unheard speech by observing lip and facial movements.

Manual Alphabet A separate hand shape using the fingers to represent the signs in the English word order. Although signs were originally created to represent concepts and not words, PSE is an acceptable method of communication. This signing system is combined with speech and fingerspelling. Known as simultaneous communication, it is used often by hearing people to communicate with deaf people. The signs for definite and indefinite articles (*a, an,* and *the*) are not used. It is acceptable to deaf people for hearing people to learn their language and use it in English syntax.

each letter of the written alphabet.

Manual Communication The use of sign language and fingerspelling to convey thoughts and ideas.

Manually Coded English or Manual English Using sign language and fingerspelling to represent the English language word for word.

Nonmanual Behavior Communication features used with sign language that are not conveyed with the hands—body posture, head and body movement, and facial expression.

Oral Method, Oral Training, Oralism Using a system of speech and speechreading to educate a deaf person. Signs and fingerspelling are not used.

Pidgin Sign English (PSE) The use of American Sign Language in English syntax or word order; articles (*a, an,* and *the*) and inflections are usually omitted.

Receptive Skill To understand sign language and fingerspelling expressed by another.

Sign Language A visual language using either one or both hands formed into unique shapes and movements to represent concepts and ideas, including fingerspelling.

Signer A person who expresses their ideas and thoughts through sign language.

Sign English A pidgin language using American Sign Language in English syntax or word order. In some forms of Sign English all words are signed, while other Sign English systems favor ASL.

Simultaneous Method of Communication The use of manual (signing and fingerspelling) and oral (speech) communication simultaneously to convey thoughts and ideas.

Syntax The order or arrangement in which words are used to form sentences in a language.

Total Communication The educational philosophy that all deaf people have the right to all information through all possible means including sign language, fingerspelling, pantomime, speech, lipreading, writing, pictures, gestures, facial expression, reading, and hearing aids.

ASL Word Order

With its own syntax and grammar, ASL is the natural language used by the deaf community. It is usually used when hearing people are not involved in the exchange. The signs often represent concepts and not words. In ASL, the definite and indefinite articles (*a, an,* and *the*) are not signed. Fingerspelling is used mainly for people and places. Speech is not used although some lip movement may be used. Even though most hearing people who sign do not know ASL and some deaf people don't know it either, it is the prime identifying characteristic of the deaf community.

GETTING STARTED: THE BASICS

Using the Manual Alphabet and Fingerspelling

Fingerspelling is used to spell out words one letter at a time with the manual alphabet. The importance of learning to fingerspell cannot be overstated since it plays a key role in communicating with deaf people. Fingerspelling (also known as dactylology) is used in combination with sign language for names of people, places, and words for which there are no signs, or as a substitute when the sign has not been learned. Therefore, it is recommended that the manual alphabet be memorized at the beginning of learning sign language. Many of the manual alphabet hand shapes are easy to remember because they resemble the configuration of English letters. The entire manual alphabet can be memorized in just an hour or two. Look at each illustration carefully, being sure to form the hand shape correctly. Then start fingerspelling two- and three-letter words (see words list on page 37) before moving on to larger words.

Fingerspelling
Position

When fingerspelling, hold your hand in a comfortable, natural position near the shoulder, with the palm facing forward and at a slight angle (see art at left). Don't make exaggerated hand or arm movements. Strive to combine the letters smoothly and at a comfortable rate. Don't worry about speed. It will come with practice. Instead, developing a smooth rhythm helps to make the signs readable. Most people prefer a reasonable rate for fingerspelling because of the amount of concentration needed to receive and understand it. Pause slightly at the end of each word but do not drop the hands between words. It is important to speak or mouth the word, not the letter, as you begin to fingerspell it.

When fingerspelling words with double letters (for instance, *keep*), open the hand slightly between letters. For words with double open letters, such as *will*, move the *L* hand to the right with a small bounce to sign the second letter *L*.

When receiving or reading fingerspelling, learn to read words in syllables, rather than individual letters. This may be difficult at first but it will help you to grasp the word more quickly.

Size of Signs

Do not make signs overly large but use a size proportional to the audience; smaller for one or two people and somewhat larger for a group. If possible, use less fingerspelling for large groups, as fingerspelling can't be enlarged and is difficult to see from a distance.

When signing to music, strive to express the meaning and rhythm, while maintaining the sign for as long as the word is sung. Make the signs large enough for the audience to see clearly, without distorting the signs.

Knowing the Signing Area

Most signs are made within an imaginary rectangle in front of the body—an area extending from the top of the head to the waist, and from shoulder to shoulder. This allows the eyes to follow the sign's movement more readily and makes the signs easier to understand. Pause when you are in between thoughts or sentences, or waiting for a response, by holding your hand in a comfortable position at chest level or at your side. It is extremely important to maintain eye contact and use appropriate facial expressions and body language when signing to deaf people for they rely upon the combination of these elements.

The signing area

Understanding Present, Past, and Future Time

It is important to understand the sign language concept of present, past, and future time. Think of the area immediately in front of the body as representing *present* time. Therefore, signs dealing with present time are made in front of the body, such as *now* (at right). Signs referring to the future, such as *tomorrow* (at right) and *next* (page 244) have a forward movement away from the body. Signs that deal with the past, such as *last year* (at right) and *yesterday* (page 244) move backward from the present time reference place.

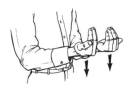

Now

Pronouns

In sign language, pronouns can be indicated by pointing to an imaginary spot or location. Each time you mention a particular person, point to them, if present, or to their imaginary location. Several people can be discussed at the same time using this method, by pointing to their respective spots or locations.

Tomorrow

Questions and Punctuation

Punctuation, such as the period and question mark, are not always used in American Sign Language. A quizzical or questioning facial expression and body language will help convey that you are asking a question. Holding the last sign of a sentence a little longer helps also. If you like, you can add the question mark (see page 270) at the beginning or end of a sentence.

To indicate the end of a thought or sentence, just pause for a moment before beginning the next sentence. If you are signing in English word order, and need to use punctuation signs, they can be found on page 38.

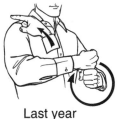

Last year

Signing Capitals

When capitals or abbreviations are fingerspelled, such as *U.S.A.*, they need to be differentiated from other letters or words. This is done by circling (clockwise) each letter slightly as you sign it. This applies to all forms of capitalization, such as used for names of people, organizations, businesses, and places.

Understanding Possessives and Plurals

Possessives ('s) and plurals are not signed in ASL for they are generally understood within context. When plurals are needed, they can be signed in several ways. One way is to add a sign for a number or quantity after the sign; the sign for *house* followed by the sign for *many*, for example, would mean "many houses." Another way is to make a sign and repeat it several times on either side of you: the sign for *book* repeated this way would mean "many books." A third way is to make a sign and point your index finger at different locations: if you sign *horse* and

THE BASIC HAND SHAPES _____

Throughout this book you will notice certain basic hand shapes which are used in the descriptions on how to form the signs correctly. Become familiar with the following hand shapes:

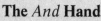

The *And* Hand
When the "*and* hand" is mentioned only the ending position is being referred to with all fingertips touching, as illustrated here.

Bent Hand
The fingers are touching and bent at the knuckles.

Clawed Hand
The fingers are held apart and bent.

Closed Hand
The hand is closed like a fist in the shape of an *S* hand.

Curved Hand
The fingers are curved and touching. Sometimes a term such as "curved *open* hand" is used, in which case the fingers are kept bent but spread apart.

Flat Hand
The hand is held flat with fingers touching. Sometimes a term such as "flat *open* hand" is used, in this case fingers are separated.

Open Hand
The hand is held flat, fingers apart.

point—there, there, there—the meaning is "many horses."

Possessives('s) and plurals may be signed for the purpose of conveying exact English syntax, such as when teaching deaf pupils English. You will find the possessive and plural signs under "Markers" on page 38, if you decide to use them.

Using the *Person Ending* **Sign**

The *person (personalizing word ending)* sign is used to indicate a person's occupation, position in life, or nationality and is always used at the end of another sign. It is made by holding both flat open hands to the front with palms facing; then move them down simultaneously. Some examples of its use are: sign *art* plus the *person ending* for *artist* (page 183); sign *America* plus the *person ending* for *American* (page 201).

Person (PWE)

Signing Negatives

Signers can show the negative by signing *not,* such as for negative prefixes (*un-, im-, in-, dis-*) or simply shake the head back and forth to signify "no" and omit the sign for *not.* Example: If you sign *not* and *like* it becomes *dislike* or *don't like.* Making the sign for *want* and shaking the head "no" means *don't want.*

Another way to make a sign negative is to twist the hand out to a forward position or to turn it downward. Example: Sign *like* and twist the palm outward while maintaining the *like* handshape. The sign for *don't want* is made by turning the hands down.

Signing Contractions

Contractions (Example: *don't, isn't,* and *won't*) are often used in the English language to form a negative. Instead of signing both words that form the contraction, the signer only needs to sign *not* and say the contraction with a questioning facial expression.

Definite and Indefinite Articles

Definite and indefinite articles (*a, an,* and *the*) are not used in American Sign Language. Hearing people sometimes use them when signing in English word order, especially when deaf pupils are being taught English. They are on page 38, if you decide to use them.

Intensity and Degree of Signs

It is not necessary to use another sign to show the intensity of feelings, actions, or colors when using ASL. Instead, the sign itself is made with varying degrees of intensity or forcefulness to emphasize "deep feelings," "fast or slow actions," or "bright colors." This is accomplished with a combination of facial expressions, and the size and speed of the sign. A sad countenance and eyes looking downward help emphasize the sign for *sad.* Wide open eyes or a quick twist of the wrist for initialized color signs help to emphasize that they are bright or strong. *Walk* can be signed quickly or slowly to illustrate what is intended.

Numbers, Money, and Years

Money amounts, years, addresses, and telephone numbers are signed as they are spoken in English. To express the amount $18.32, sign *eighteen (18) dollars three two (3 2) cents.* For the year 1989, sign *nineteen (19) eight nine (8 9).* The address 776 Wildwood Road is signed *7 7 6 Wildwood Road* (the words are signed and/or fingerspelled). The digits of a telephone number are signed as they are spoken; the number 555-4948, for example, is signed *5 5 5* (pause) *4 9 4 8.*

HINTS FOR BETTER SIGNING

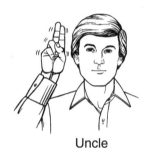

Uncle

Aunt

Gender Signs and Their Locations

The male and female gender signs are identified more easily by their locations. Many male-related signs are made near the forehead, while many female-related signs are made near the cheek or chin (see *uncle* and *aunt* at left).

Opposites

You will soon discover that there are a number of pairs of signs that have the same hand shape, but have a reverse movement and, quite often, are opposite in meaning. Two examples are: *come* and *go*; and *open* and *close.*

The Iconicity of Some Signs

Some signs have shapes and movements that resemble what they describe and remind one of the actual physical concept portrayed. This is known as "iconicity;" meaning, the signs are a "picture of the action." For example: the sign for *deer* portrays the deer's antlers, while the sign for *baseball* portrays the use of a baseball bat.

Name Signs

When a proper name is first mentioned in a conversation, it is fingerspelled. Since it is impractical to fingerspell a name each time it is used, the *name sign* provides the solution. Name signs are short gestures using an initial from a person's name and/or incorporating some aspect of a person's features or personality. They are a form of shorthand to indicate a particular person. A name sign for *Sarah,* who has long black hair, could be the fingerspelled letter *S* touching the signer's hair, then moved down several inches. Another possibility would be the fingerspelled letter *S* moving across the right eyebrow (similar to the sign for *black*). Try to make all your name signs flattering, avoiding ones which are derogatory.

Getting Someone's Attention

Starting a conversation with a deaf person is different from starting a conversation with a hearing person. In spoken language, you can begin a conversation with someone who is not looking at you. In sign language you must get the person's visual attention. Either look them in the face until they look at you or you can tap the person on the shoulder or touch the person's arm. Then, maintain eye contact for effective manual communication. Deaf people consider breaking eye contact as interrupting or ending the conversation.

The Symmetry of Signs

Whenever a sign requires both hands to move or to be active, both hands will have the same hand shape. Conversely, when both hands have a different hand shape, only the dominant hand moves. This principle also holds true for the motion of the sign as well. When both hands move—in any direction—the type of motion, even if alternating, will be the same for both hands. Example: The sign for *game* (at right) has two *A* hands and the motion, or movement, of each hand is the same.

Game

Signs That Deal with Thinking and Feeling

Signs that deal with thinking or mental activity are usually made at or near the head. Two examples: *imagination* (at right) and *smart* (page 136).

Another group of signs are those that deal with *feelings*. Many of these signs are done in the chest area near or at the heart. Here are two examples: *happy* (at right) and *proud* (page 148).

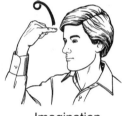

Imagination

Initialized Signs

As you begin to learn signing, you will notice that a number of signs are "initialized." The term refers to a sign formed with the fingerspelled hand shape of the first letter of the English word. An example is *education* (page 176), made with *E* hands. Other examples are the signs for *cousin:* made with a *C* hand and *imagination:* made with an *I* hand (see art at right).

Happy

Clothing

If you plan to sign in front of a group, or when interpreting, wear a solid color (shirt, blouse, or dress) that contrasts with the skin color of your hands. Busy patterns on clothing make reading the signs difficult and can tire the eyes quickly.

You Are Ready to Begin

As you begin your journey into the beautiful and expressive language of deaf people, you may, at times, find it to be challenging. Yet, it will be filled with excitement and enjoyment as your signing abilities increase and you learn to communicate with your hands. May your learning of sign language be a rewarding one. Welcome to *Signing Illustrated*.

Cousin

THE MANUAL ALPHABET

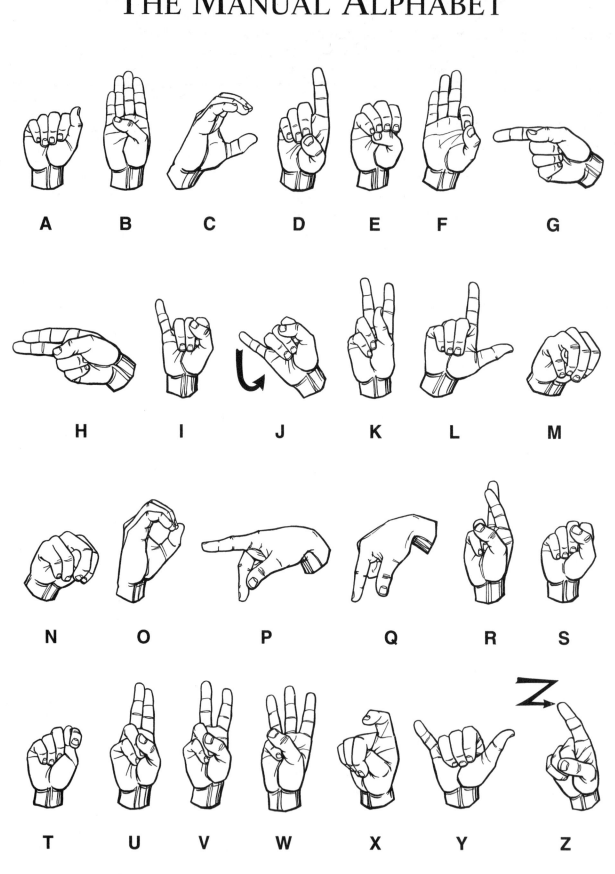

Chapter

Family, People, and Pronouns

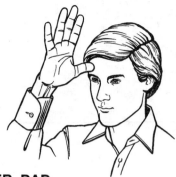

FATHER, DAD

Touch the forehead with the thumb of the right open hand. The fingers may be wiggled slightly.

Memory aid: Indicates the head male of the family unit.

MOTHER, MOM, MAMA

Touch the right chin or cheek with the thumb of the right open hand. The fingers may be wiggled slightly. The sign for *mama* is similar except that the thumb touches the cheek several times.

Memory aid: Indicates the head female of the family unit.

GRANDFATHER

Touch the forehead with the thumb of the right open hand which has its palm facing left. Move the right hand in two forward arcs.

Memory aid: The combination of the sign for *father* and the double hand movements of both signs suggest the reference to someone of the older generation.

GRANDMOTHER

Touch the chin with the thumb of the right open hand which has its palm facing left. Move the right hand in two forward arcs.

Memory aid: The combination of the sign for *mother* and the double hand movements of both signs suggest the reference to someone of the older generation.

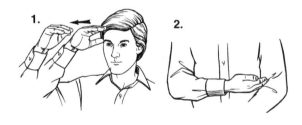

SON

Move the right hand to the forehead as though gripping the peak of a hat between the fingers and thumb; then move it forward a few inches. Next move the right flat hand with palm facing up into the crook of the bent left elbow.

Memory aid: Indicates a male baby cradled in the arms.

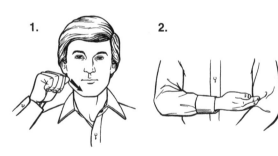

DAUGHTER

Trace the right jawbone from ear to chin with the palm side of the right *A* thumb. Then move the right flat hand with palm facing up into the crook of the bent left elbow.

Memory aid: Indicates a female baby cradled in the arms.

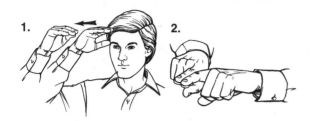

BROTHER

Move the right hand to the forehead as though gripping the peak of a hat between the fingers and thumb; then move it forward a few inches. Next, point both index fingers forward and bring them together. The latter is the sign for *same.*

Memory aid: The two signs combined suggest a male of the same family.

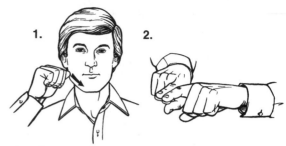

SISTER

Trace the right jawbone from ear to chin with the palm side of the right *A* thumb. Then point both index fingers forward and bring them together. The latter movement is the sign for *same.*

Memory aid: The two signs combined suggest a female of the same family.

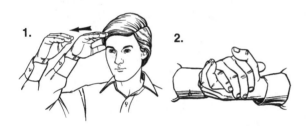

HUSBAND

Move the right hand to the forehead as though gripping the peak of a hat between the fingers and thumb; then move it forward a few inches. Clasp the hands with the right hand above the left. The latter position is the sign for *marriage.*

Memory aid: Indicates a married male.

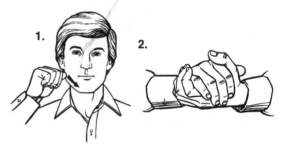

WIFE

Trace the right jawbone from ear to chin with the palm side of the right *A* thumb. Then clasp the hands in a natural position with the right hand above the left. The latter is the sign for *marriage.*

Memory aid: Indicates a married female.

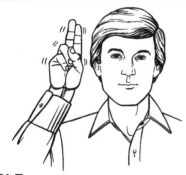

UNCLE

With the palm facing forward, place the right *U* hand close to the right temple and shake back and forth from the wrist.

Memory aid: The initial *U* is placed near the *male* sign position.

AUNT

Place the right *A* hand close to the right cheek and shake back and forth from the wrist.

Memory aid: The initial *A* is placed near the *female* sign position.

NEPHEW

Place the right extended *N* fingers close to the right temple and shake back and forth from the wrist.

Memory aid: The initial *N* is placed near the male sign position.

NIECE

Place the right extended *N* fingers close to the right side of the chin and shake back and forth from the wrist.

Memory aid: The initial *N* is placed near the *female* sign position.

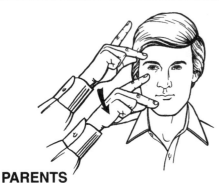

PARENTS

Place the middle finger of the right *P* hand at the right temple, then at the right side of the chin.

Memory aid: The initial indicates the word, and the two locations refer to the basic male and female positions.

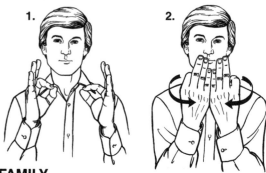

FAMILY

Place both upright *F* hands to the front with the palms facing each other. Make an outward circular movement with each hand simultaneously until the little fingers touch.

Memory aid: The two *F* hands describe the circle of a *family*.

COUSIN

Place the right *C* hand either close to the right temple for a male or close to the right cheek for a female; then shake back and forth from the wrist. Place between the *male* and *female* positions for neuter reference.

Memory aid: The initial *C* is placed wherever appropriate.

IN-LAW

Place the index and thumb side of the right *L* hand on the front of the palm-forward left hand. Begin near the top; then move the right hand downward in a small arc to the base of the left hand. Some prefer to sign *in* first.

Memory aid: This is the sign for *law*.

MAN

Touch the thumb of the right open hand on the forehead, then on the chest.

Memory aid: This sign is a combination of *father* and *fine.*

WOMAN

Touch the thumb of the right open hand on the chin, then on the chest.

Memory aid: The sign is a combination of *mother* and *fine.*

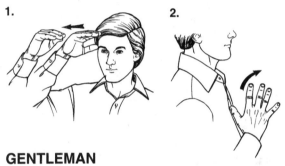

GENTLEMAN

Move the right hand to the forehead as though gripping the peak of a hat between the fingers and thumb; then move it forward a few inches. Place the right thumb of the right open hand on the chest with palm facing left, then tilt the hand in a slight up-forward-down movement.

Memory aid: Old-fashioned tipping of hat.

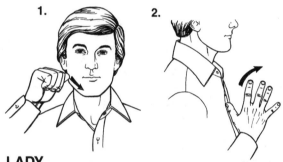

LADY

Trace the right jawbone from ear to chin with the palm side of the right *A* thumb. Then place the right thumb of the right open hand on the chest with palm facing left; then tilt the hand in a slight up-forward-down movement.

Memory aid: Indicates a *lady's* dress or blouse with frilly ruffles.

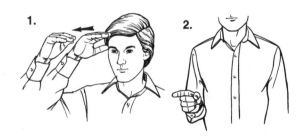

HE, HIM

Move right hand to forehead as though gripping the peak of a hat between fingers and thumb; then move it forward a few inches. Next point the index finger forward. If it is obvious that a male is being referred to, the sign for *male* can be omitted.

Memory aid: The signer directs attention by pointing.

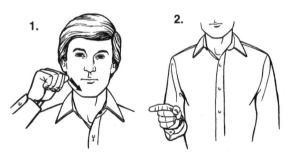

SHE, HER

Trace the right jawbone from ear to chin with the palm side of the right *A* thumb; then point the index finger forward. If it is obvious that a female is being referred to, the sign for *female* can be omitted.

Memory aid: The signer directs attention by pointing.

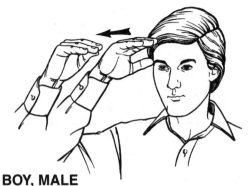

BOY, MALE

Move the right hand to the forehead as though gripping the peak of a cap or hat between the fingers and thumb; then move it forward a few inches.

Memory aid: Old-fashioned tipping of caps by men, especially when greeting women.

GIRL, MAIDEN, FEMALE

Trace the right jawbone from ear to chin with the palm side of the right *A* thumb.

Memory aid: The thumb follows the location of the old-fashioned bonnet string.

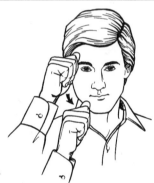

ADULT

Place the right *A* hand thumb first at the right temple, then at the right side of the chin.

Memory aid: The initial indicates the word, and the two locations refer to the basic positions for *male* and *female*.

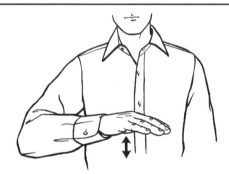

CHILD, CHILDREN

Place the right flat downturned hand before the body and motion as if patting the head of a child. When referring to more than one child, move the hand to another position and repeat the sign.

Memory aid: *Children* are shorter than adults.

BABY, INFANT

Hold the arms in the natural position for cradling a baby and rock the arms sideways.

Memory aid: The natural movement of comforting a *baby* in the arms.

KID

Extend the index and small finger of the right hand. With the palm facing down, put the index finger under the nose. The hand is then pivoted up and down slightly and often moved to the right simultaneously.

Memory aid: Suggests the runny nose of a young child.

BACHELOR

Put the index finger of the right *B* hand first on the right side of the mouth, then on the left. *Note:* Some signers reverse this action.

Memory aid: The *B* hand suggests the word, and the action can symbolize a mouth that has not yet spoken to end the state of *bachelorhood.*

SWEETHEART, BEAU, LOVER

Bring the knuckles of both *A* hands together with palms facing inward; then raise and lower both thumbs simultaneously.

Memory aid: Suggests two lovebirds billing and cooing.

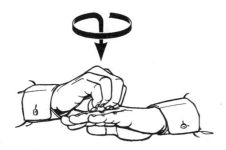

ENGAGED (prior to marriage)

Circle the right *E* hand over the left palm-down flat hand; then place the right *E* on the left ring finger.

Memory aid: The *engagement* ring finger is given prominence.

MARRY, MARRIAGE

Clasp the hands in a natural position with the right hand above the left.

Memory aid: A couple joins hands during their wedding ceremony.

WEDDING

Point the fingers of both flat hands down from the wrists in the front. Swing the hands toward each other until the left fingers and thumb grasp the right fingers.

Memory aid: Suggests a bride and groom joining hands.

DIVORCE

Hold both *D* hands with palms facing and knuckles touching. Twist both hands outward and sideways until the palms face forward.

Memory aid: Two people once close to each other now separate.

TWINS

Place the thumb side of the right *T* hand first on the left side of the chin, then on the right.

Memory aid: The two *T* positions on the same chin indicate the meaning.

CUTE

Stroke the chin several times with the fingers of the right *U* hand. Assume a smiling expression.

Memory aid: The sound of *U* rhymes with *cute.*

OTHER, ANOTHER

Hold the right *A* hand in front of the chest with upturned thumb. Pivot the hand from the wrist so that the thumb points to the right.

Memory aid: Pointing away from oneself with the thumb indicates *another.*

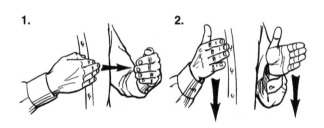

NEIGHBOR

Hold the left curved hand away from the body with palm facing in. Move the back of the right curved hand close to the palm of the left. Bring both flat hands down simultaneously with palms facing each other.

Memory aid: This is a combination of *near* and *person (personalizing word ending).*

PERSON

Place both *P* hands forward and move them downward simultaneously.

Memory aid: Suggests outlining the form of another *person.*

PEOPLE

Make inward circles alternately from the sides with both *P* hands. *Note:* Some signers prefer to direct the circles forward.

Memory aid: The *P* hands suggest the word, and the action suggests people milling around.

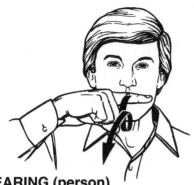

HEARING (person)

Place the right index finger in front of the mouth and make a few small forward circular movements.

Memory aid: The sign is similar to the one for *say* and indicates that a *hearing* person can learn to speak easily.

PERSON (personalizing word ending)

Hold both flat open hands to the front with palms facing; then move them down simultaneously.

Memory aid: Suggests outlining the form of another *person*.

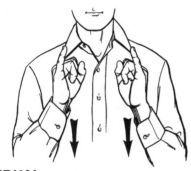

INDIVIDUAL

Drop both *I* hands simultaneously in front of the chest with palms facing.

Memory aid: The movement is the same as for *person,* but here it is identified by the initial *I*.

GROUP, ASSOCIATION, TEAM, CLASS, AUDIENCE, COMPANY, SOCIETY, DEPARTMENT, ORGANIZATION

Hold both *C* hands upright before chest with palms facing. Move hands outward in a circle until little fingers touch. Initialize each sign if desired.

Memory aid: The circle suggests an area encompassing several people.

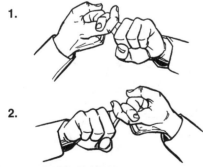

FRIEND, FRIENDSHIP

Interlock the right and left index fingers and repeat in reverse.

Memory aid: Suggests the link of *friendship*.

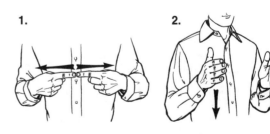

ENEMY, FOE, OPPONENT, RIVAL

Point the two index fingers toward each other with palms facing in. Move them outward sharply in opposite directions; then add the sign for *person (personalizing word ending)*.

Memory aid: Symbolizes *enemies* drawing further and further apart.

NAME, CALLED, NAMED
Cross the middle-finger edge of the right *H* fingers over the index-finger edge of the left *H* fingers. To sign *called* or *named,* move the crossed *H* hands in a small forward arc together.

Memory aid: Reminds one that those who cannot write have to sign their *name* with an *X*.

WHO, WHOM
Make a counterclockwise circle in front of the lips with the right index finger.

Memory aid: Attention is drawn to the lips as they form the word shape.

FAMOUS, FAME
Point both index fingers toward the mouth and move them outward and upward in small spiraling circles.

Memory aid: Suggests that news about someone or something is being broadcast far and wide.

CHARACTER (individual)
Put the thumb side of the right *C* hand against the left flat hand and rotate forward in a clockwise circle.

Memory aid: The initial indicates the word, and the action suggests a circle of personal activities.

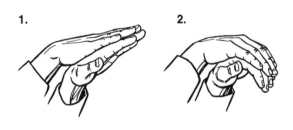

HYPOCRITE, FAKE, IMPOSTER
Place the right flat hand over the back of the left flat hand, with all fingers pointing forward. Bend the hands downward as one.

Memory aid: Suggests a covering, as in the use of a mask.

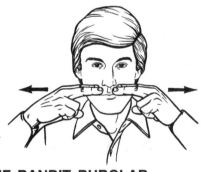

THIEF, BANDIT, BURGLAR, CROOK, ROBBER
Place the index-finger side of both *H* hands under the nose; then draw both hands outward.

Memory aid: Suggests a false mustache that can be used as a disguise.

GENERATION, ANCESTORS, DESCENDANTS

Start with both slightly cupped hands at the right shoulder; then roll them one over the other in a downward-forward movement. Reverse the action if the past generation is referred to.

Memory aid: The movement symbolizes descending or ascending steps.

ASSOCIATE, EACH OTHER, MINGLE, FELLOWSHIP, MUTUAL, SOCIALIZE, ONE ANOTHER

Point the left *A* thumb upward while the right *A* thumb points downward and revolves in a counterclockwise direction around the stationary left thumb.

Memory aid: Suggests the *mingling* of people.

POLITE, COURTEOUS, MANNERS

Place the thumb edge of the right flat open hand at the chest and pivot the hand forward a few times or wiggle the fingers instead of pivoting the hand.

Memory aid: Symbolizes the old-fashioned ruffled shirt or blouse of a refined person.

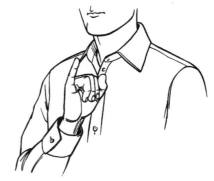

I

Position the right *I* hand with palm facing left and thumb touching the chest.

Memory aid: The initial *I* in close proximity to the body suggests the individual.

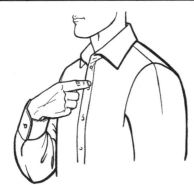

ME

Point the right index finger toward the chest.

Memory aid: The signer directs attention to himself.

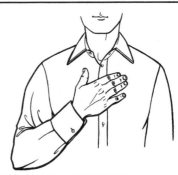

MY, MINE, OWN, PERSONAL

Place the palm of the right flat hand on the chest.

Memory aid: The hand over the heart suggests protection of *personal* belongings.

MYSELF, SELF

Bring the *A* hand against the center of the chest with palm facing left.

Memory aid: The thumb can be thought of as representing *self.*

YOU

Point the right index finger to the person being addressed. Or, if referring to several people, make a sweeping motion from left to right.

Memory aid: The person being pointed to clearly understands the reference to self.

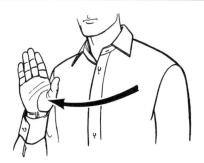

YOUR, YOURS (plural)

Move the flat hand across the front of the body from left to right with the palm facing outward.

Memory aid: The flat hand and the left to right movement symbolizes possession by several people.

YOURSELF, HERSELF, HIMSELF, ITSELF, ONESELF, THEMSELVES, YOURSELVES

Hold the right *A* hand thumb up and make several short forward movements in the direction of the person or object referred to.

Memory aid: The jerking movement can suggest the individual nature of persons or things.

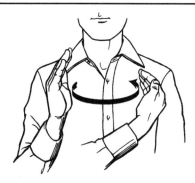

OUR

Place the slightly cupped right hand on the right side of the chest with palm facing left. Move the right hand forward in a circular motion, bringing it to rest near the left shoulder with the palm facing right.

Memory aid: The circular movement suggests the inclusion of others.

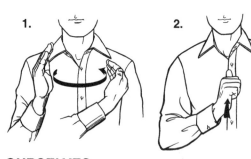

OURSELVES

Place the slightly cupped right hand on the right side of the chest, palm left. Move the right hand forward in a circular motion, bringing it to rest near the left shoulder with the palm facing right. Place the right *A* hand against the center of the chest, palm left.

Memory aid: The signs for *our* and *self.*

HIS, HER, THEIR, YOUR, YOURS (singular)

Push the right flat hand forward with palm facing out toward the person or persons being referred to. The signs for *male* and *female* can precede *his* and *her* if it is not obvious from the context.

Memory aid: Suggests the idea of something separate or apart from the signer.

WE, US

Touch the right index finger on the right shoulder; then move it in a forward semi-circle until it touches the left shoulder. Sometimes the *W* or *U* hand is used instead of the index finger to indicate either *we* or *us* respectively.

Memory aid: Touching two shoulders suggests more than one person.

THEY, THEM, THESE, THOSE

Point the right index finger forward or in the direction of the persons or objects referred to, then move it to the right.

Memory aid: The signer directs attention by pointing.

SOMEONE, SOMEBODY, SOMETHING

Hold the right index finger up with palm facing forward and shake it slightly back and forth from left to right.

Memory aid: The index finger represents *someone* or *something*.

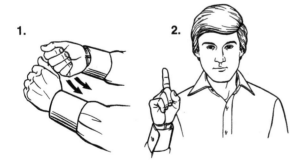

EVERYONE, EVERYBODY

Hold the left *A* hand to the front with palm facing right. The knuckles and thumb of the right *A* hand rub downward on the left thumb a few times. Add the numerical sign for *one*.

Memory aid: The right thumb seems to be giving recognition to the left thumb.

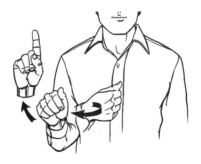

ANYONE, ANYBODY

Place the right *A* hand in front of the body with the palm facing in. Move the *A* hand forward to the right until the palm faces forward. Point up with the right index finger.

Memory aid: The hand seems to be engaged in a wide-angled search for something or someone.

ANY

Place the right *A* hand in front of the body with the palm facing in. Move the *A* hand forward to the right until the palm faces forward.

Memory aid: The thumb seems to be searching for something or someone.

EACH, EVERY

Hold the left *A* hand to the front with palm facing right. The knuckles and thumb of the right *A* hand rub downward on the left thumb a few times.

Memory aid: The right thumb seems to be giving recognition to the left thumb.

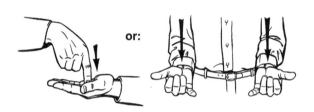

THIS

Put the right index fingertip into the palm of the flat left hand if something specific is indicated. Drop both *Y* (or flat) hands together with palms facing up if something more abstract is indicated.

Memory aid: The right index finger points to an object in the left hand. Or both hands seem to be holding something.

THAT

Place the right *Y* hand on the left upturned palm. *Note:* When signing in English syntax order, many signers omit the sign for *that* when it is a conjunctive, as in the sentence, It is good *that* you trust me.

Memory aid: *That* is often used in relation to either asking or answering a question. The *Y* hand suggests the interrogative *why?*

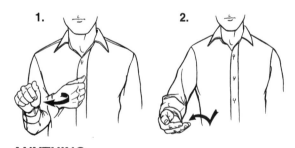

ANYTHING

Place the right *A* hand in front of the body with the palm facing in. Move the *A* hand forward to the right until the palm faces forward. Drop the right hand slightly a few times as it is moved to the right.

Memory aid: The hand movements suggest the idea of presenting several alternatives.

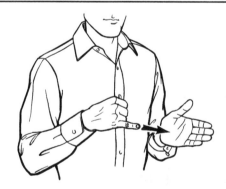

IT

Hold the flat left hand to the front with the palm facing right; then move the little finger of the right *I* hand into the left palm.

Memory aid: The initialized right hand indicates the word and seems to be pointing out something specific.

NAME THE SIGN

To reinforce the vocabulary you have already learned, identify the following signs from this chapter by writing the names underneath the signs.

1. Mom   2. Son   3. Cousin   4. Aunt

5. Dad   6. Cute   7. Kid   8. married

9. Husband   10. famous   11. Boy   12. Bachelor

Answers are on page 285.

FINGERSPELLING PRACTICE

Once you are comfortable with the manual alphabet, practice the following words at a steady and comfortable rate. Don't worry about speed; developing a rhythm and accuracy are more important.

Fingerspelling Words

ad	ant	act	cash	bash	boat	back	chasm	follow
an	are	aid	curl	cent	fine	lack	front	garden
at	but	dap	hope	dash	from	land	guild	hazard
be	buy	dip	hurl	dine	goat	rack	happy	hijack
by	cab	fry	lash	done	halt	sand	hitch	homage
do	can	lab	mash	gent	lane	slap	honey	hurtle
is	car	mop	pope	gone	note	slim	impel	import
it	cat	pad	rash	line	rank	slip	knack	monkey
no	doe	sad	ship	pine	salt	than	print	scrawl
or	dog	sea	shoe	rent	sank	that	spasm	scream
so	foe	sob	shop	sash	shop	then	spoil	script
to	sow	too	soap	sent	tame	they	spoke	scurry
up	toe	try	twin	tone	vote	this	sport	speech

MARKERS, ARTICLES, AND PUNCTUATION

The following markers (inflections or word endings), articles, and punctuation are used as "teaching tools" to teach deaf students English. Most are not used in ASL.

MARKERS

They are added to the basic sign to express a word exactly.

-MENT
Place the modified *M* hand near the top of the flat left hand; then move the modified *M* hand down to the base of the hand.

-NESS
Place the modified *N* hand near the top of the flat left hand and move the modified *N* hand down to the base of the hand.

-ER (Comparative Degree)
Face both *A* hands in front, right *A* hand lower and move the right *A* hand up slightly above the left hand.

-EST (Superlative Degree)
Place both *A* hands in front, facing each other, with right hand lower than left and move the right *A* hand high above the left.

-ING
The *I* hand faces left, then twist it to the right.

-'S or S' (possessives)
The *S* hand faces left, then twist it to the right (use after a sign or fingerspelled word).

-S
S hand.

-ED
Sign *past* by moving the right upraised flat hand backward over the right shoulder with palm facing the body.

-ED (alternative)
D hand.

-EN
N hand.

-Y
Y hand.

-LY
Sign "I love you" hand shape and move downward in a wavy movement.

-LY (alternative)
Sign *L*; then sign *Y*.

ARTICLES

A (indefinite article)
Hold the right *A* hand to the front with palm facing forward, and make a small arc to the right.

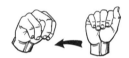

AN (indefinite article)
Fingerspell *A–N*.

THE (definite article)
Hold the right *T* hand up with palm facing left and rotate it counterclockwise.

PUNCTUATION MARKS

PERIOD, APOSTROPHE, COLON, COMMA, EXCLAMATION POINT, SEMICOLON
Draw the shape of the appropriate punctuation mark in the air with the right index finger or with the right index finger and thumb, which touch at the tips. The other fingers are closed.

Chapter

2

Home,
Clothing,
and
Colors

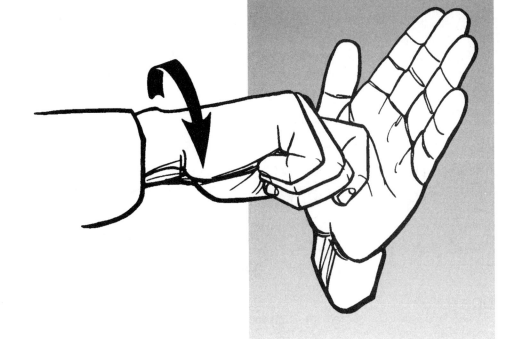

HOME

Place the fingertips of the right *and* hand first at the mouth, then at the right cheek. Sometimes the position at the cheek is made with a slightly curved hand.

Memory aid: Suggests the place where one eats and sleeps.

HOUSE, RESIDENCE

Form the point of a triangle at head level with both flat hands; then move them apart and straight down simultaneously with the fingers pointing up.

Memory aid: Suggests the roof and walls of a *house.*

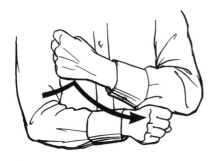

FOUNDATION, SUPPORT

With the palm facing in, hold the left closed hand to the front with the forearm horizontal. Place the right *S* hand first under the left hand, then under the forearm.

Memory aid: Suggests the pillars that *support* a building.

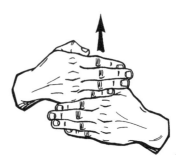

WINDOW

Place the little-finger edge of the right flat hand on the index-finger edge of the left flat hand with palms facing in. Move the right hand up a short distance.

Memory aid: Suggests raising a sliding *window.*

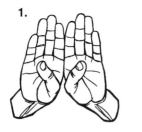
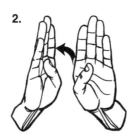

DOOR

Hold both *B* hands to the front with palms facing out and index fingers touching. Twist the right hand back and forth from the wrist.

Memory aid: Symbolizes the opening and closing of a *door.*

FLOOR

Place the index-finger edge of both flat hands together with palms facing down; then move both hands apart to the sides. The sign can be repeated further to the right.

Memory aid: Symbolizes *flooring* boards placed side by side.

GATE

Point the fingertips of both flat hands together with palms facing in. Move the right hand back and forth a few times.

Memory aid: Symbolizes the action of a *gate*.

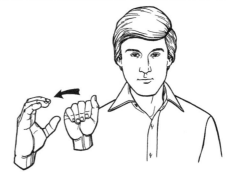

AIR CONDITIONING

Fingerspell *A* and *C*.

Memory aid: The initials indicate the words.

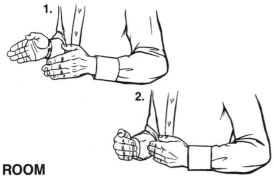

ROOM

Place both flat hands to the front with palms facing; then move the left hand close to the body and the right hand further away with both palms facing the body. This sign can also be done with *R* hands.

Memory aid: The hands outline a rectangular shape.

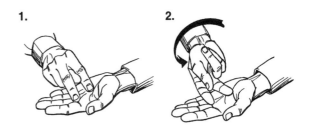

KITCHEN

Place the right *K* hand first palm down, then palm up on the upturned left palm.

Memory aid: The action suggests food being turned over in a pan.

RESTROOM

Move the right *R* hand in a short arc to the right.

Memory aid: The initial indicates the word, and the movement suggests that the direction of the *restroom* is indicated.

TOILET, BATHROOM

Shake the right *T* hand in front of the chest with the palm facing forward.

Memory aid: The shaking motion suggests the need to meet a physical requirement.

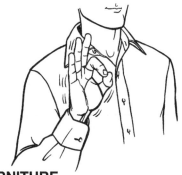

FURNITURE

Shake the *F* hand back and forth near the right shoulder or in front of the chest.

Memory aid: The initialized sign indicates the word.

DRAWER

Hold both hands to the front with palms facing up and fingers almost completely curved. Pull both hands to self.

Memory aid: Symbolizes opening a *drawer*.

BED

Hold both hands palm to palm and place the back of the left hand on the right cheek.

Memory aid: The sign symbolizes resting the head on a pillow.

MIRROR

Hold up the slightly curved right hand at eye level, and look at the palm while pivoting the hand slightly from the wrist.

Memory aid: Suggests looking at one's reflection in a *mirror*.

TABLE

Place both arms to the front in a similar position to that of folding them, but put the right forearm over the left. The right flat hand can pat the top of the left forearm a few times.

Memory aid: Can suggest resting the arms on a *table* surface.

CHAIR

Place the palm side of the right *H* fingers on the back of the left *H* fingers.

Memory aid: Symbolizes a person sitting on a *chair*.

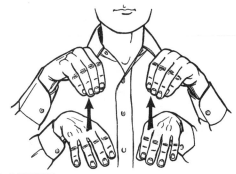

BLANKET

Hold both open hands to the front with palms facing down and fingers pointing down. Lift both hands to shoulder level while closing the thumbs on the index fingers.

Memory aid: Symbolizes pulling up a *blanket* to cover oneself.

REFRIGERATOR

With palms facing forward, hold both *R* hands up and shake them.

Memory aid: The initial indicates the word, and the action symbolizes coldness.

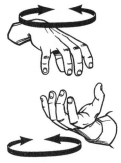

WASHING MACHINE

Hold both curved open hands with palms facing each other vertically. Make twisting circular motions with both hands, which rotate in opposite directions.

Memory aid: Suggests the swirling water and clothes in a *washing machine.*

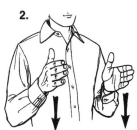

DRYER (clothes)

Move the right curved index finger across the mouth from left to right (the sign for *dry*). Next, hold both flat open hands to the front with palms facing each other and move them simultaneously downward a short distance.

Memory aid: Suggests that drying is purposely activated by a person.

WASH DISHES, DISHWASHING

With palms facing, rub the right flat hand in a clockwise circle over the left flat hand.

Memory aid: Symbolizes *washing* a plate with a dishcloth.

WASH

Rub the knuckles of both closed hands together with circular movements.

Memory aid: Suggests *washing* clothes by hand.

TELEPHONE, CALL
Position the *Y* hand at the right of the face so that the thumb is near the ear and the little finger near the mouth.

Memory aid: The natural position for using the *telephone.*

UMBRELLA
Hold the right closed hand over the left closed hand; then raise the right hand a short distance.

Memory aid: Symbolizes opening an *umbrella.*

KEY, LOCK, LOCK UP
Place right crooked index finger into left flat palm and twist clockwise.

Memory aid: The sign symbolizes the use of a *key.*

SCISSORS, CLIPPERS, SHEARS, CUT
Open and close the right *H* fingers several times.

Memory aid: Symbolizes the *scissor* action.

STRING, CORD, THREAD, TWINE
Touch the fingertips of both *I* hands with palms facing in. Draw them apart while simultaneously making small spirals.

Memory aid: Suggests the twisted fibers that make up a piece of *string.*

RUBBER
Rub the thumb side of the right *X* hand down the right cheek a few times.

Memory aid: The rubbing action and the resiliency of the cheek suggest the meaning.

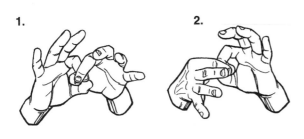

CHAIN

Interlock both index fingers and thumbs a few times. Alternate the position of each thumb so that one thumb is first above, then beneath.

Memory aid: Pictures the links of a *chain*.

CANDLE

Hold the left open hand up with palm facing forward and the right index finger at the base of the left hand. Wiggle the fingers of the left hand.

Memory aid: Suggests the flickering flame of a *candle*.

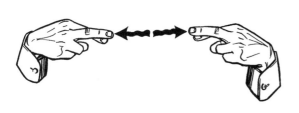

ROPE

Touch the fingertips of both *R* hands; then draw them apart to the sides with a slight wavy motion.

Memory aid: The initial suggests the word, and the movement suggests the twisted strands that make up a *rope*.

THING, SUBSTANCE

Drop the right flat hand slightly a few times as it moves to the right.

Memory aid: The hand movements suggest the idea of presenting several alternatives.

CLOTHES, DRESS, GARMENT, GOWN, SUIT, WEAR

Brush the fingertips of both flat open hands down the chest a few times.

Memory aid: Suggests the smoothing of *clothes* over the body.

HANG UP, HANGER, SUSPEND

With palm facing forward, move the right *X* hand up and forward a short distance.

Memory aid: The sign suggests the use of a *hanger* or hook.

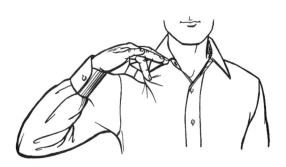

SHIRT
Grasp the *shirt* between thumb and index and pull slightly. Two hands may be used.

Memory aid: Identifies the *shirt* directly.

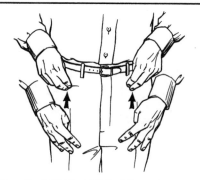

PANTS, SLACKS, TROUSERS
Place the curved open hands just below the waist and move them up to the waist while simultaneously forming *and* hands.

Memory aid: The sign symbolizes pulling up *pants*.

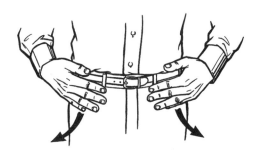

SKIRT
Brush the fingers of both flat open hands downward and outward just below the waist.

Memory aid: Can suggest the smoothing of a *skirt*.

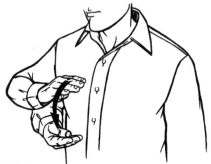

BLOUSE
Place the thumb side of the right flat hand on the upper part of the chest with the palm facing down. Move the hand down to the waist while turning it, so that the little-finger edge rests against the body with the palm facing up.

Memory aid: Suggests the area covered by a *blouse*.

COAT, JACKET, OVERCOAT
Move the thumbs of both *A* hands downward from either side of the base of the neck to the center of the lower chest.

Memory aid: The movement follows the lines of *jacket* lapels.

HAT
Pat the top of the head with the right flat hand.

Memory aid: The location of a *hat*.

NECKTIE
Hold both extended *N* fingers in front of the neck. Rotate the right *N* fingers forward around the left *N* fingers; then move the right hand down a short distance with palm facing up.

Memory aid: Symbolizes the movements necessary in hand-tying a *necktie.*

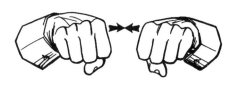

SHOES
Strike the thumb sides of both closed hands together a few times.

Memory aid: Can suggest the clicking of military heels.

1.   **2.**

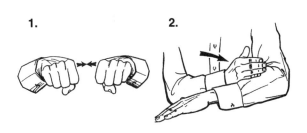

BOOTS
Strike the thumb sides of both closed hands together a few times; then place the right flat hand at the bent left elbow.

Memory aid: Suggests heels clicking together in military fashion followed by the length of the left forearm shown to indicate the length of the *boots.*

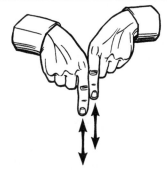

SOCKS, HOSE, STOCKINGS
Point both index fingers down. Rub them up and down against each other alternately.

Memory aid: Suggests the use of needles for hand knitting *socks.*

GLOVES
Hold the left open hand up with palm facing self. Move the curved right hand down over the back of the left hand a few times.

Memory aid: The sign mimics putting on *gloves.*

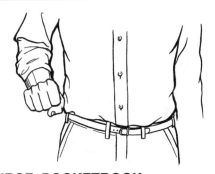

PURSE, POCKETBOOK
Place the right *S* hand near the waist with palm facing down.

Memory aid: A common position for holding the strap or handle of a *purse.*

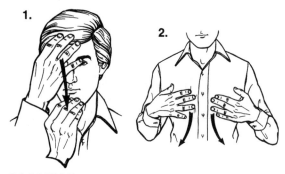

PAJAMAS

Place the palm side of the right open hand in front of the face and move it down to chin level while forming an *and* hand; then brush the fingertips of both flat open hands down the chest a few times.

Memory aid: A combination of the signs for *sleep* and *clothes.*

COLLAR

Move the index and thumb of the right *Q* hand along the side of the neck from back to front. Sometimes two hands are used to perform the same movement on either side of the neck.

Memory aid: Outlines the area and shape of a *collar.*

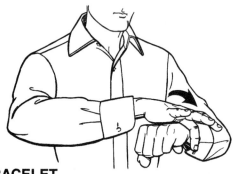

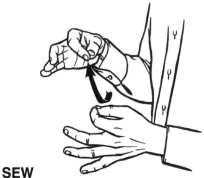

BRACELET

Place the right index finger and thumb around the left wrist and rotate the right hand forward around the left wrist.

Memory aid: Indicates the position of a *bracelet* around the wrist.

SEW

Pivot the right *F* hand from a palm-down position to palm facing self as it moves down, and then up a short distance above the left *F* hand. Repeat as desired.

Memory aid: The movement for *sewing* with a needle.

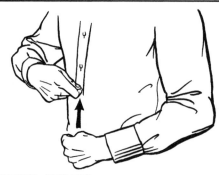

ZIPPER, ZIP UP

Hold both modified *A* hands (thumb tips in the crook of both index fingers) at waist level with palms facing in and the right hand just above the left. Move the right hand straight upward to the upper chest.

Memory aid: Suggests the action of *zipping up* a jacket.

TEAR, RIP, SEVER

Place both thumb tips in the crook of their respective index fingers. The remaining fingers are closed, with the palms facing each other. Move the right hand sharply toward self and the left hand forward.

Memory aid: Suggests the action of *tearing* paper.

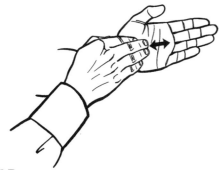

SOAP

Brush the right fingertips across the left palm several times. *Note:* Variations in the direction and manner of rubbing exist for this sign.

Memory aid: The action of rubbing the hands on *soap*.

SHAMPOO

Form *A* hands with both hands and rub them on the sides of the head.

Memory aid: The movement suggests the natural action of *shampooing* one's hair.

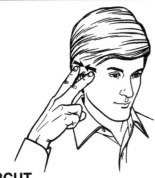

HAIRCUT

Open and close the right *H* fingers near the hair several times.

Memory aid: The action of cutting hair.

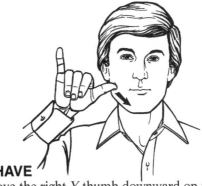

SHAVE

Move the right *Y* thumb downward on the right cheek a few times.

Memory aid: Suggests use of the old-fashioned single-blade straight razor.

IRONING

Hold the flat left hand in front, palm up, and slide the right *A* hand, palm down, back and forth over the left palm.

Memory aid: Resembles the act of *ironing*.

COLOR

Point the fingertips of the open right hand toward the mouth and wiggle them as the hand moves slightly out. Some signers begin this sign by touching the lips with the fingertips.

Memory aid: The fingers can suggest the different *colors* of a rainbow.

RED
Stroke the lips downward with the right index finger (or *R* fingers).

Memory aid: Suggests *red* lips or lipstick.

GREEN
Move the right *G* hand to the right while shaking it from the wrist.

Memory aid: The initial indicates the word.

ORANGE (color and fruit)
Slightly open and squeeze the right *S* hand in front of the mouth a few times.

Memory aid: Suggests squeezing an *orange* to obtain the juice.

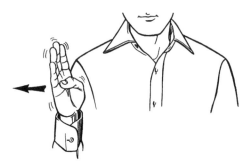

BLUE
Move the right *B* hand to the right while shaking it from the wrist.

Memory aid: The initial indicates the meaning.

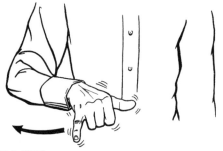

YELLOW
Move the right *Y* hand to the right while shaking it from the wrist.

Memory aid: The initial indicates the meaning, which requires context and simultaneous lipreading for full comprehension.

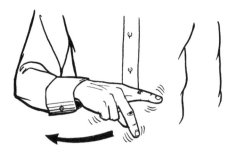

PURPLE
Hold the right *P* hand to the front and shake it at the wrist as the hand moves to the right.

Memory aid: The initial indicates the word, which requires context and simultaneous lipreading for full comprehension.

WHITE

Place the fingers and thumb of the right curved hand on the chest; then move it forward while simultaneously forming the *and* hand.

Memory aid: Can suggest reference to a clean *white* shirt.

BLACK

Move the right index finger sideways across the right eyebrow.

Memory aid: Suggests the cosmetic makeup of the eyebrow.

PINK

Stroke the lips downward with the middle finger of the right *P* hand.

Memory aid: Suggests *pink* lips.

BROWN

Move the index finger of the right *B* hand down the right cheek.

Memory aid: Suggests the skin color.

TAN

Move the right *T* hand down the right cheek.

Memory aid: Suggests the skin color.

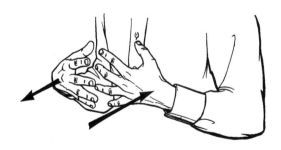

GRAY

Pass the fingers of both open hands back and forth through the open spaces between the fingers.

Memory aid: The merging fingers suggest the mixture of black and white to produce *gray*.

MATCHING SKILL

Look at the words at the left side of the page. Then match the signs with the words by writing the correct word next to the sign.

1.

_____

2.

_____

3.

_____

4.

_____

5.

_____

6.

_____

7.

_____

8.

_____

9.

_____

10.

_____

11.

_____

12.

_____

13.

_____

14.

_____

MATCHING WORDS

scissors

shave

shoes

rope

home

bed

candle

clothes

orange

window

purple

hat

mirror

black

Answers are on page 285.

Chapter

3

Food
and
Eating

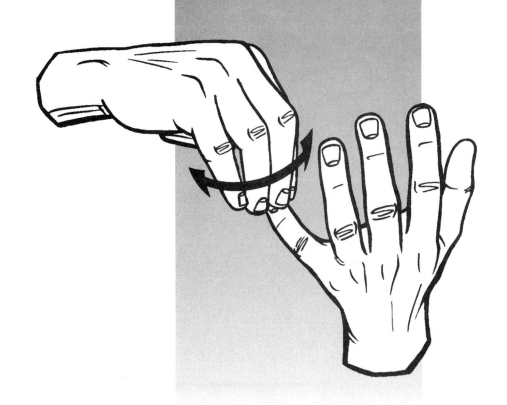

BREAD

Draw the little-finger edge of the right hand downward a few times over the back of the flat left hand, which has its palm facing the body.

Memory aid: Symbolizes cutting slices of *bread.*

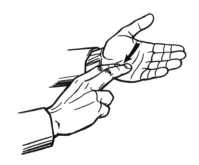

BUTTER

Quickly brush the fingertips of the right *H* hand across the left palm a few times.

Memory aid: Suggests spreading *butter* on bread.

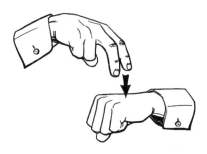

POTATO

Strike the tips of the right curved *V* fingers on the back of the left downturned *S* hand.

Memory aid: Suggests piercing a *potato* with a fork.

GRAVY, FAT, GREASE, OIL

Hold the left flat hand with fingers pointing right, and pinch the little-finger edge of the left hand with the right thumb and index finger. Draw the right index and thumb downward from this position a few times.

Memory aid: Suggests *gravy* or *oil* dripping.

MEAT, BEEF, FLESH

Using the right thumb and index finger, pinch the flesh of the left hand between the thumb and index finger.

Memory aid: A *fleshy* part of the hand is indicated.

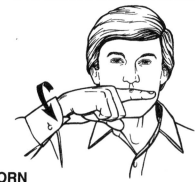

CORN

Rotate the right index finger back and forth in front of the mouth. The movement is from the wrist.

Memory aid: Suggests the action of eating an ear of *corn.*

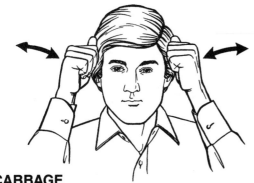

CABBAGE

Strike both *A* (or *S*) hands simultaneously against the sides of the head.

Memory aid: The emphasis on the head suggests the head shape of the *cabbage*.

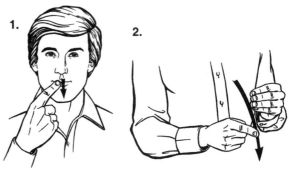

TOMATO

Stroke the lips downward with the right index finger. Hold the left *and* hand with fingers pointing right; then bring the right index finger down past the fingers of the left *and* hand.

Memory aid: Suggests the red color of a *tomato* followed by the action of slicing it with a knife.

CHEESE

Place the heels of both hands together and rotate them back and forth in opposite directions.

Memory aid: Suggests the action of shaping *cheese*.

PIZZA

Outline the shape of a *Z* in front of the chest with the *P* hand.

Memory aid: Emphasizes the *P* and *Z*s of *pizza*.

SOUP

Hold the left curved hand with palm facing up; then move the slightly curved right *H* fingers into the left palm and upward a few times.

Memory aid: Suggests using a spoon to eat *soup*.

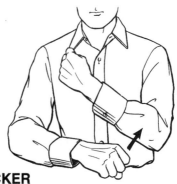

CRACKER

Strike the right *S* near the left elbow.

Memory aid: Suggests an old European method of crumbling *crackers* into soup.

SPAGHETTI, STRING, THREAD, WIRE
Touch the tips of both *I* fingers; then make small spirals as both hands are drawn apart to the sides.

Memory aid: Suggests the length of *spaghetti, string,* or *wire.*

SANDWICH
Place the fingertips of both palm-to-palm hands near the mouth.

Memory aid: The two hands suggest two slices of bread.

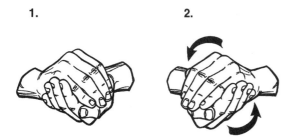

HAMBURGER
Cup the right hand on top of the left cupped hand; then reverse.

Memory aid: Suggests the shaping of *hamburger* patties.

FRENCH FRIES
Sign the right *F* hand once, then again a second time slightly to the right.

Memory aid: The two initials are used.

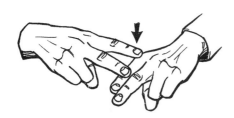

SALT
Tap the right *V* fingers on the left *H* fingers a few times. Sometimes each of the right *V* fingers is used alternately for the tapping movement. Some prefer the left hand also be in the *V* shape.

Memory aid: Suggests the old-fashioned custom of putting *salt* on a knife and tapping it to distribute the *salt.*

PEPPER
Hold the right *O* hand to the front with the *O* pointing down to the left. Shake down to the left a few times.

Memory aid: Symbolizes the use of a *pepper* shaker.

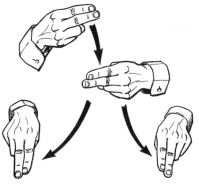

EGG

Bring the middle finger of the right *H* hand down upon the index finger of the left *H* and move both hands down and out. Most of the latter movement can be done from the wrists.

Memory aid: Suggests the action of removing an *egg* from its shell by breaking the shell.

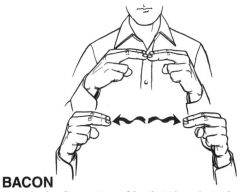

BACON

Touch the fingertips of both *U* hands in front of the chest. Move both hands out sideways in opposite directions while waving the *U* fingers up and down.

Memory aid: Suggests the wavy shape of *bacon* as it is being cooked.

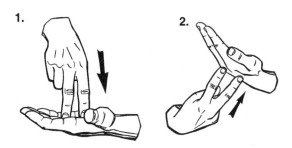

TOAST

Thrust the right *V* fingers into the left palm; then into the back of the left flat hand.

Memory aid: Suggests the old-fashioned method of using a special long fork to *toast* bread in front of a fire.

JELLY, JAM

Rub the fingertip of the right *J* across the left palm once or twice.

Memory aid: Suggests spreading *jelly* on bread.

BISCUIT

Place the right *C* thumb and fingertips into the left flat palm and raise right hand a few times.

Memory aid: Suggests a *biscuit* rising.

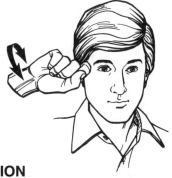

ONION

Pivot the knuckle of the right bent index finger back and forth at the side of the right eye.

Memory aid: Suggests wiping away tears created by the odor of *onions*.

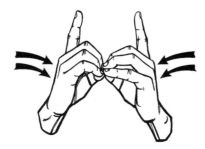

DESSERT

Bring the thumbs of both upright *D* hands together a few times.

Memory aid: The *D* hands suggest the word, and the repetition can suggest the desire for something in addition to the main course.

CAKE

Move the fingertips and thumb of the right *C* hand forward across the left flat hand from wrist to fingertips.

Memory aid: Suggests sliding a piece of *cake* from a serving dish onto someone's plate.

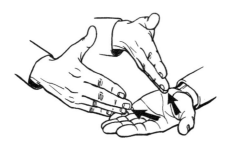

PIE

Pull the little-finger edge of the right flat hand across the palm of the left flat hand twice. Use a different angle the second time.

Memory aid: The movement of cutting a *pie*.

ICE CREAM, LOLLIPOP

Pull the right *S* hand toward the mouth with a downward twist a few times. The tongue may also be shown.

Memory aid: The action of licking an *ice cream* cone.

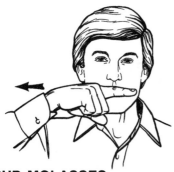

SYRUP, MOLASSES

Move the right index finger across the lips from left to right.

Memory aid: Suggests wiping sticky lips.

COOKIE

Place the right *C* thumb and fingertips into the left flat palm and twist. Repeat a few times.

Memory aid: Suggests using a *cookie* cutter.

DOUGHNUT
Beginning at the lips, make a forward circle with both *R* hands.

Memory aid: Suggests the ring shape of a *doughnut*.

VANILLA
Shake the right *V* hand.

Memory aid: The *V* hand indicates the word, which requires context and simultaneous lip-reading for full comprehension.

CHOCOLATE
Make a few small circles with the thumb of the right *C* hand over the back of the left flat hand.

Memory aid: The *C* hand indicates the word, and the action suggests mixing *chocolate* icing.

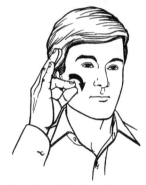

FRUIT
Place the thumb and index fingers of the right *F* hand on the right cheek. Twist forward or backward.

Memory aid: The sign is similar to the one for *apple*.

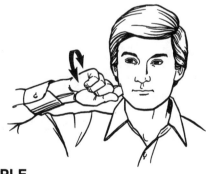

APPLE
Pivot the knuckle of the right closed index finger back and forth on the right cheek two times. *Alternative* (not illustrated): The right *A* thumb is sometimes used.

Memory aid: Can relate to the expression Rosy red cheeks, which reminds one of *apples*.

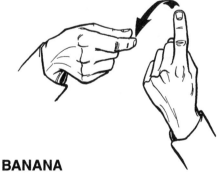

BANANA
Hold the left index finger up with the palm facing in; then make a few grasping downward movements around it with the fingers and thumb of the right hand.

Memory aid: Suggests peeling a *banana*.

GRAPES

Place the fingertips of the right curved hand on the back of the closed left hand. Move the right hand down on the left hand with several small hops.

Memory aid: Can suggest the number of *grapes* in a bunch.

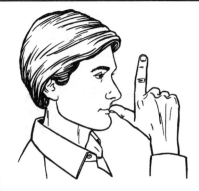

LEMON

Hold the thumb of the right *L* hand at the lips. Assume an expression indicating sourness.

Memory aid: The initial *L* and the facial expression indicate the meaning.

PINEAPPLE

Place the middle finger of the right *P* hand on the cheek and twist forward.

Memory aid: Initialized sign for *apple*.

PEAR

Hold the left *and* hand in front with the palm facing in. Place the right thumb and fingers over the left hand; then slide the right fingers off to the right until they also form an *and* hand.

Memory aid: Suggests the broad-to-narrow shape of a *pear*.

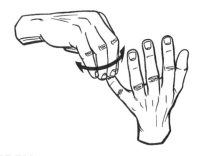

BERRY

Make a twisting motion with the right fingers and thumb while they hold the left little finger.

Memory aid: Suggests the action of picking a *berry*.

STRAWBERRY

Grasp the left index finger with the right thumb and fingers and twist back and forth. *Alternative* (not illustrated): Pull the right closed thumb and index finger forward from the mouth.

Memory aid: The sign suggests the removal of the *strawberry* stem.

BLACKBERRY

Move the right index finger sideways across the right eyebrow. Make a twisting motion with the right fingers and thumb while they hold the left little finger.

Memory aid: The signs for *black* and *berry*.

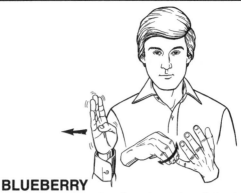

BLUEBERRY

Move the right *B* hand to the right while shaking it from the wrist. Make a twisting motion with the right fingers and thumb while they hold the left little finger.

Memory aid: The signs for *blue* and *berry*.

PEACH

Touch the right cheek with the fingertips of the right open hand; then draw it down a short distance while simultaneously forming the *and* hand.

Memory aid: Suggests feeling a man's beard and being reminded of the fuzz on a *peach*.

WATERMELON

Flick the right middle finger on the back of the palm-down closed left hand a few times.

Memory aid: Suggests testing a *watermelon* for ripeness.

CANDY

Brush the tips of the right *U* fingers downward over the lips and chin a few times.

Memory aid: Suggests tasting something sweet.

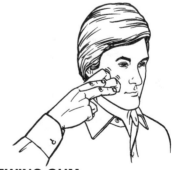

CHEWING GUM

Place the right *V* fingertips on the right cheek and move the right hand up and down. The fingertips of the right *V* remain in place on the right cheek during this movement.

Memory aid: Suggests constant chewing.

NUTS, PEANUTS
Move the right *A* thumb forward from behind the upper teeth.

Memory aid: Suggests the use of teeth to break a *nut's* shell.

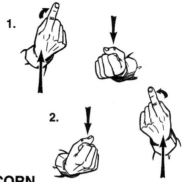

POPCORN
Hold both *S* hands in front with the palms facing up. Flick both index fingers up alternately several times.

Memory aid: Symbolizes the popping of corn kernels.

WATER
Touch the mouth with the index finger of the right *W* hand a few times.

Memory aid: The initial indicates the word, and the movement points to the location for drinking.

JUICE
At shoulder level, make a *J* two times.

Memory aid: The initialized sign suggests the meaning.

COFFEE
Make a counterclockwise circular movement with the right *S* hand over the left *S* hand.

Memory aid: Symbolizes grinding *coffee* beans by hand.

TEA
Rotate the right thumb and index finger over the *O*-shape of the left hand.

Memory aid: Symbolizes stirring *tea* in a cup.

MILK

Squeeze one or both slightly open *S* hands with a downward motion. Do it alternately if two hands are used.

Memory aid: Symbolizes the act of *milking* a cow.

CREAM

Move the little-finger edge of the curved right hand across the left flat palm from fingertips to wrist.

Memory aid: Suggests skimming the *cream* off the top of milk.

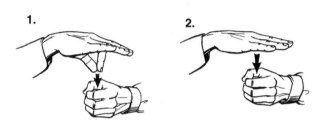

SODA, POP, SODA WATER

Put the thumb and index finger of the right *F* hand into the left *O* hand. Open the right hand and slap the left *O* with it.

Memory aid: Symbolizes inserting a cork into a bottle and forcing it down.

WINE

Make a forward circular movement with the right *W* hand on the right cheek.

Memory aid: Symbolizes the redness of cheeks caused by drinking too much alcohol.

BEER

Draw the index-finger side of the right *B* hand down at the right side of the mouth.

Memory aid: The initial *B* suggests the word, and the downward action suggests drinking.

LIQUOR, WHISKEY

Strike the back of the closed left hand with the extended little finger of the right hand a few times while keeping the right index finger extended.

Memory aid: Suggests the size of the small glass used for a shot of *whiskey*.

SWEET, SUGAR
Brush the right fingertips downward over the lips. Sometimes this is done on the chin.

Memory aid: Suggests licking something *sweet* on the fingers.

SOUR, ACID, BITTER, TART
Place the tip of the right index finger at the corner of the mouth and twist it. It can be twisted back and forth a few times. Assume an appropriate facial expression.

Memory aid: Suggests that the lips resist something *sour* passing through them.

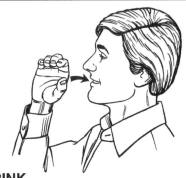

DRINK
Move the right *C* hand in a short arc toward the mouth.

Memory aid: Suggests the action of *drinking* from a glass.

THIRSTY, PARCHED
With the palm facing in, trace a downward line with the right index finger by starting under the chin and ending near the base of the neck.

Memory aid: Suggests the direction liquid flows when swallowed.

DRUNK, INTOXICATE
Move the thumb of the right *A* (or *Y*) hand backward and downward toward the mouth.

Memory aid: Symbolizes pouring alcohol into the mouth.

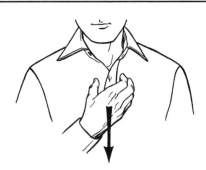

HUNGRY, HUNGER, APPETITE, CRAVE, FAMINE, STARVE
Move the thumb and fingers of the right *C* hand down the center of the chest from just below the throat.

Memory aid: Suggests the direction that food travels to the stomach.

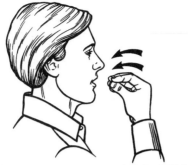

EAT, CONSUME, DINE, FOOD, MEAL

The right *and* hand moves toward the mouth a few times.

Memory aid: Putting *food* into the mouth.

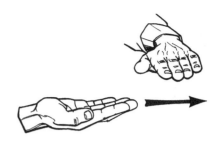

BAKE, OVEN

Slide the right flat (or *B*) hand under the left downturned flat hand.

Memory aid: Symbolizes placing bread in an *oven*.

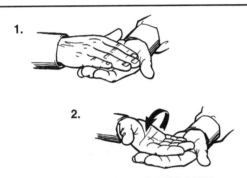

COOK (verb), FRY, PANCAKE

Place first the palm side and then the back of the right flat hand on the upturned palm of the left flat hand.

Memory aid: Suggests the turning over of food in a *frying* pan.

BOIL, COOK (verb)

Hold the horizontal left arm in front, palm down and wiggle the fingers of the right curved hand under the left palm.

Memory aid: Suggests fire under a pan.

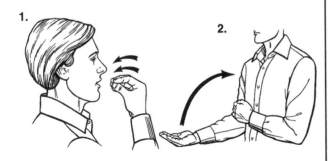

BREAKFAST

Move the fingers of the right closed *and* hand to the mouth a few times. Place the left flat hand into the bend of the right elbow; then raise the right forearm upward. *Note:* This sign is a combination of *eat* and *morning*.

Memory aid: The nighttime fast is broken by eating in the morning.

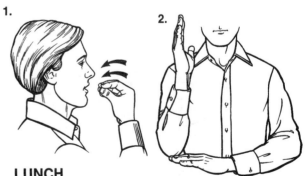

LUNCH

Move the fingers of the right closed *and* hand to the mouth a few times. Place the left flat hand at the outer bend of the right elbow, and raise the right forearm to an upright position with palm facing left.

Memory aid: Suggests the meal eaten when the sun is overhead.

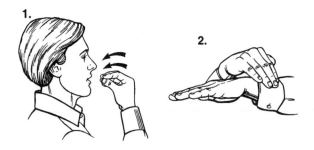

DINNER, SUPPER

Move the fingers of the right closed *and* hand to the mouth a few times and place the curved right hand over the back of the left flat hand. *Note:* This sign is a combination of *eat* and *night*.

Memory aid: Suggests the meal eaten when the sun has set.

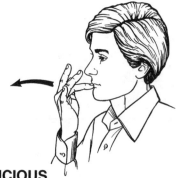

DELICIOUS

Touch the lips with the right middle finger. Sometimes the middle finger and thumb are rubbed together a few times as the hand moves forward. This is in addition to the first part of the sign.

Memory aid: Suggests that something is tasted and approved of.

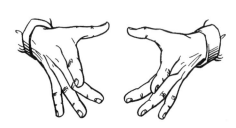

PLATE

Make a circle with the thumbs and fingers of both hands.

Memory aid: The sign symbolizes a *plate* by its shape.

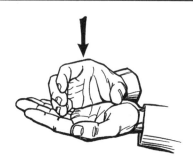

CUP

Put the little-finger edge of the right *C* hand on the left flat palm.

Memory aid: Indicates the size and shape of a *cup*.

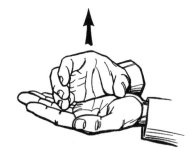

GLASS (drinking)

Place the little-finger edge of the right *C* hand on the left flat palm and raise the right hand a short distance.

Memory aid: Indicates the size and shape of a *glass*.

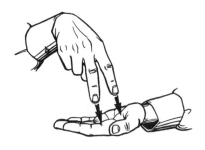

FORK

Move the fingers of the right *V* hand into the left upturned palm a few times.

Memory aid: The fingers symbolize the tines of a *fork*.

KNIFE

Move the right *H* (or index) fingers downward across the left *H* (or index) fingers several times.

Memory aid: The basic sign symbolizes an action similar to sharpening a pencil by hand, while the alternative sign suggests cutting by its action.

SPOON

Lift the right curved *H* fingers upward toward the mouth a few times from the palm of the slightly curved left hand.

Memory aid: Symbolizes use of a *spoon*.

NAPKIN

Wipe the fingertips of the right flat hand across the mouth; then move it forward a few inches.

Move the right hand to the forehead as though gripping the peak of a cap or hat between the fingers and thumb; then move it forward a few inches.

BOY, MALE

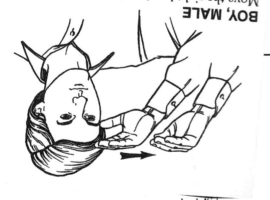

RESTAURANT

With the palm facing left, move the right *R* fingers from the right to the left of the mouth.

Memory aid: The initial *R* at the mouth suggests the meaning.

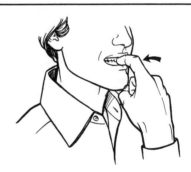

GLASS (substance), CHINA, DISH, PORCELAIN

Touch the teeth with the right index finger.

Memory aid: The teeth are breakable, just like *glass*.

1. **2.**

  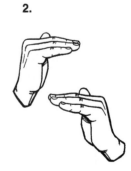

BOX

Point the fingertips of both flat hands up with the palms facing each other in front of the chest. Bend both hands with the right hand positioned over the left. Can also be done with hands in the horizontal position.

Memory aid: The hands outline the shape of a *box*.

FIND THE FOOD SIGNS

There are 13 food signs on this page. How many can you
find? Circle the number next to each one.

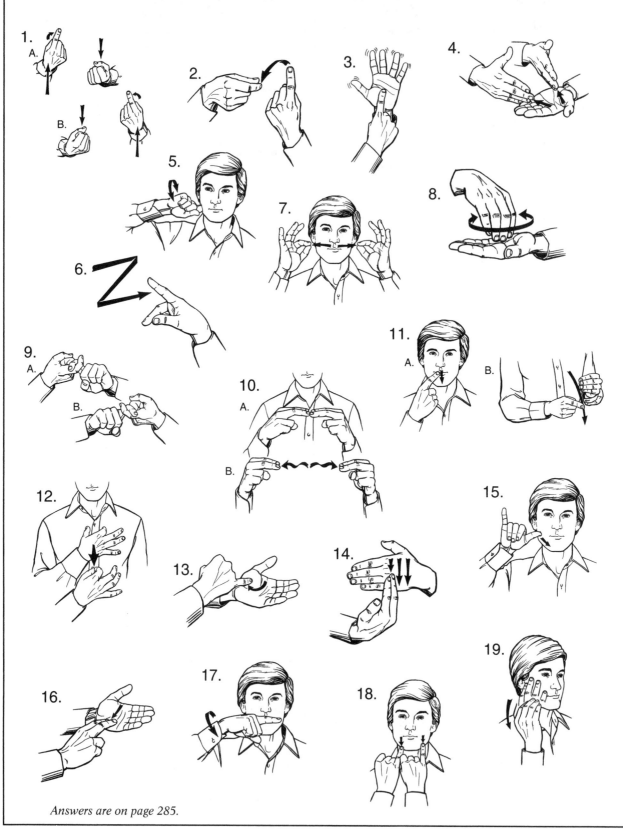

Answers are on page 285.

Chapter

4

Actions
and
Related
Words

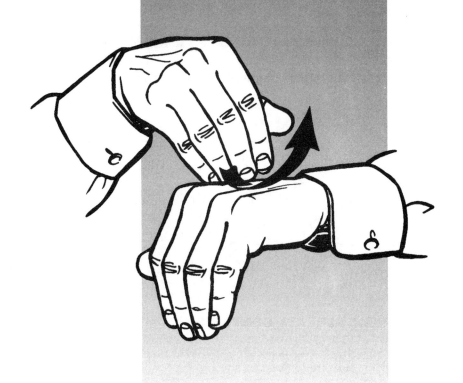

DO, ACTION, CONDUCT, DEED, DONE, PERFORM

Point both *C* hands down to the front and move them simultaneously first to one side and then the other.

Memory aid: Suggests being busy with one thing and another.

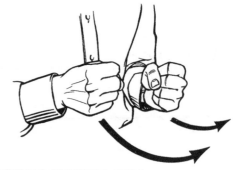

ATTEMPT, EFFORT, TRY

Hold both *S* hands to the front with palms facing; then move them forward with a pushing motion. *Effort* and *try* may be initialized.

Memory aid: Pushing takes *effort.*

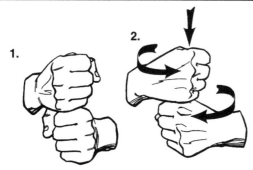

MAKE, FASHION, FIX

Strike the right *S* hand on the top of the left *S* hand and twist the hands slightly inward. Repeat for emphasis as needed.

Memory aid: Suggests the action of unscrewing something.

COMPLETE, CONCLUDE, DONE, END, FINISH

Hold the left flat hand with fingers pointing forward and palm facing right. Move the fingers of the right flat hand outward along the index-finger edge of the left until it drops off the end.

Memory aid: Suggests coming to the *end.*

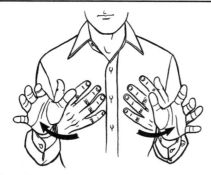

FINISH, ALREADY, COMPLETE

Hold both open hands to the front with palms facing self and fingers pointing up. Shake them quickly outward to the sides a few times.

Memory aid: Symbolizes something being shaken off by the hands.

PUT, MOVE

Point both curved open hands down to the left. Form *and* hands and move them simultaneously up and over to the right.

Memory aid: Suggests picking something up and changing its location.

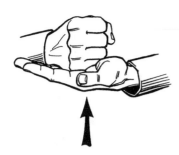

HELP, AID, ASSIST, BOOST

Place the closed right hand on the flat left palm and lift both hands together.

Memory aid: Suggests the giving of a *helping* hand.

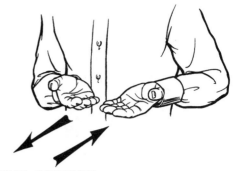

SERVE, SERVICE

Move both upturned flat hands back and forth alternately.

Memory aid: Suggests that something is being offered to another.

SHARE

Move the little-finger edge of the right flat hand back and forth on the left flat hand between the fingers and wrist.

Memory aid: Suggests *sharing* by separating something into two portions.

VOLUNTEER, APPLY, CANDIDATE

Take a piece of clothing near the right shoulder between the thumb and index finger of the right hand, and pull it away from the body a few times. If a jacket or suit is worn, the lapel may be used.

Memory aid: Making oneself prominent.

SUPERVISE, CARE, TAKE CARE OF

Cross the wrist of the right *V* hand over the wrist of the left *V* hand. Move both hands in a counter-clockwise circle.

Memory aid: The fingers can symbolize four eyes watchful over all.

SUPPORT, ENDORSE, UPHOLD

Bring the right *S* hand up under the left *S* hand and move both hands upward together a short distance.

Memory aid: The left hand is *supported* by the right.

ESTABLISH, BASED, FOUNDED

Hold the left closed hand in front with palm facing down. Make a clockwise circle with the right *A* hand above the left hand; then bring the little-finger edge of the right *A* hand down onto the back of the left hand.

Memory aid: The right hand finds a solid resting place on the back of the left hand.

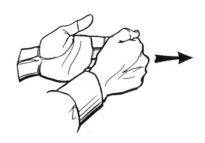

GUIDE, CONDUCT, LEAD

Pull the left flat hand forward with the right hand, which grasps the fingers of the left.

Memory aid: One hand is *leading* the other.

PLAN, ARRANGE, ORDER, PREPARE, READY, SYSTEM

Place both flat hands to the front and off to the left with palms facing and fingers pointing forward. Move both hands simultaneously to the right while moving them up and down slightly.

Memory aid: Suggests placing things in correct sequence.

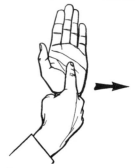

SHOW, DEMONSTRATE, EXPRESS, EXAMPLE, REPRESENT, REVEAL

Hold the left flat hand up, palm facing forward. Place the tip of the right index finger in the left palm and move both hands forward together. All the words may be initialized with the right hand.

Memory aid: The right hand seems to be *showing* the left hand.

CHECK, EXAMINE, INSPECT, INVESTIGATE

Point the right index finger to the right eye, then move it forward and down, and then forward across the upturned left palm until it goes beyond the fingers.

Memory aid: The right index finger is *checking* the left hand.

ALIGN, LINE UP

Place both open hands in front of chest with the left palm facing right and the right palm facing left. Put one hand in front of the other and touch the little finger and thumb. Both hands may pivot back and forth slightly in opposite directions.

Memory aid: The fingers can suggest people *lined up*.

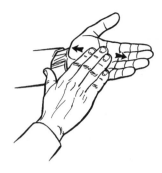

RUB
Place the fingertips of the right flat downturned hand in the palm of the upturned left hand and *rub* back and forth.

Memory aid: The natural movement of *rubbing*.

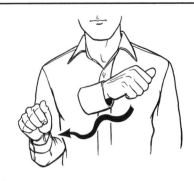

DUST
The *A* hand, facing left with palm down, sweeps across the front of the body in a wavy motion.

Memory aid: Suggests the movement of *dusting* with a cloth.

LEAVE, DEPART, RETIRE, WITHDRAW
Bring both flat hands up from the right and close to *A* hands.

Memory aid: The hands *leave* one position for another.

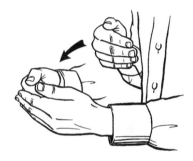

ARRIVE, GET TO, REACH
Move the back of the right curved hand forward into the palm of the left curved hand.

Memory aid: Destination is *reached*.

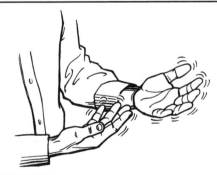

WAIT, PENDING
With palms facing up, hold both curved open hands up to the left with the right hand behind the left. Wiggle all the fingers.

Memory aid: The wiggling fingers suggest impatience.

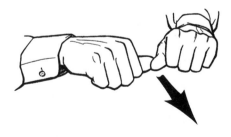

CONTINUE, ENDURE, LASTING, PERMANENT, PERSEVERE
Place the tip of the right *A* thumb behind the left *A* thumb and move both hands forward together. The palms face down.

Memory aid: Suggests a determination to *continue* forward.

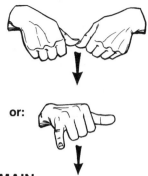

or: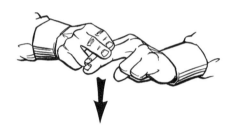

STAY, REMAIN

Place the tip of the right *A* thumb on top of the left *A* thumb and move both hands downward together. *Alternative:* Move either one (or both) *Y* hands firmly downward.

Memory aid: The movement suggests remaining in one spot.

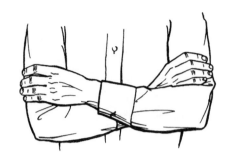

REST, RELAX, UNWIND

Fold the arms in a natural position. Sometimes the *R* hands are used.

Memory aid: The sign suggests a natural position of *rest.*

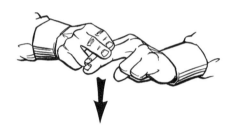

SIT, BE SEATED, SEAT

Place the palm side of the right *H* fingers on the back of the left *H* fingers; then move both hands down slightly.

Memory aid: Symbolizes a person *sitting* on a chair.

STAND

Place the fingers of the right *V* hand on the left upturned palm.

Memory aid: The two fingers of the *V* hand represent a person's legs.

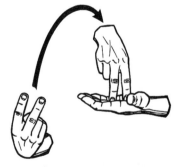

STAND UP, ARISE, GET UP, RISE

Begin with the right *V* fingers pointing up and the palm facing in. Make an arc with the *V* fingers until they rest in an upright position on the left upturned palm.

Memory aid: The *V* fingers represent a person's legs.

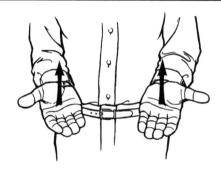

RISE, ARISE, GET UP

Place both flat hands to the front with palms up, and move them upward once or twice.

Memory aid: Indicates the request for an audience to stand.

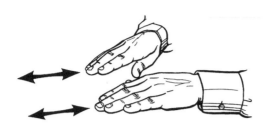

WALK, STEP

Hold both flat hands in front with palms down; then imitate walking by moving each hand forward alternately.

Memory aid: Symbolizes the movement of feet.

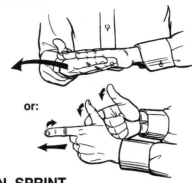

RUN, SPRINT

Place both flat hands palm to palm with left hand on top. Slide the right hand quickly forward. *Alternative:* Point *L* hands forward and hook right index around left thumb. Wiggle thumbs and index fingers as both hands move forward quickly.

Memory aid: The movement suggests the meaning.

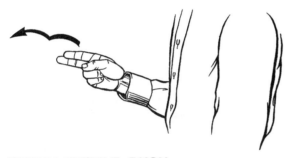

HURRY, HUSTLE, RUSH

Move one or both *H* hands quickly forward in short arcs. *Note:* If two hands are used, they can be quickly raised up and down alternately.

Memory aid: Suggests someone walking rapidly.

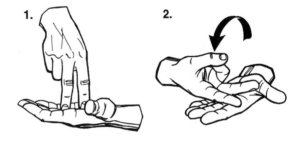

FALL

Stand the right *V* fingers in the left flat palm. Flip them over so that the backs of the *V* fingers rest on the left palm.

Memory aid: Symbolizes a person *falling* flat on the back.

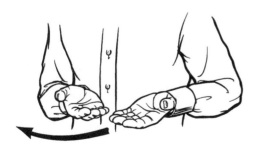

BRING, FETCH

Hold both open hands to the front with palms facing up and one hand slightly in front of the other. Move both hands toward self, another, or to the right or left, depending on who is indicated.

Memory aid: Symbolizes something being *brought* closer.

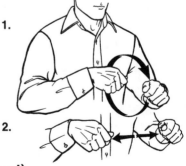

TIE (a knot)

Place both thumb tips in the crook of their respective bent index fingers, with the other fingers closed. Move the hands alternately in small forward circles; then pull the hands apart to the sides.

Memory aid: Symbolizes the movements of tying a *knot*.

ACCEPT

Hold both open hands to the front of the body. Move them toward the chest while simultaneously forming *and* hands, which then come to rest on the chest.

Memory aid: Suggests bringing something toward oneself.

REJECT

Brush the little-finger edge of the right flat hand over and beyond the hand and fingers of the left flat hand, which is palm up.

Memory aid: Suggests pushing something aside.

GIVE, DISTRIBUTE

Hold both *and* hands to the front with palms facing down. Move them forward simultaneously while forming flat hands with fingers pointing forward and palms facing up.

Memory aid: Suggests the act of *giving*.

KEEP

Cross the wrist of the right *V* hand over the wrist of the left *V* hand.

Memory aid: The fingers can symbolize four watchful eyes.

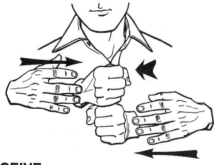

RECEIVE

Bring both open hands together while simultaneously forming *S* hands and place the right hand on top of the left hand; then bring both hands toward the body.

Memory aid: Suggests *receiving* something and drawing it to oneself.

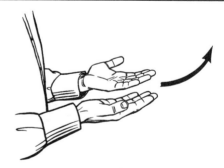

OFFER, PRESENT, PROPOSE, SUGGEST

Move both flat hands in an upward-forward movement with palms facing up.

Memory aid: The gesture represents giving a gift to someone.

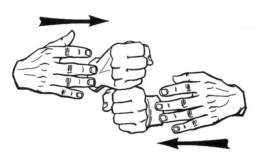

GET, ACQUIRE, OBTAIN

Bring both open hands together while simultaneously forming *S* hands and place the right on top of the left.

Memory aid: Suggests taking hold of something.

HOLD

Place both *S* hands in front of the body, palms in, right hand over left hand, and move them a short distance toward the body.

Memory aid: Suggests *holding* an object and pulling it to oneself.

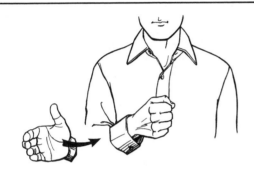

TAKE

Place the right open hand forward and draw it into the chest while simultaneously forming a closed hand.

Memory aid: Symbolizes reaching out and *taking* something.

USE, USEFUL, UTILIZE

With the palm facing forward, make a clockwise circle with the right *U* hand.

Memory aid: The letter *U* is put to work.

INCLUDE, INVOLVE

Hold the left *C* hand to the front with palm facing right. Make a sweeping circular movement from right to left (or left to right) with the right open hand; then form the *and* position and place it in the left *C* hand.

Memory aid: The movement suggests a gathering together into one.

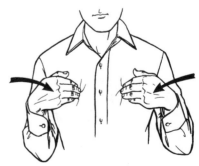

HAVE, HAS, HAD, OWN, POSSESS

Place the fingertips of both bent hands on the chest.

Memory aid: Symbolizes pointing out personal *ownership*.

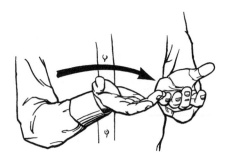

CARRY, TRANSPORT
Hold both slightly curved hands to the front with palms facing up. Move them both simultaneously in an arc from right to left, or vice versa.

Memory aid: Symbolizes *carrying* something from one side of the body to the other.

SEND
Touch the back of the left bent hand with the fingertips of the right bent hand; then swing the right hand forward.

Memory aid: A common gesture used when *sending* someone on his way.

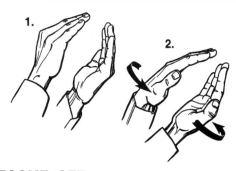

BECOME, GET
Place the curved hands in front with the right palm facing forward and the left palm facing self; then reverse positions.

Memory aid: Suggests a change around.

ABANDON, DISCARD, FORSAKE, LEAVE, NEGLECT
With the palms facing each other, point both flat hands to the left (or to the right); then pivot both hands downward from the wrists.

Memory aid: Suggests putting something to the side.

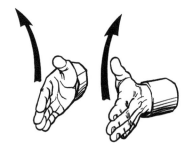

ALLOW, GRANT, LET, PERMIT
Hold both flat hands forward with palms facing. Swing them upward simultaneously so that the fingertips point slightly outward. The *L* hands may be used for *let* and the *P* hands for *permit*.

Memory aid: The slight widening of the hands suggests flexibility.

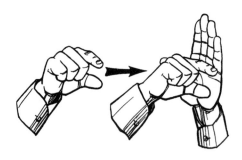

FORBID, BAN, PROHIBIT
Point the fingers of the left flat hand upward with palm facing right. Slap the right *G* hand into the left palm.

Memory aid: Suggests that a person may come up against the strong hand of the law. Note the similarity to the sign for *law*.

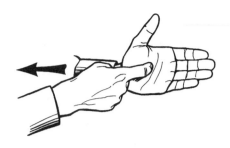

DEMAND, INSIST, REQUIRE

Thrust the bent right index finger into the left flat palm, which is facing right; then pull both hands toward the body.

Memory aid: Can symbolize putting a hook into something and drawing it to oneself with determination.

FORCE, COMPEL, MAKE

Place the right C hand in front of the right shoulder. The palm can face either forward or to the left. Move the right hand sharply forward and down until the forearm is horizontal.

Memory aid: Suggests trying to hold someone down.

PREVENT, BLOCK, HINDER, OBSTRUCT

Bring the little-finger edge of the right flat down-turned hand against the index finger of the left flat vertical hand. This may be repeated while both hands move forward.

Memory aid: The left hand is *blocking* the right.

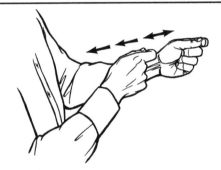

PERSUADE, COAX, PROD, URGE

Place both closed hands to the front, palms facing, and both thumb tips in the crook of the respective bent index fingers. Position the left hand slightly in front of the right; move both hands firmly toward the body in short back-and-forth stages.

Memory aid: Can symbolize the pulling action required to lead an unwilling mule.

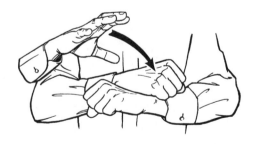

CATCH, CAPTURE, SEIZE, GRAB, GRASP

The curved open hand moves quickly into an *S* hand as it rests on the back of the closed left hand.

Memory aid: The act of *catching* an object.

AVOID, EVADE, SHUN

Place both *A* hands to the front with palms facing and the right hand slightly behind the left. Move the right hand backward away from the left with a wavy motion.

Memory aid: The sign suggests that the right hand is attempting to *avoid* the left.

DENY

Move the thumb tips of both *A* hands forward alternately from under the chin.

Memory aid: A stronger form of *not*.

DENY (self)

Point the thumbs of both *A* hands downward in front of the chest, then move them down a short distance.

Memory aid: Suggests keeping one's own desires under control.

CANCEL, ANNUL, CORRECT, CRITICIZE

Trace an *X* on the left palm with the right index finger.

Memory aid: Suggests the idea of crossing something out.

STRAY, DEFLECT, DEVIATE, WANDER

Point both index fingers forward and place them side by side with palms down. Slide the right index finger forward and off to the right.

Memory aid: Suggests the idea of a train leaving the track.

DISMISS, LAY OFF

Slide the fingers of the right flat hand quickly over and off the lower edge of the left flat hand.

Memory aid: The right hand leaves the left hand.

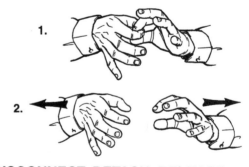

DISCONNECT, DETACH, RELEASE

Interlock the index fingers and thumbs of both hands with all other fingers extended. Pull them apart.

Memory aid: Suggests the links of a chain breaking.

DELAY, POSTPONE, PROCRASTINATE, PUT OFF

Place both *F* hands to the front with palms facing and fingers pointing forward. Make a few short forward arcs.

Memory aid: Suggests moving an appointment further into the future.

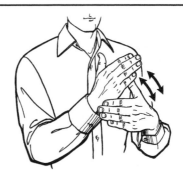

DISTURB, BOTHER, INTERFERE, MEDDLE

Strike the little-finger edge of the right flat hand into the opening between the left thumb and index finger a few times.

Memory aid: The right hand jars the left.

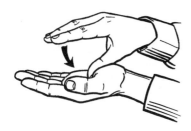

DEFLATE, FLAT TIRE

Put the thumb of the right *C* hand either on the palm or back of the left hand. Bring the right fingers down upon the right thumb.

Memory aid: Symbolizes the air going out of a tire.

MATCH, FIT, COMBINE

Hold both curved open hands to the front with palms facing self. Move the hands together until the fingers interlock.

Memory aid: Suggests two gears coming together.

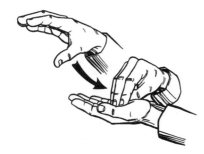

COPY, DUPLICATE, IMITATE

Move the right open hand into the left flat palm while simultaneously closing into the *and* hand shape.

Memory aid: The right hand seems to be impressing its message onto the left hand.

DEVELOP

Place the *D* hand against the left flat palm, which faces right. Slide the *D* hand up to the left fingertips.

Memory aid: The initialized sign indicates the word.

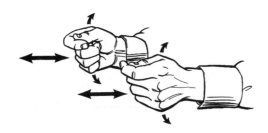

CONTROL, DIRECT, GOVERN, MANAGE, OPERATE, REGULATE, REIGN, RULE

Close both hands with the thumb tips in the crook of the index fingers. Hold both hands parallel; then move them back and forth with wrists slightly pivoting.

Memory aid: Suggests holding horse reins.

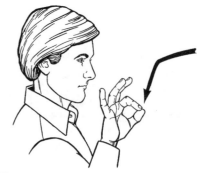

APPOINT

Extend the right open hand and close the index finger and thumb. Move the right hand back, then down while maintaining the same hand shape.

Memory aid: Selecting something and putting it in its place.

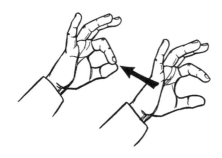

CHOOSE, PICK, SELECT

Use the right thumb and index finger to make a picking motion from the front as the hand is drawn back toward self. The remaining right fingers are extended.

Memory aid: An item is *selected* with great care.

EXCUSE, EXEMPT

Stroke the lower part of the left flat hand with the right fingertips several times.

Memory aid: Suggests a wiping movement and the expression A clean slate.

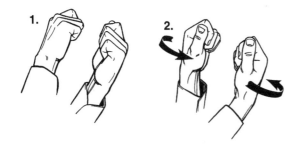

CHANGE, ADJUST, ADAPT, ALTER

Place the thumb tips of both closed hands into the crook of the bent index fingers. Hold the palms facing with the left palm facing the chest and the right palm facing out; then reverse positions so that the right palm faces in. *A* hands can be used.

Memory aid: Suggests a *change* around.

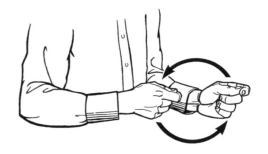

EXCHANGE, REPLACE, SUBSTITUTE, TRADE, SWITCH

Hold the right modified *A* hand a few inches behind the left modified *A* hand. Move both hands in a backward circle, right hand under left hand and left hand over right hand, until both hands have exchanged places.

Memory aid: One thing *exchanges* place with another.

DEPEND, RELY

Cross the right index finger over the top of the left index finger with palms facing down, then move both hands down a short distance.

Memory aid: Suggests that the right finger can *rely* upon the support of the left.

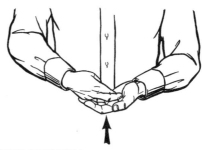

REHABILITATION

Hold the left flat hand, palm up, to the front. Place the right *R* hand on top of the left hand and lift both hands together.

Memory aid: Initialized sign for *help.*

LOOK, LOOK AT, LOOK AT ME, LOOK BACK, LOOK DOWN, GAZE, OBSERVE, WATCH

Point the fingers of the right *V* hand at the eyes and then in the particular direction desired.

Memory aid: The two fingers represent the two eyes.

SEARCH, EXAMINE, QUEST, RESEARCH, SEEK

Make a few circular motions across the face from right to left with the right *C* hand.

Memory aid: Can symbolize the use of binoculars to enhance vision.

CALL, SUMMON

Place fingers of right slightly curved hand on the back of the left flat hand. Pull right hand up toward the body while forming an *A* hand.

Memory aid: The sign indicates that deaf persons may need to be touched to get their attention.

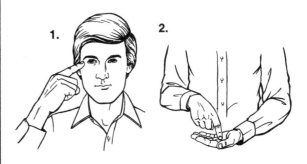

NOTICE, NOTE, OBSERVE

Point toward the right eye with the right index finger; then place it in the palm of the left flat hand.

Memory aid: Suggests directing the attention to a particular point.

ADVERTISE, COMMERCIAL, PUBLICIZE

Place the left *S* hand in front of the mouth area with the palm facing right and the right *S* hand in front of the left. Move the right *S* hand forward and backward a few times.

Memory aid: Suggests the expression Blowing one's horn, which is used to boast of personal accomplishment.

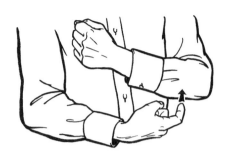

TEMPT, ENTICE

Tap close to the left elbow with the right curved index finger.

Memory aid: Suggests a secretive and persistent method of attracting attention.

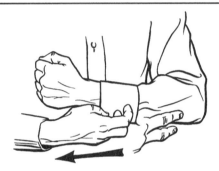

STEAL, EMBEZZLE

Slide the curved fingers of the right *V* hand along the left forearm from the elbow to wrist. Curve the right *V* fingers even more during the action.

Memory aid: Suggests trying to remove something secretly from under the arm by pulling it with the fingers.

KILL, MURDER, SLAY

Place the slightly curved left hand to the front with palm facing down. Move the right index finger under the left hand while simultaneously giving it a clockwise twist.

Memory aid: Suggests stabbing someone with a knife.

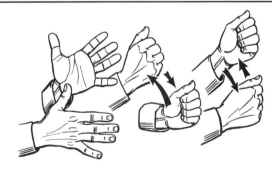

DESTROY, ABOLISH, DAMAGE, DEMOLISH

Put both open hands to front with palms facing and right hand lower than the left. Reverse hands while forming *A* hands; then reverse them again to original position while maintaining *A* hands.

Memory aid: Suggests pulling something up and down with *destructive* force.

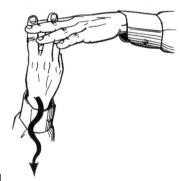

DROWN

Move the right *V* fingers down from between the left index and middle finger with a slight wavy movement.

Memory aid: The *V* fingers represent a person's legs, and the left hand symbolizes the water surface.

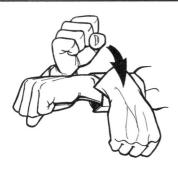

CONQUER, BEAT, DEFEAT, OVERCOME, SUBDUE

Move the right *S* hand forward and down across the wrist of the left *S* hand.

Memory aid: The right hand dominates the left.

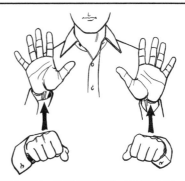

SURRENDER, FORFEIT, GIVE UP, SUBMIT, YIELD

Hold both *A* hands to the front with palms facing down. Move both hands upward simultaneously while forming open hands with the palms facing forward.

Memory aid: Symbolizes raising hands in *surrender.*

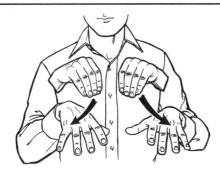

SCATTER, SPREAD

Hold both *and* hands together in front of the body, move them forward and to the sides as they open.

Memory aid: The movement is similar to *scattering* seed.

BURY, CEMETERY, GRAVE

Place both downturned curved hands forward and move them in a backward arc toward the body. *Note:* Sometimes the *A* hands are used in the starting position before changing to curved hands.

Memory aid: Symbolizes a mound of earth over a *grave.*

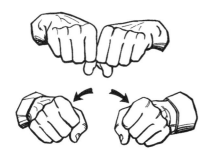

BREAK, FRACTURE, SNAP

Hold the thumb and index-finger sides of both *S* hands together; then twist them both sharply outward and apart.

Memory aid: Can symbolize *breaking* a stick.

STUCK, CHOKE, TRAPPED

Place the fingertips of the right *V* hand on the neck.

Memory aid: The *V* shape around the neck suggests constriction.

ESCAPE, FLEE, RUN OFF

Point the right index finger forward and place it under the left flat palm. Move the right index finger quickly forward and to the right.

Memory aid: Symbolizes someone breaking away from cover.

DEFEND, GUARD, PROTECT

With palms facing down, place the little-finger edge of the left *S* hand on the thumb side of the right *S* hand (or vice versa) and move both hands forward.

Memory aid: Suggests a fending-off action.

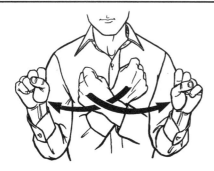

RESCUE, DELIVER, FREE, REDEEM, INDEPENDENT, LIBERTY

Cross the closed hands on the chest with palms facing in; then rotate them to the sides with palms facing forward. Most signers prefer to initialize each word.

Memory aid: Suggests breaking a rope tied around the wrists.

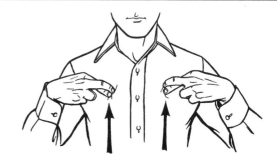

REVIVE

Bring the *R* hands straight up the chest.

Memory aid: The increasing height of the fingers suggest something getting better.

HIDE

Touch the lips with the right *A* thumb; then move the right *A* hand forward under the left curved hand, which has its palm facing down.

Memory aid: The right hand *hides* under the left.

COVER

Slide the curved right hand over the back of the curved left hand from fingertips to wrist.

Memory aid: Shows one hand *covering* the other.

TURN

Hold the left index finger upward with palm facing in. Move the right index finger around the left index finger in counterclockwise circles while simultaneously turning the left index finger slowly around in the same direction.

Memory aid: Can symbolize two gears *turning* at different speeds.

CAREFUL

Cross the wrist of the right *V* hand over the wrist of the left *V* hand. Strike the right wrist on the left wrist a few times.

Memory aid: The fingers can symbolize four watchful eyes.

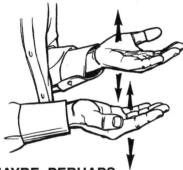

MAY, MAYBE, PERHAPS, POSSIBLY, PROBABLY

Hold both flat hands to the front and move them up and down alternately.

Memory aid: Symbolizes the weighing of one thing against another.

MUST, HAVE TO, IMPERATIVE, NEED, NECESSARY, OUGHT TO, SHOULD, VITAL

Move the right bent index finger firmly downward a few times.

Memory aid: Suggests the idea of standing with determination on a chosen position.

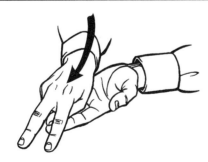

SLIDE, SLIP

Slide the right downturned *V* fingers across the left flat palm.

Memory aid: Symbolizes a person's feet *sliding*.

BACK AND FORTH

Move the right *A* hand *back* and *forth* a few times.

Memory aid: The movement indicates the meaning.

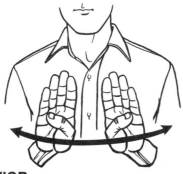

BEHAVIOR

Hold both *B* hands, side by side with palms forward, in front of the body and swing them simultaneously back and forth.

Memory aid: Displaying one's actions for all to see.

HAPPEN, EVENT, OCCUR

Point both index fingers up with palms facing. Pivot both hands forward from the wrists so that the palms face forward.

Memory aid: Two pointing hands suggest the importance of noticing something.

RESTLESS

Place the back of the right *V* fingers in the left palm and pivot back and forth from the wrist.

Memory aid: Symbolizes a person tossing and turning in bed.

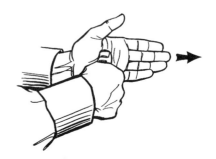

IMPRESS, EMPHASIZE, STRESS

Press the right thumb into the palm of the left flat hand. Sometimes the right hand is rotated forward slightly while the thumb is being pressed into the left palm, and sometimes both hands are moved forward slightly.

Memory aid: An *impression* is made in the left palm.

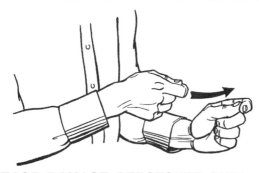

TEASE, DAMAGE, PERSECUTE, RUIN, SPOIL, TORMENT

Hold both closed hands to the front with both thumb tips in the crooks of their respective index fingers. Move the knuckles of the right hand forward across the top of the left hand.

Memory aid: The use of the knuckles suggests repeated harassment.

WARN, CAUTION

Pat the back of the left flat hand with the right flat hand a few times.

Memory aid: Suggests slapping the hand as a disciplinary measure.

PUSH

Place both open hands to the front with palms facing forward. Push both hands forward with simulated effort.

Memory aid: The act of *pushing.*

HIT

Strike the knuckles of the right closed hand against the left upright index finger.

Memory aid: Symbolizes aggressive contact.

STRIKE, REBELLION, REVOLT

Hold up the right *S* hand at the right temple with palm facing in. Twist it sharply so that the palm faces out.

Memory aid: Suggests a mind that is turning away and *striking* out with new thoughts.

BLAME, ACCUSE, FAULT, MY FAULT, YOUR FAULT

Strike the back of the closed left hand with the little-finger edge of the right *A* hand. Point the right knuckles and thumb to self or another depending on who is being referred to.

Memory aid: Suggests that someone needs to have the back of the hand slapped.

PUNISH

Strike the right index finger along the underside of the left forearm to the elbow.

Memory aid: Can suggest pain at a sensitive part of the body.

SPANK

Hold up the left *A* hand at shoulder level with palm facing right. Move the right flat hand sharply from right to left under the left hand a few times.

Memory aid: Suggests holding someone at the neck and *spanking* the person.

MEET, ENCOUNTER
Bring both extended index finger hands together from the sides with palms facing.

Memory aid: Suggests two persons *meeting*.

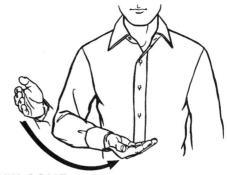

WELCOME
Position the right flat hand forward and to the right with the palm facing left. Sweep the hand in toward the body until the palm is facing in front of the abdomen.

Memory aid: A common gesture of politeness and acceptance.

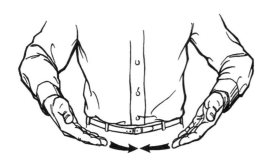

INTRODUCE
Move both flat hands in from the sides with palms up until the fingertips almost touch.

Memory aid: Suggests bringing two people together.

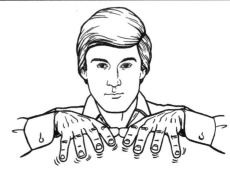

FLIRT, PHILANDERER
With the palms facing down, touch the thumbs of both open hands, leaving the fingers pointing forward. Wiggle the fingers.

Memory aid: Suggests the *flirtatious* batting of the eyelashes.

KISS
Place the fingers of the right hand on the lips and then on the cheek.

Memory aid: Suggests two common locations for *kissing*.

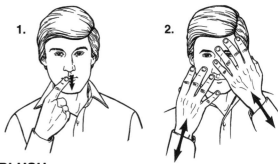

BLUSH
Stroke the right index finger down across the lips. Raise both open hands in front of the face with palms facing in.

Memory aid: Suggests red coming over the face in embarrassment.

SMILE, GRIN
Move the fingers (or just the index fingers) upward and backward across the cheeks from the corners of the mouth. Assume an appropriate facial expression.

Memory aid: The upturned mouth suggests the meaning.

LAUGH, CHUCKLE, GIGGLE
Starting near the corners of the mouth, move both index fingers upward over the cheeks a few times. Assume an appropriate facial expression.

Memory aid: Suggests the upturned mouth.

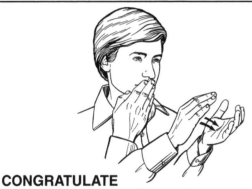

CONGRATULATE
Touch the lips with the fingers of the right flat hand and then clap the hands as much as desired.

Memory aid: A combination of *good* and *praise*.

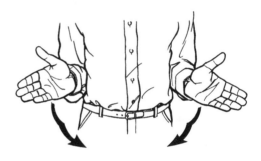

ENCOURAGE, MOTIVATE
Move both flat (or open) hands forward with several short dipping movements. The fingertips of both hands point out to the sides.

Memory aid: Suggests the natural action of *encouraging* someone by pushing the person forward.

CLAP, APPLAUD, OVATION, PRAISE
Clap the hands as many times as desired.

Memory aid: The action represents the word.

CELEBRATE, CHEER, TRIUMPH, CELEBRATION, VICTORY
Hold up one or both closed hands with the thumb tips and index fingertips touching. Make small circular movements. The *V* hands can be used for *victory*.

Memory aid: Symbolizes the waving of small flags.

NAME THE SIGN

To reinforce the vocabulary you have already learned, identify the following signs from this chapter by writing the names underneath the signs.

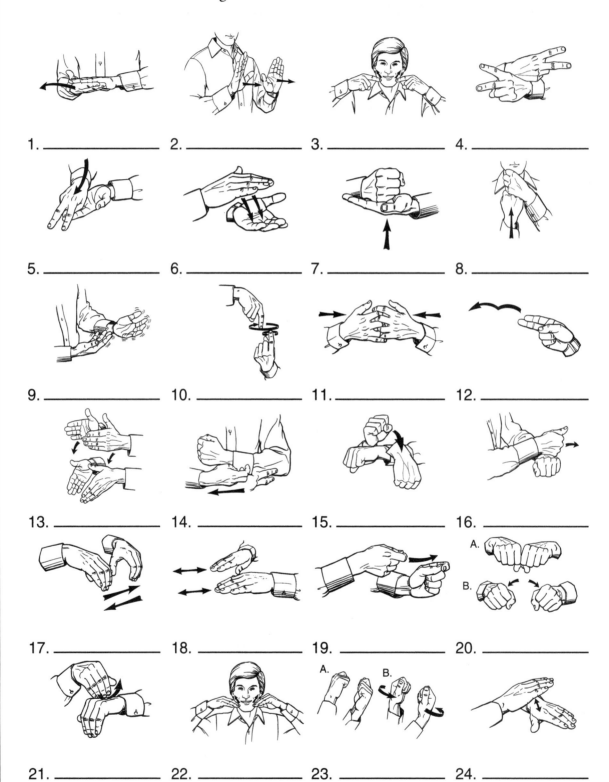

1. _____ 2. _____ 3. _____ 4. _____

5. _____ 6. _____ 7. _____ 8. _____

9. _____ 10. _____ 11. _____ 12. _____

13. _____ 14. _____ 15. _____ 16. _____

17. _____ 18. _____ 19. _____ 20. _____

21. _____ 22. _____ 23. _____ 24. _____

Answers are on page 285.

Chapter 5

Sports, Recreation, and Hobbies

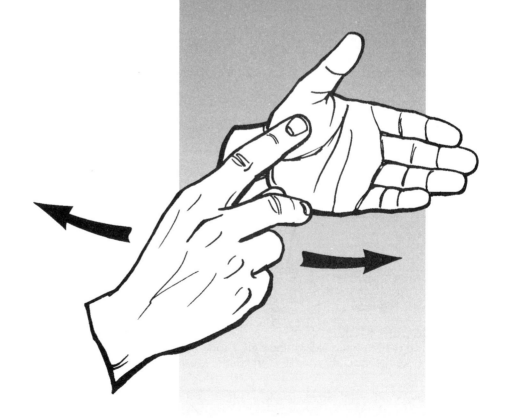

BASEBALL, BAT, SOFTBALL
Place the right *S* hand above the left *S* hand and swing them forward together from the right of the body to the center of the body.

Memory aid: The position and action of a *baseball* batter.

BASKETBALL
Hold both curved open hands at head level and move them forward and upward.

Memory aid: The natural position and action for throwing a *basketball*.

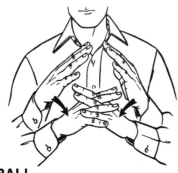

FOOTBALL
Interlock the fingers of both hands vigorously a few times.

Memory aid: Suggests the strong physical contact made in *football*.

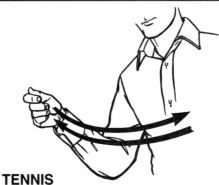

TENNIS
Extend the right arm out to the right side with the hand closed. Move it forward across to the left and back to the right again.

Memory aid: The position and action of a *tennis* player.

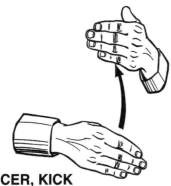

SOCCER, KICK
Sweep the flat index side of the right hand upward to strike the little-finger edge of the flat or closed left hand.

Memory aid: Symbolizes *kicking* a ball.

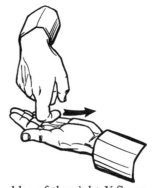

HOCKEY
Brush the knuckles of the right *X* finger across the left flat palm a few times.

Memory aid: Suggests the shape and action of a *hockey* stick.

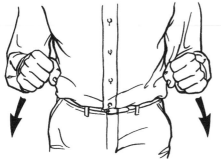

SKIING
Hold both S hands to the front and sides.
Push down and backward with both hands
simultaneously.

Memory aid: The position for holding and using
ski poles.

GOLF
Point the right A hand down at waist level with
the thumb side of the left A hand touching the
little-finger side of the right hand. Swing both
hands from right to left.

Memory aid: The position and action of a *golf*
player.

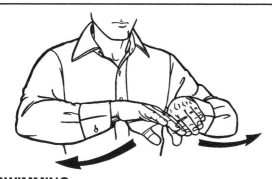

SWIMMING
Place the slightly curved hands to the front with
the backs of the hands partially facing each other
and the fingers pointing forward. Move the hands
simultaneously forward and to the sides.

Memory aid: The action simulates the
breaststroke.

VOLLEYBALL
Hold both flat hands at head level with palms facing forward. Move them forward and upward.

Memory aid: The position and action for playing
volleyball.

FISHING
Place both thumb tips in the crooks of their
respective index fingers with the other fingers
closed. Position the left hand above the right as if
holding a *fishing* rod. Pivot the hands quickly up
and backward from the wrists.

Memory aid: The action performed when a *fish*
is caught.

BOXING, FIGHTING
Place the right S hand close to the body and the
left S hand a short distance from the body.
Reverse positions a few times.

Memory aid: The position and action for *boxing.*

ROLLER SKATING

Hold both curved *V* fingers to the front with palms facing up. Move the hands alternately forward and backward.

Memory aid: The *V* fingers symbolize the front two wheels of a *roller skate.*

ICE SKATING

Hold both *X* hands to the front with palms facing up. Move the hands alternately forward and backward.

Memory aid: The *X* fingers symbolize the metal runner on an *ice-skating* boot.

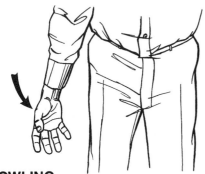

BOWLING

Swing the right curved hand forward from behind the body to the front.

Memory aid: The action for *bowling.*

ARCHERY

Stretch the left *S* hand out sideways; then bring the right curved *V* fingers backward from behind the left hand to a closed-hand position just under the chin.

Memory aid: Symbolizes an arrow being pulled back in a bow.

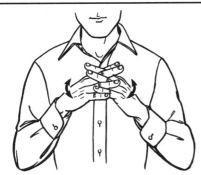

WRESTLING, WRESTLER

Interlock the fingers of both hands and move them back and forth in front of the chest. To sign *wrestler,* add *person (personalizing word ending).*

Memory aid: Symbolizes the way *wrestlers* grip each other.

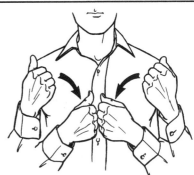

GAME, CHALLENGE

Hold both *A* hands in front and to the sides of the chest with palms facing self. Bring the hands firmly together until the knuckles touch.

Memory aid: Suggests that the hands are competing with each other.

RACE, COMPETE, COMPETITION, CONTEST, RIVALRY

Hold both *A* hands to the front with palms facing. Move them quickly back and forth alternately.

Memory aid: The hands can symbolize two runners *competing.*

HORSEBACK RIDING

Point the fingers of the left *B* hand to the front with palm facing right. Straddle the inverted right *V* fingers over the left hand. Move the hands with a forward-up-down movement.

Memory aid: The right hand rides the left hand.

TICKET

Squeeze the little-finger edge of the left palm between the right curved *V* fingers.

Memory aid: The sign symbolizes the punching of a *ticket* by an official.

OLYMPICS

Form *F* hands and interlock the thumbs and index fingers a few times as the hands move to the right.

Memory aid: Represents the five Olympic rings.

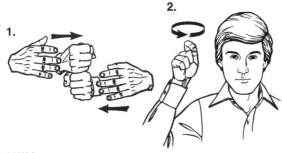

WIN

Bring both open hands together while simultaneously forming *S* hands, and place the right hand on top of the left. Hold up either one or both closed hands with the thumb tip and index fingertip touching. Make small circular movements.

Memory aid: This sign is a combination of *get* and *celebration.*

PLAY, RECREATION, ROMP

Hold both *Y* hands in front of the chest and pivot them from the wrists a few times.

Memory aid: The flexibility of the movement suggests that the hands are free to *play.*

PARTY

Hold both *P* hands in front and swing them back and forth from left to right.

Memory aid: The initial indicates the word, and the movement indicates lively action.

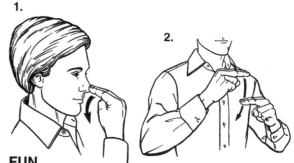

FUN

Brush the tip of the nose with the fingers of the right *U* hand. Move the right *U* hand down and brush the left and right *U* fingers up and down against each other a few times.

Memory aid: Suggests that people's noses wrinkle when they laugh.

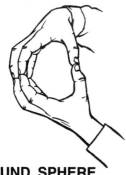

BALL, ROUND, SPHERE

Curve both hands with fingertips touching as if holding a ball. Let the thumbs and index fingers face the observer.

Memory aid: The round shape identifies a *ball*.

THROW, TOSS

Place the right *A* hand beside the right side of the head. Move the right hand quickly forward while simultaneously opening it.

Memory aid: A common motion for *throwing*.

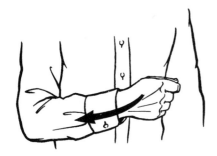

PING-PONG, TABLE TENNIS

Place the right thumb tip in the crook of the right index finger with the other fingers closed. Move the hand back and forth, with most of the movement from the wrist.

Memory aid: The action of playing with a *Ping-Pong* paddle.

PLAYING CARDS

Place both thumb tips in the crooks of their respective index fingers with the other fingers closed. Position the right hand slightly above the left; then move it forward a few times while simultaneously changing it to a 3 hand with palm facing up.

Memory aid: The action of dealing *cards*.

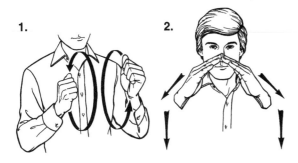

THEATER

Rotate both *A* hands alternately toward the body with the palms facing each other. Form the point of a triangle at head level with both flat hands; then move them apart and straight down simultaneously with the fingers pointing up.

Memory aid: This sign is a combination of the signs for *drama* and *house*.

STAGE

Move the right *S* hand across the back of the left downturned flat hand from wrist to fingertips.

Memory aid: The initial indicates the word, and the action suggests someone moving across a *stage*.

DRAMA, ACT, PERFORM, PLAY, SHOW

Rotate both *A* hands inward toward the body with the palms facing each other.

Memory aid: The initialed hands suggest the word *act,* and the movement suggests the action that accompanies *drama*.

MOVIE, CINEMA, FILM

Place both flat open hands palm to palm with the left palm facing somewhat forward. Slide the right hand back and forth over the left hand a few times. Most of the movement is from the right wrist.

Memory aid: Symbolizes the rapidly moving *film* frames.

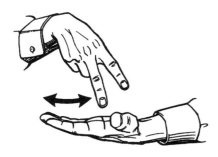

DANCE, BALL

Point the left flat upturned hand to the right; then swing the downturned fingers of the right *V* hand from side to side over the left palm.

Memory aid: The fingers of the *V* hand represent the *dancing* legs of a person.

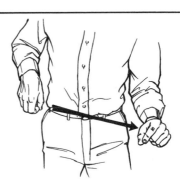

POOL, BILLIARDS, SNOOKER

Hold the left *X* hand forward at waist level with palm facing down and the right *O* hand close to the right side of the waist with the palm facing self. Move the right hand back and forth toward the left hand.

Memory aid: Symbolizes the use of a *billiards* cue.

CAMP

Form the point of a triangle with the fingers of both *V* hands, then separate them by moving them down and to the sides a short distance. Repeat the sign a few times while moving the hands to the right.

Memory aid: Symbolizes the shape of a tent used for *camping*.

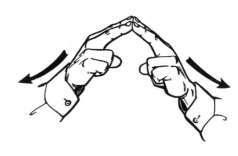

TENT

Form the point of a triangle with the fingers of both *V* hands, then separate them by moving them down and to the sides a short distance.

Memory aid: Symbolizes the shape of a *tent*.

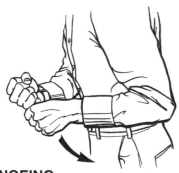

CANOEING

Hold the right *S* hand over the left *S* hand to the right or left of the body. Move them simultaneously down and backward.

Memory aid: The natural action for paddling a *canoe*.

ROWING

Hold both S hands to the front with palms facing down. Move them simultaneously in backward circles.

Memory aid: The action of *rowing* a boat with oars.

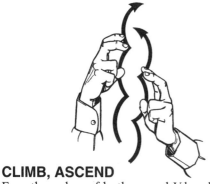

CLIMB, ASCEND

Face the palms of both curved *V* hands, then make a *climbing* motion with each hand alternately. *Alternative* (not illustrated): The hands can simulate *climbing* the rungs of a ladder or up a rope.

Memory aid: Upward action indicates the meaning.

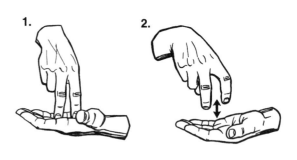

JUMP, HOP, LEAP

Imitate a jumping motion with the right *V* fingers on the left flat palm.

Memory aid: Symbolizes a person's legs *jumping*.

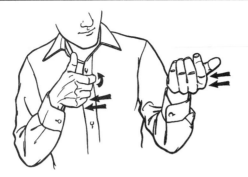

HUNT, GUN, RIFLE, SHOOT

Hold the left *A* hand out to the front at shoulder level, with the palm facing up and the thumb slightly extended. Place the right hand just below the chin with the palm facing in. Jerk both hands backward slightly as the right index finger is crooked.

Memory aid: Symbolizes the use of a *rifle*.

JOGGING

Place both partially open *A* hands to the front with palms facing. Move them back and forth alternately.

Memory aid: The motion of the arms when *jogging*.

BICYCLE, CYCLE, TRICYCLE

Move both downturned *S* hands forward in alternate circles.

Memory aid: Symbolizes the action of pedaling a *bicycle*.

BALLOON

Hold both *C* hands upright before the mouth with palms facing. Move the hands outward in a circle until the fingers touch.

Memory aid: The hands suggest the shape of a *balloon*.

RHYTHM

Move the right *R* hand back and forth with *rhythm* in front of the chest.

Memory aid: The initial and the *rhythmic* movement suggest the meaning.

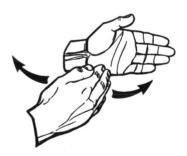

SING, HYMN, MELODY, MUSIC, SONG

Wave the right flat hand from left to right in front of the left flat hand, which has its palm facing right. The *M* hand can be used for *music*.

Memory aid: Symbolizes the action of a conductor.

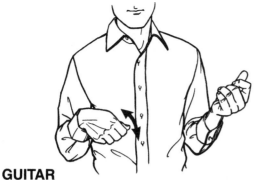

GUITAR

Hold the left hand forward and to the left with thumb extended and fingers partially curled. Place the thumb of the right *A* hand in the crook of the index finger and pivot the hand up and down in front of the chest.

Memory aid: The position and movement for playing a *guitar*.

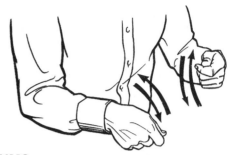

DRUMS

Place both *A* hands to the front with the thumbs in the crooks of their respective index fingers. Pivot the hands sharply up and down from the wrists.

Memory aid: The action of using *drumsticks*.

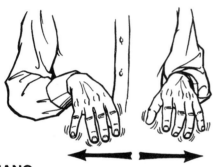

PIANO

Hold both downturned curved open hands to the front; then move them to the left and right while making simultaneous downward striking movements with various fingers.

Memory aid: The movement of playing a *piano*.

VIOLIN

Hold the left hand up with thumb and fingers curled. Move the right *O* hand back and forth over the bent left elbow.

Memory aid: The position and movement for playing a *violin*.

XYLOPHONE

Hold both modified *A* hands (thumb tips in the crooks of both index fingers) with palms facing. Move the hands up and down alternately.

Memory aid: Suggests the action of striking the bars of a *xylophone* with the hammers.

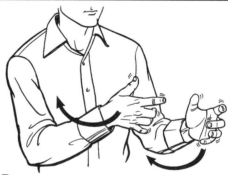

HARP

Place both curved open hands to the front with palms facing. Move the hands backward with slight circular movements while bending and unbending the fingers. Both hands may also move toward the body at the same time.

Memory aid: The movement of playing the *harp*.

TROMBONE

Place the thumbs of both *A* hands in the crooks of their respective index fingers. Hold the left hand near the mouth and move the right hand forward and backward in front of the left hand.

Memory aid: The position and movement for playing a *trombone*.

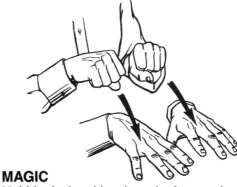

MAGIC

Hold both closed hands to the front and open them suddenly with a forward movement. Repeat a few times.

Memory aid: Suggests a *magician's* hands when performing a trick.

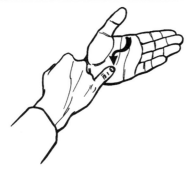

ART, DESIGN, DRAW

Trace a wavy line over the left flat palm with the right *I* finger.

Memory aid: Symbolizes the use of a pencil or brush.

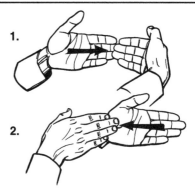

PAINT

Brush the fingertips of the right hand back and forth on the left palm.

Memory aid: Symbolizes *painting* with a brush.

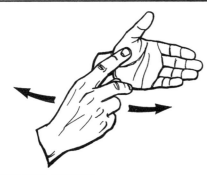

POETRY, POEM

Move the right *P* hand back and forth with rhythm in front of the left flat hand.

Memory aid: Suggests the rhythmic nature of rhyming *poetry* lines.

DOLL

Place the bent index finger across the bridge of the nose and move both head and hand downward simultaneously.

Memory aid: A *doll's* nose can be pulled, but a real person cannot be fooled the same way.

MATCHING SKILL

Look at the words at the left side of the page. Then match the signs with the words by writing the correct word next to the sign.

MATCHING
WORDS

guitar

jogging

paint

climb

tent

baseball

drums

golf

ball

sing

jump

tennis

fishing

piano

1. _____

2. _____

3. _____

4. _____

5. _____

6. _____

7.

8. _____

9. _____

10. _____

11. _____

12. _____

13. _____

14.

Answers are
on page 285.

Chapter

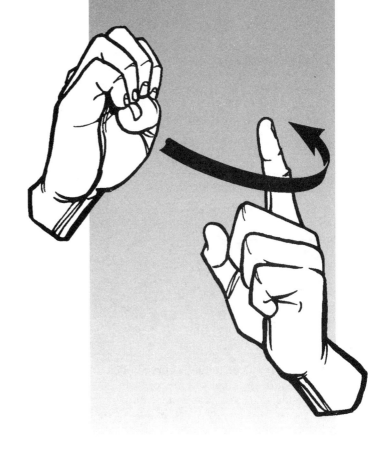

6

Animals, Nature, and Science

ANIMAL

Place the fingertips of both bent hands on the chest. Maintain the position of the fingertips while rocking both hands in and out sideways.

Memory aid: Suggests the often pronounced breathing movements of an animal that has exerted itself physically.

HORSE

Extend the thumb of the right *U* hand and place it on the right temple with palm facing forward. Bend and unbend the *U* fingers a few times.

Memory aid: Suggests the movement of a *horse's* ears.

CAT

Place the index fingers and thumbs of the *F* hands under the nose with the palms facing, then move them out sideways. This sign may also be done with the right hand only.

Memory aid: Suggests a *cat's* whiskers.

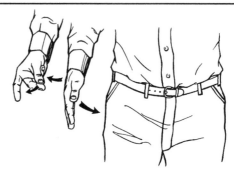

DOG

Slap the right flat hand against the right leg and snap the right middle finger.

Memory aid: A common gesture for attracting a *dog's* attention.

TIGER

Place the fingers of both slightly curved open hands in front of the face, with palms facing in. Pull the hands apart sideways while simultaneously changing to claw-shape hands. Repeat a few times.

Memory aid: Symbolizes a *tiger's* stripes and clawed paws.

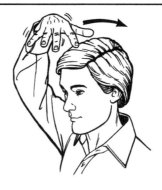

LION

Shake the right curved open hand as it moves backward over the head.

Memory aid: Suggests the shaggy mane of a male *lion.*

DEER, ANTLERS, MOOSE, ELK

With palms facing forward, touch the temples with the thumbs of both open hands a few times. *Note: Moose* can be signed with the same movement but with the fingers closed rather than open.

Memory aid: Symbolizes the *antlers.*

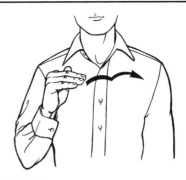

KANGAROO

Hold the right bent hand to the front with palm facing forward. Move the hand forward with several up and down movements. *Note:* This sign is sometimes done with two hands making identical movements.

Memory aid: Symbolizes the shape and jumping action of a *kangaroo.*

GIRAFFE

Place the thumb and index finger of the left *C* hand on the neck. Touch the neck with the thumb and index finger of the right *C* hand, then move the right hand in a forward-upward direction. This sign is often made using only the right hand.

Memory aid: Suggests a *giraffe's* long neck.

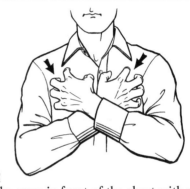

BEAR

Cross the arms in front of the chest with palms facing self. Make a few downward and inward clawing movements with both hands.

Memory aid: Symbolizes the action of a *bear's* claws while grasping at something.

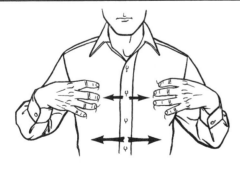

ZEBRA

Place both slightly curved open hands on the abdomen with palms touching the body. Draw both hands toward the sides and repeat the action on the chest.

Memory aid: The fingers symbolically outline the stripes of a *zebra.*

FOX, SLY

Place the circle formed by the thumb and index fingers of the right *F* hand over the nose with the palm facing left. Twist the hand so that the palm faces down.

Memory aid: The initial indicates the word, and the location suggests the pointed nose of a *fox.*

MONKEY, APE

Scratch the sides of the chest with both claw-shaped hands.

Memory aid: The scratching of a *monkey* to relieve pest infestation in its fur.

ELEPHANT

Place the back of the right curved hand in front of the mouth. Move the right hand down and then forward and upward. Let the fingertips lead the way throughout the movement.

Memory aid: Symbolizes an *elephant's* trunk.

RABBIT

Cross the *H* hands at the wrists with the palms facing self. Bend and unbend the *H* fingers a few times.

Memory aid: The sign suggests a *rabbit's* ears.

SQUIRREL, CHIPMUNK

Hold the curved fingers of both *V* hands to the front with palms facing. Tap the fingertips of both *V* hands against each other a few times.

Memory aid: Suggests the teeth of a *squirrel* at work on a nut.

SKUNK

Point the right *K* fingers down in front of the forehead with the palm facing the head. Move the right hand backward over the top of the head.

Memory aid: The action illustrates a *skunk's* white stripe.

DINOSAUR

Point the left flat hand to the right with palm facing down. Rest the right elbow on the back of the left hand with the right arm in a vertical position and move the right *and* hand back and forth a few times.

Memory aid: The arm and the *and* hand suggest the neck and head of a *dinosaur*.

GOAT

Place the thumb side of the right *S* hand on the point of the chin. Move the right hand up to the forehead while changing to a *V* hand with palm facing left.

Memory aid: Suggests the beard and horns of a *goat.*

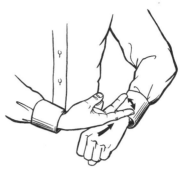

SHEEP, LAMB

Place the back of the right *V* fingers on the left forearm, which is held to the front with its hand closed and palm facing down. Open and close the right *V* fingers as they move up the forearm. To sign *lamb,* add the sign for *small.*

Memory aid: Suggests the shearing of *sheep.*

COW

Place the thumb tips of both *Y* hands against the temples and twist upward so that the little fingers point up (sometimes the action is reversed). This sign is often done with the right hand only.

Memory aid: Suggests a *cow's* horns.

PIG, HOG

Place the back of the right flat hand under the chin with the fingers pointing to the left. Bend and unbend the hand several times from the knuckles.

Memory aid: Can represent the *pig's* snout constantly dipping for more food.

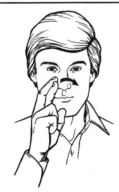

RAT

Brush across the nose tip with the right *R* fingers a few times.

Memory aid: The initial indicates the word, and the action suggests the twitching of a *rat's* nose.

MOUSE

Brush the right index finger to the left across the nose tip a few times.

Memory aid: Suggests the twitching nose of a *mouse.*

BIRD

Place the right *Q* hand at the right side of the mouth with the fingers pointing forward. Close and open the *Q* fingers a few times.

Memory aid: Suggests the movement of a *bird's* beak.

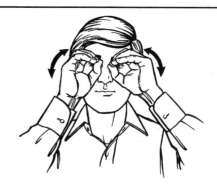

OWL

Look through both *O* hands and twist them toward the center and back a few times.

Memory aid: Symbolizes an *owl's* large eyes.

EAGLE

Place the right *X* hand in front of the nose with palm facing forward.

Memory aid: Symbolizes the hooked beak of an *eagle*.

DUCK

Point the right *N* fingers and thumb forward in front of the mouth. Open and close the *N* fingers and thumb a few times.

Memory aid: Suggests the shape and movement of a *duck's* bill.

TURKEY

With the palm facing down, shake the right *Q* fingers back and forth in front of the chin; then move the *Q* hand forward and down with a few small spiraling movements.

Memory aid: Symbolizes the shaking wattle that hangs from a *turkey's* throat.

ROOSTER, COCK

Place the right thumb of the 3 hand against the forehead with the palm facing left.

Memory aid: Symbolizes the *rooster's* comb.

CHICKEN, HEN

Open and close the right index finger and thumb in front of the mouth. Sometimes these fingers are also brought down into the upturned left palm with a pecking motion.

Memory aid: Indicates a *chicken's* beak.

TURTLE, TORTOISE

Place the right *A* hand under the palm-down left curved hand. Expose the right *A* thumb from under the little-finger edge of the left hand and wiggle it up and down.

Memory aid: Symbolizes the head of a *turtle* looking out from under its shell.

FROG

Hold the closed right hand under the chin with palm facing in. Flick out the right index and middle fingers of the closed right hand.

Memory aid: The flicking fingers picture the jumping nature of a *frog*. The location suggests the expression A *frog* in the throat.

FISH (noun)

Place the fingertips of the left flat hand at the right wrist or elbow. Point the right flat hand forward with palm facing left, and swing from right to left a few times. Most of the movement is at the wrist.

Memory aid: Suggests the swimming motion of a *fish's* tail.

SNAKE

Move the right index finger forward in small spiral circles as it passes under the downturned palm of the left flat hand.

Memory aid: The sign suggests a *snake* slithering out from under a rock.

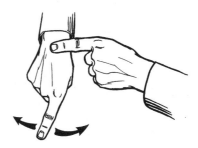

TAIL, WAG

Place the left index finger on the right wrist. Point the right index finger down and swing it from side to side.

Memory aid: Symbolizes an animal's *tail* swinging or *wagging*.

ZOO

Hold the left flat open hand up with palm facing forward. Trace the letter *Z* across the front of the left hand with the right index finger. This sign is often fingerspelled.

Memory aid: The initial indicates the word, and the open left hand suggests the bars on animal cages.

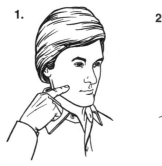

BEE

Touch the right cheek with the right index finger. Quickly brush the index-finger side of the right flat hand downward across the cheek.

Memory aid: Suggests that a *bee* landing on the cheek is quickly brushed off.

BUTTERFLY

Interlock the thumbs of both open hands in the crossed position in front of the chest with the palms facing self. Wiggle the fingers and flap the hands.

Memory aid: Symbolizes the shape and flying motion of a *butterfly*.

SPIDER

Interlock the little fingers of both curved open hands with the palms facing down. Move the hands forward while simultaneously wiggling the fingers.

Memory aid: Suggests a *spider's* legs in action.

WORM

Wiggle the right index finger as it moves forward along the palm side of the left flat hand from heel to fingertips.

Memory aid: Symbolizes the crawling motion of a *worm*.

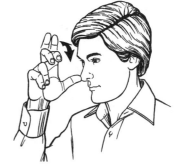

BUG, INSECT

Touch the nose with the thumb tip of the right 3 hand. Bend and unbend the index and middle fingers a few times.

Memory aid: Suggests the moving antennae or feelers of many *insects*.

FLY (insect)

Move the right flat hand quickly onto the left forearm. End with the right hand closed.

Memory aid: Symbolizes the act of catching a *fly*.

PLANT, SOW

Move the right downturned curved hand from left to right while simultaneously moving the right thumb across the inside of the fingers from little finger to index finger.

Memory aid: Suggests holding seeds between the fingers and thumb and gradually dropping them into the ground.

 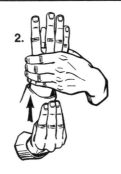

GRASS

Move the right *G* hand to the right while shaking it from the wrist, then open the fingers of the right *and* hand as they pass up through the left *C* hand. These are the signs for *green* and *grow*.

Memory aid: The sign suggests that something green is growing.

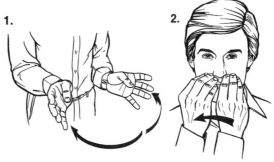

GARDEN, YARD

Hold the upright open hands close together with palms facing in. Describe a half circle with each hand toward the body until the hands meet. Then place the fingertips of the right *and* hand under each nostril separately.

Memory aid: Suggests an enclosed space where plants or flowers grow.

FLOWER

Place the fingertips of the right *and* hand under each nostril separately.

Memory aid: Suggests smelling a *flower*.

BLOSSOM, BLOOM

Point both curved hands upward with palms facing and fingertips touching. Move the hands outward and upward while forming open curved hands.

Memory aid: Suggests the process of budding and *blooming*.

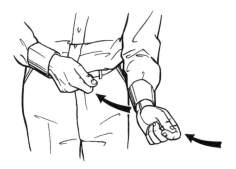

GARDENING, HOEING, RAKING
Place both thumb tips into the crooks of both curved index fingers with the other fingers closed. Hold the left hand in front of the right and pull toward self with both hands in unison. *Note: Raking* can be signed by pulling the right downturned open curved hand toward self.

Memory aid: Suggests working with a *hoe.*

SOIL, DIRT, GROUND
Hold both curved hands to the front with palms facing up and rub the fingertips with the thumbs.

Memory aid: Symbolizes the feeling of *soil.*

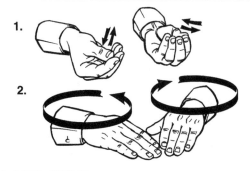

LAND, FIELD
Hold both curved hands to the front with palms facing up and rub the fingertips with the thumbs. Then make circles in opposite directions with both downturned flat hands.

Memory aid: Symbolizes the feeling and leveling of *soil.*

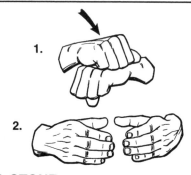

ROCK, STONE
Strike the closed right hand on the back of the closed left hand; then hold both *C* hands slightly apart with palms facing.

Memory aid: Suggests the hardness and size of a *rock.*

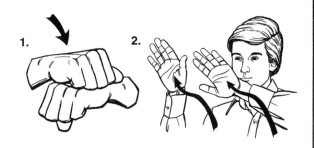

MOUNTAIN, HILL
Strike the closed right hand on the back of the closed left hand (the sign for *rock*), then move both open hands upward to the front with a wavy motion.

Memory aid: Suggests the substance and shape of a *mountain.*

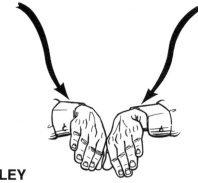

VALLEY
With the palms facing out to the sides, move both flat hands downward from shoulder level until they meet in front of the waist.

Memory aid: Suggests the shape of a *valley.*

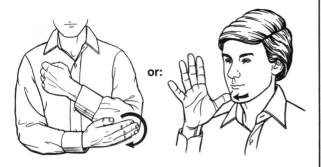

FARM, COUNTRY (rural)

Bend the left arm and rub the left elbow with the right flat hand. *Alternative:* Place the thumb of the right open hand on left side of chin with palm facing in. Rub thumb across chin to the right.

Memory aid: The first sign indicates the wear and tear on the elbows of a *farm* worker, and the second sign suggests an unshaven *farm* worker.

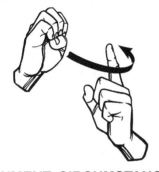

ENVIRONMENT, CIRCUMSTANCE, SITUATION

Circle the right *E* hand in a counterclockwise direction around the front of the left vertical index finger. Initialize with a *C* for *circumstance* and an *S* for *situation*.

Memory aid: Suggests the surrounding area.

WOOD, LUMBER, SAW

Move the little-finger edge of the right flat hand back and forth across the back of the left hand.

Memory aid: Suggests a *saw* cutting *wood*.

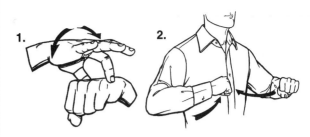

EARTHQUAKE

Grasp the back of the left closed hand between the right index finger and thumb; then pivot the right hand back and forth (toward the left fingers and elbow). Move both fists forward and backward in front of the body with forceful movements.

Memory aid: These movements combine the signs for *earth* and *thunder*.

TREE, BRANCH, FOREST, WOODS

Place the right elbow in the left palm with the right fingers pointing up. Pivot the right wrist and wiggle the fingers. Initials can be used for *branch, forest,* and *woods*.

Memory aid: The forearm symbolizes a *tree* trunk, while the moving hand and fingers suggest the *branches* and leaves.

ISLAND

With the palms facing in, touch the *I* fingers and make a circle toward the body until the *I* fingers touch again.

Memory aid: The initial indicates the word, and the movement suggests the shape of an *island*.

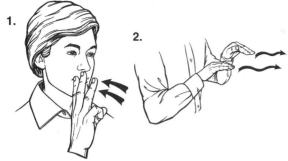

OCEAN, SEA

Touch the mouth with the index finger of the right *W* hand a few times (the sign for *water*). Move both downturned curved hands forward with a wavy motion.

Memory aid: Symbolizes the waves of the *ocean*.

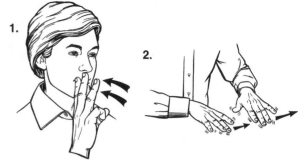

RIVER

Touch the mouth with the index finger of the right *W* hand a few times (the sign for *water*). Place both open hands with palms facing down and wiggle the fingers as both hands move either to the right or to the left.

Memory aid: The sign suggests the rippling of moving water.

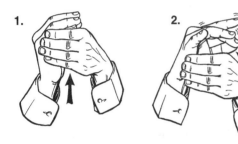

FOUNTAIN, SPRING

Bring the right *and* hand up through the left *C* hand. Wiggle the right open fingers as the hand appears above the left *C*, and continue to wiggle them as they are moved down the outside edge of the *C* hand a short distance.

Memory aid: Symbolizes water bubbling up from a *spring* or over a *fountain*.

CLOUD, GALE, STORM

Hold both open curved hands to the front at head level with palms facing. Move both hands from one side to the other while making circular and up-and-down movements from the wrists. Make more vigorous movements for *gale* and *storm*.

Memory aid: Symbolizes the movement and formation of *clouds*.

SKY, HEAVENS, SPACE

Hold the right flat hand slightly above head level with the palm facing in. Move it in an arc from left to right. The hand may also be pivoted slightly from left to right during the movement.

Memory aid: Suggests the wide open *space* above.

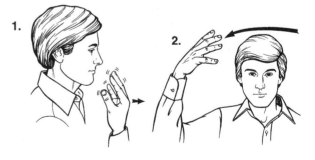

RAINBOW

Point the fingers of the right open hand toward the mouth and wiggle them (the sign for *color*). Move the right open hand over the head from left to right in an arc.

Memory aid: Suggests the colors and shape of a *rainbow*.

SUN

Point the right index finger forward just above head level and make a clockwise circle.

Memory aid: Symbolizes the position and shape of the *sun.*

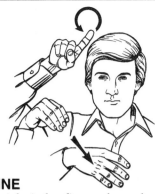

SUNSHINE

Point the right index finger above the head and make a clockwise circle; then sweep the right hand down and to the left, starting with the *and* hand and ending with an open hand.

Memory aid: Symbolizes the sun and its rays.

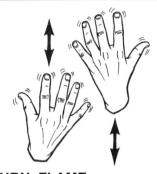

FIRE, BURN, FLAME

With palms facing in, move both slightly curved open hands up and down alternately in front of the body while wiggling the fingers.

Memory aid: Symbolizes leaping *flames.*

ELECTRICITY, PHYSICS

Strike the bent index and middle fingers of each hand (or just the index fingers) together a few times. The other fingers are closed.

Memory aid: Suggests *electrical* lines being brought together.

EARTH, GEOGRAPHY, GLOBE, TERRESTRIAL

Grasp the back of the left closed hand between the right index and thumb and pivot the right hand from left to right (toward the left fingers and elbow).

Memory aid: The left hand symbolizes the *earth,* and the right thumb and finger identify the poles.

MOON

Hold the shape of the right *C* hand around the right eye.

Memory aid: The initial shape represents the shape of the *moon,* and the locality of the eye suggests that people can see by the *moon's* light.

STAR, STARRED

Point both index fingers upward at eye level. Move them alternately upward, striking the side of one index finger a glancing blow against the side of the other index finger.

Memory aid: Can suggest the suns in the universe shooting out newly created *stars.*

UNIVERSE

Make a forward circle with the right *U* hand around the left *U* hand. End with the little-finger edge of the right *U* hand resting on the thumb side of the left *U* hand.

Memory aid: The initials indicate the word, and the action symbolizes the movement of the *universe.*

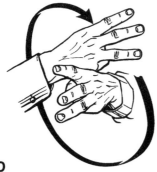

WORLD

Make a forward circle with the right *W* hand around the left *W* hand. End with the little-finger edge of the right *W* hand resting on the thumb side of the left *W* hand.

Memory aid: The initials indicate the word, and the action symbolizes the revolving *world.*

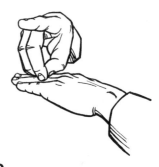

DIAMOND

Place the thumb and middle finger of the right *D* hand on the fourth finger of the left downturned hand.

Memory aid: The initial indicates the word, and the action draws attention to the ring finger.

GOLD

Touch the right ear with the right index finger, or grasp the right earlobe between the right index finger and thumb. Shake the right *Y* hand as it moves down and forward.

Memory aid: Suggests both the idea of earrings and the color of *gold.*

SILVER

Touch the right ear with the right index finger. Move the right hand forward to an *S* position and shake it.

Memory aid: The movement suggests earrings, and the initial indicates the word.

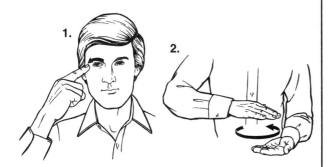

SHADOW

Move the right index finger outward across the right eyebrow (the sign for *black*). Hold the left hand with upturned palm and move the down-turned right hand over the left hand from right to left in a partial circle.

Memory aid: Suggests a black *shadow.*

SCIENCE, BIOLOGY, CHEMISTRY, EXPERIMENT

Place both *A* hands in front of the shoulders and move them alternately in and down a few times. Use initialized hands for *biology, chemistry,* and *experiment.*

Memory aid: Symbolizes the use of test tubes when preparing and testing a solution.

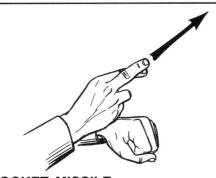

ROCKET, MISSILE

Place the right *R* hand on the back of the closed downturned left hand, and move the right hand forward and up.

Memory aid: Suggests a *rocket* taking off.

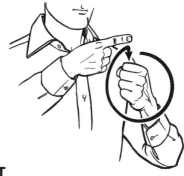

ORBIT

Make a forward circle around the left closed hand with the right index-finger hand. End with the right index resting on top of the left hand.

Memory aid: Suggests a space craft which *orbits* around the earth before landing.

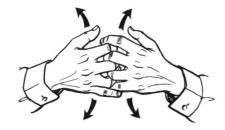

MACHINE, ENGINE, FACTORY, MECHANISM, MOTOR

Intertwine the fingers of both open hands and pivot at the wrists a few times.

Memory aid: Suggests the meshing of gears.

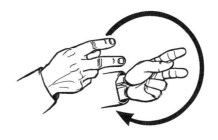

KIND (type), SORT, VARIETY

Point both *K* hands forward and rotate the right *K* forward around the left.

Memory aid: The initials indicate the word, and the circular movement suggests a world full of diversity.

NAME THE SIGN

To reinforce the vocabulary you have already learned, identify the following signs from this chapter by writing the names underneath the signs.

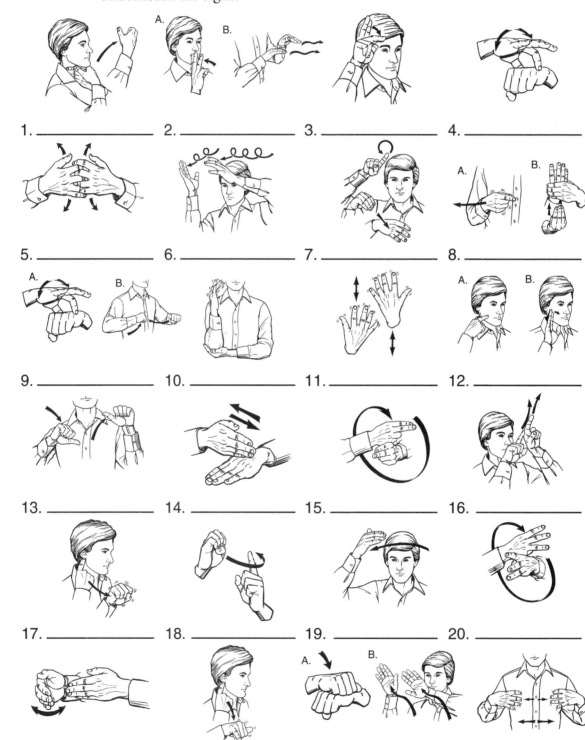

1. _____

2. _____

3. _____

4. _____

5. _____

6. _____

7. _____

8. _____

9. _____

10. _____

11. _____

12. _____

13. _____

14. _____

15. _____

16. _____

17. _____

18. _____

19. _____

20. _____

21. _____

22. _____

23. _____

24. _____

Answers are on page 285.

Chapter

7

Travel,
Holidays,
Location,
and
Direction

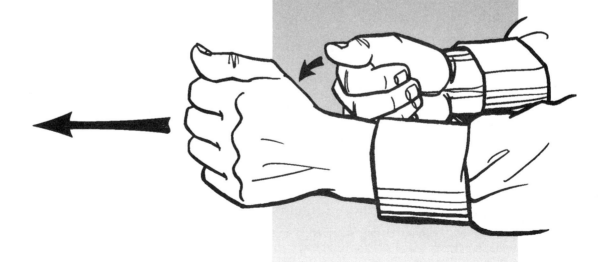

TRAVEL, JOURNEY, TRIP
With right palm facing down, imitate traveling along a winding road with right curved *V* fingers.

Memory aid: The *V* hand represents the legs of a person who is going somewhere.

HOTEL
Rest the little-finger edge of the right *H* hand on the left vertical index finger while moving the *H* fingers back and forth.

Memory aid: The initialized right hand indicates the word, and the movement can suggest a *hotel* sign revolving on a pole.

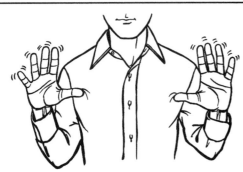

VACATION, HOLIDAY, LEISURE
Place both thumbs at the armpits and wiggle all the fingers.

Memory aid: A common symbol of *leisure*.

VISIT
Hold both *V* hands up with palms facing in. Rotate them forward alternately.

Memory aid: The action symbolizes a mingling of people among each other.

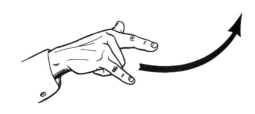

AIRPLANE, JET, FLY
Use the *Y* hand with index finger extended and palm facing down. Make a forward-upward sweeping motion.

Memory aid: Suggests the wings and fuselage of an *airplane* taking off.

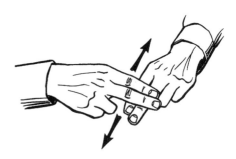

TRAIN, RAILROAD
With palms facing down, rub the right *H* fingers back and forth over the length of the left *H* fingers a few times.

Memory aid: Suggests *trains* going up and down the tracks.

BOAT

Form a cupped shape with both curved hands and move forward with a bouncing motion.

Memory aid: Suggests the hull of a *boat* going over waves.

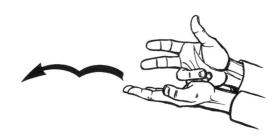

SHIP

Put the right 3 hand on the palm of the left curved hand and move both hands forward simultaneously with a wavy motion.

Memory aid: Suggests a *ship* going over the waves.

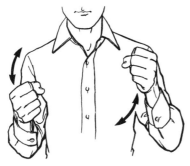

CAR, AUTOMOBILE, DRIVE

Use both closed hands to manipulate an imaginary steering wheel.

Memory aid: Holding a steering wheel.

MOTORCYCLE

Hold both S hands to the front with palms down and rotate them forward and backward from the wrists.

Memory aid: Symbolizes holding a *motorcycle's* handlebars.

RIDE (in a vehicle)

Place the right curved U fingers in the left O hand and move both hands forward.

Memory aid: Suggests a passenger being carried.

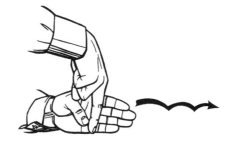

RIDE (on an animal)

Place the right upside-down V hand astride the index-finger side of the left flat hand. Move both hands forward together in short arcs.

Memory aid: Symbolizes a horse and its rider.

BRIDGE

Hold the left closed hand to the front with the forearm almost horizontal. Touch the underside of the forearm with the tips of the right *V* fingers, first under the wrist and then under the forearm.

Memory aid: Suggests the pillars supporting a *bridge.*

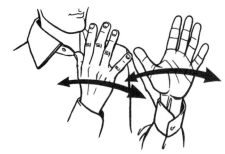

TRAFFIC

With the palms facing, move the open hands back and forth a few times.

Memory aid: Symbolizes two-way *traffic.*

STREET, WAY, AVENUE, HIGHWAY, PATH, ROAD

Hold both flat hands with palms facing; then move them forward together while simultaneously winding from side to side. *Note:* All these words may be signed by using the initial. Thus, *way* could be signed with *W* hands, and so on.

Memory aid: Symbolizes the direction of a *road.*

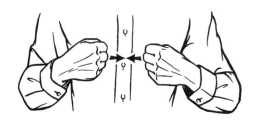

ACCIDENT, COLLISION, CRASH, WRECK

Strike the knuckles of both clenched hands together.

Memory aid: Symbolizes a *collision.*

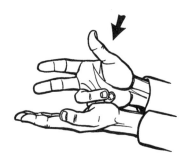

PARK (a vehicle)

Bring the right *3* hand down onto the left flat palm. Movements suggesting the parking of a vehicle can also be made with the right *3* hand on the left palm.

Memory aid: The *3* hand symbolizes a person in a car.

GASOLINE

Bring the right *A* thumb down into the left *O* hand.

Memory aid: Symbolizes putting *gas* into an automobile tank.

CAMERA

Hold both hands with the thumbs and bent index fingers in front of the face. Keep the other fingers closed. Raise and lower the right index finger.

Memory aid: The position and action for operating a *camera*.

PICTURE, PHOTOGRAPH

Hold the right *C* hand close to the face; then move it forward until the thumb side of the right *C* hand is against the left flat palm. The left palm can face either to the right or to the front.

Memory aid: Suggests that a facial likeness is transferred to the flat surface of a *photograph*.

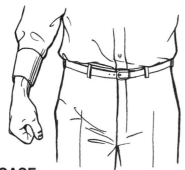

SUITCASE

Use the right hand to imitate the movement of picking up a *suitcase*.

Memory aid: Symbolizes picking up a *suitcase*.

EASTER

Move the right *E* hand in a sideways arc to the right with the palm facing forward.

Memory aid: The initial suggests the word, and the arc can be symbolic of the resurrection.

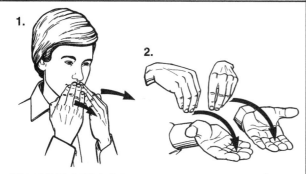

THANKSGIVING

Touch the lips with the fingertips of one or both flat hands; move the hands forward until palms are facing up. Hold both curved hands to the front with palms facing down; move them forward while simultaneously forming flat hands that point forward with the palms facing up.

Memory aid: A combination of *thanks* and *give*.

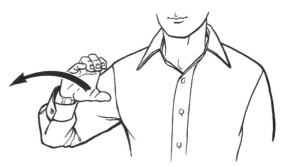

CHRISTMAS

Move the right *C* hand in a sideways arc to the right with the palm facing forward.

Memory aid: The initialized movement requires context and simultaneous lipreading for full comprehension.

FIREWORKS

With palms facing forward, open and close both *S* hands alternately with upward movements.

Memory aid: Suggests *fireworks* bursting in the air.

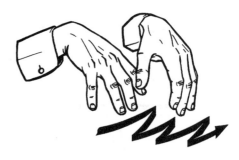

PARADE, MARCH

Swing the fingers of both bent hands back and forth sideways as they are moved forward with one hand behind the other.

Memory aid: Symbolizes organized *marching*.

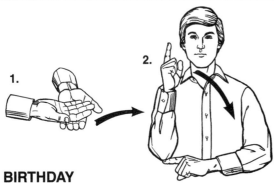

BIRTHDAY

Place back of right flat hand into upturned left palm. Move hands forward and upward together. Point left index finger to right, palm down. Rest right elbow on left index finger with right index finger pointing upward. Move right index finger and arm in partial arc across body from right to left.

Memory aid: The signs for *birth* and *day*.

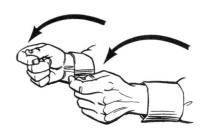

GIFT, AWARD, BESTOW, CONFER, CONTRIBUTE, PRESENT, REWARD

With the palms facing each other, place both closed hands to the front with the thumb tips touching the inside of their respective crooked index fingers. Move both hands forward simultaneously in an arc.

Memory aid: *Giving* something to someone.

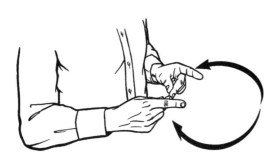

PLACE, AREA, LOCATION, SITE

With the palms facing, hold both *P* hands a short distance in front of the chest and touch the middle fingers. Make a circle toward self with both hands and touch the middle fingertips again. Each word may be initialized in a similar manner.

Memory aid: The action suggests that the hands are describing the *location* of something.

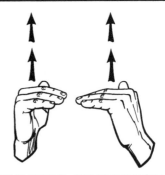

HIGH, ADVANCED, PROMOTION

Point the fingertips of both bent hands toward each other and raise both hands simultaneously.

Memory aid: Suggests going up to a *higher* level.

HERE
Hold both flat hands to the front with palms facing up. Make forward semicircles in opposite directions.

Memory aid: A natural gesture.

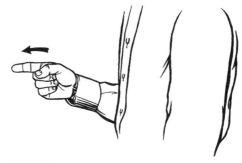

THERE
Point with the right index finger when being specific. For a more general reference, move the right flat hand to the right with palm facing forward.

Memory aid: A gesture indicating location.

ON
With both palms facing down, place the right flat hand on the back of the left flat hand.

Memory aid: Indicates something *on* top of something else.

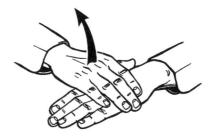

OFF
Move the flat downturned right hand upward a few inches, *off* the back of the flat downturned left hand.

Memory aid: Moving one item *off* another.

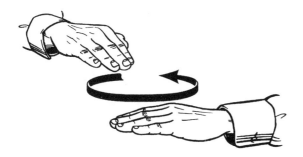

ABOVE, OVER
Make a counterclockwise circle with the right flat hand over the left flat hand.

Memory aid: Suggests one level that is higher than another.

BELOW, BENEATH, UNDER
Make a counterclockwise circle with the right flat hand below the left flat hand.

Memory aid: Suggests one level lower than another.

IN

Move the closed fingers of the right *and* hand into the left *C* hand.

Memory aid: The right hand is going *in* through an opening.

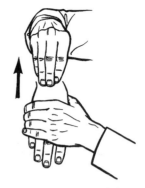

OUT

Place the downturned fingers of the open right hand in the left *C* hand with the right fingers protruding below the left *C*. Draw the right hand up and *out*.

Memory aid: Symbolizes coming up *out* of a hole.

AROUND, SURROUND

Make a counterclockwise circle with the right index finger around the left upturned *and* hand.

Memory aid: Suggests circling *around* something.

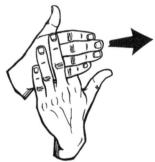

THROUGH, VIA

Pass the little-finger edge of the right flat hand forward between the left index and middle fingers.

Memory aid: Suggests finding an opening and going *through*.

AHEAD

Hold both *A* hands together with palms facing each other. Move the right hand in front of the left.

Memory aid: The right hand moves *ahead* of the left.

BEHIND

Hold both *A* hands together with palms facing. Move the right hand backward *behind* the left.

Memory aid: The right hand moves *behind* the left.

BEFORE (location), PRESENCE, FACE TO FACE

Hold the left flat hand at eye level with palm facing in. Move the right flat hand upward with a sweeping motion until palms are facing.

Memory aid: Suggests one person moving in front of another.

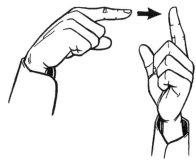

TOWARD

Hold the left index finger up and move the right index finger *toward* it, but do not touch fingertips.

Memory aid: Suggests the concept of moving closer.

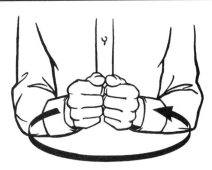

TOGETHER, ACCOMPANY

Place the knuckles of both *A* hands together and move them in a forward semi-circle to the left.

Memory aid: Suggests two people or things moving *together*.

SEPARATE, APART

Place the knuckles of both bent hands together and pull the hands apart.

Memory aid: Suggests a pulling *apart*.

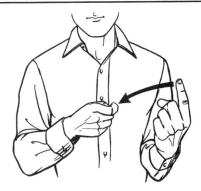

FROM

Touch the upright left index finger with the knuckle of the right *X* index finger; then move the right hand in a slight backward-downward arc.

Memory aid: Suggests pulling back *from* something.

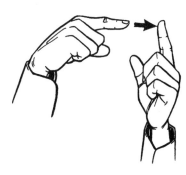

TO

Hold the left index finger up and move the right index finger toward it until the fingertips touch.

Memory aid: Suggests the concept of moving closer.

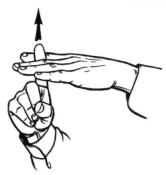

APPEAR, POP UP, RISE, SHOW UP

Move the right index finger upward between the index and middle fingers of the left flat hand, which has its palm facing down.

Memory aid: Suggests something *rising* from below.

DISAPPEAR

Move the right index finger downward between the index and middle fingers of the left palm-down flat hand.

Memory aid: Suggests something *disappearing* from view.

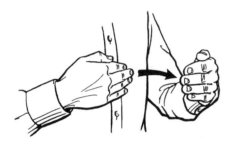

NEAR, ADJACENT, BY, CLOSE TO

Hold the left curved hand away from the body with palm facing in. Move the back of the right curved hand from a position close to the body to one near the palm of the left hand.

Memory aid: The proximity of the hands suggests the meaning.

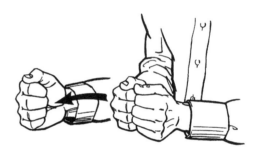

FAR, DISTANT, REMOTE

Move the right A hand well forward from an initial position beside the left A hand.

Memory aid: Symbolizes the *distance* between two points.

AWAY

Move the curved right hand away from the body and to the right, ending with the palm facing forward and downward. Sometimes the A hand is used at the beginning of the sign.

Memory aid: A natural gesture that suggests separation.

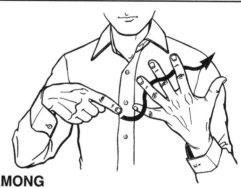

AMONG

Interweave the right index finger in and out of the fingers of the left open hand.

Memory aid: Suggests the mingling of one person *among* others.

INTO, ENTER
Push the right fingers down through the left *C* hand.

Memory aid: Symbolizes going *into* a hole.

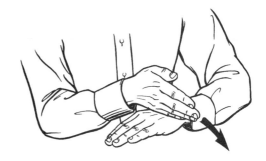

ACROSS, CROSS, OVER
With the left flat hand facing down, move the little-finger edge of the right flat hand over the knuckles of the left hand.

Memory aid: One hand crosses *over* the other.

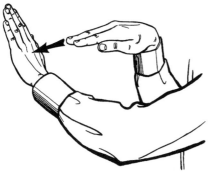

AT
Bring the fingers of the right flat hand in contact with the back of the left flat hand. This sign is often fingerspelled.

Memory aid: Suggests a meeting point.

BEYOND
Hold both flat hands to the front with palms facing in. Move the right hand over the stationary left hand and continue with the forward movement.

Memory aid: Can symbolize the other side of a wall and *beyond*.

ABOUT, CONCERNING
Move the right index finger in a forward circular direction around the fingers of the left *and* hand.

Memory aid: The circular movement suggests the meaning.

BETWEEN
Put the little-finger edge of the right flat hand between the thumb and index finger of the left flat hand. Pivot the right hand back and forth while keeping the right little-finger edge anchored.

Memory aid: The right hand is *between* two sides.

AGAINST, OPPOSE

Thrust the fingertips of the right flat hand into the palm of the left flat hand.

Memory aid: Suggests one hand attacking the other.

CENTER, CENTRAL, MIDDLE

Make a clockwise circle with the right curved hand above the left flat hand; then lower the fingertips of the right hand into the left palm.

Memory aid: Suggests something standing up in the *middle* of a circle.

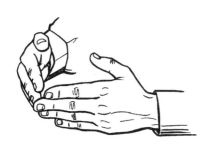

CORNER

Point either the flat-hand fingers or the index fingers at right angles to each other.

Memory aid: A *corner* is pictured.

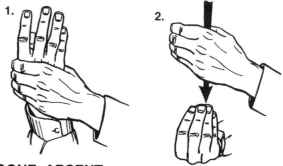

GONE, ABSENT

Draw the right open hand down through the left *C* hand and end with the right hand in the *and* position below the left hand.

Memory aid: Suggests something disappearing down a hole.

FOLLOW, DISCIPLE, SEQUEL, CHASE, PURSUE

Place both *A* hands to front, left slightly ahead of right. Move them forward, right hand following left. *Note:* Add *person (personalizing word ending)* for *follower, disciple, chaser,* or *pursuer.* Sign *chase* and *pursue* more rapidly.

Memory aid: One hand *follows* the other.

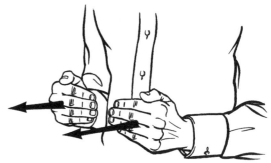

ONWARD, ADVANCE, FORWARD, PROCEED

Point the fingertips of both bent hands toward each other with palms facing in. Move both hands forward simultaneously.

Memory aid: Suggests pushing *forward.*

RIGHT (direction)
Move the right *R* hand toward the right.

Memory aid: The initial and direction indicate the meaning.

LEFT (direction)
Move the right L hand toward the left.

Memory aid: The initial and direction indicate the meaning.

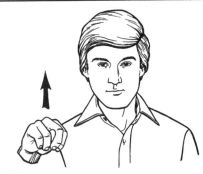

NORTH
Move the *N* hand upward.

Memory aid: Indicates the direction on a compass.

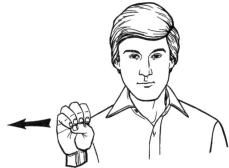

EAST
Move the right *E* hand to the right with palm facing forward.

Memory aid: The initial and direction of the movement indicate the meaning.

SOUTH
Move the *S* hand downward with palm facing forward.

Memory aid: Indicates direction.

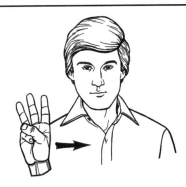

WEST
Move the *W* hand to the left.

Memory aid: Indicates direction.

MULTIPLE CHOICE

Draw a circle around or place a check mark beside the word that matches the sign to its left.

1.
A. Gone
B. Separate
C. Far

2.
A. Disappear
B. Fireworks
C. Vacation

3.
A. Street
B. Ship
C. Travel

4.
A. In
B. Gasoline
C. Center

5.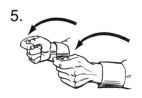
A. Gift
B. Gone
C. Here

6.
A. Across
B. High
C. Above

7.
A. Car
B. Travel
C. Street

8.
A. Visit
B. Beyond
C. Among

9.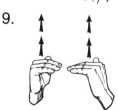
A. Onward
B. Above
C. High

10.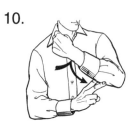
A. Corner
B. Bridge
C. Left

11.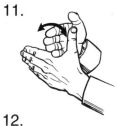
A. Appear
B. Between
C. Beyond

12.
A. Across
B. West
C. Ahead

13.
A. Into
B. In
C. At

14.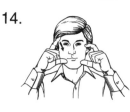
A. Christmas
B. Picture
C. Camera

Answers are on page 285.

Chapter _____

8

Thoughts, Emotions, and Abstract Ideas

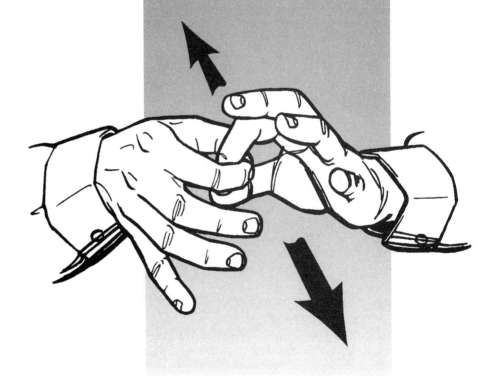

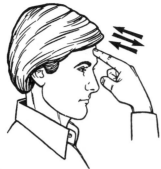

MIND, INTELLECT, MENTAL, BRAIN
Tap the right index finger on the forehead a few times.

Memory aid: The *mind* is related to the brain.

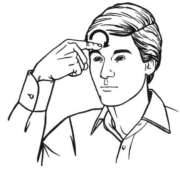

THINK, CONSIDER, REFLECT, SPECULATE
Make a counterclockwise circle with the right index finger just in front of the forehead. This can be done simultaneously with two hands if more intensity of meaning is required.

Memory aid: The circular motion indicates action in the mind.

REASON
Make a counterclockwise circle with the right *R* hand just in front of the forehead.

Memory aid: The location at the mind indicates thought processes.

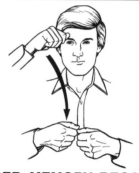

REMEMBER, MEMORY, RECALL, RECOLLECT
Place the thumb of the right *A* hand on the forehead; then place it on top of the left *A*-hand thumb.

Memory aid: Suggests knowledge that a person can keep on top of.

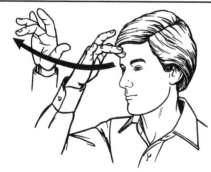

SMART, BRIGHT, BRILLIANT, CLEVER, INTELLIGENT
Touch the forehead with the right middle finger while keeping the other fingers extended. Direct the middle finger outward and upward. The index finger can also be used.

Memory aid: Suggests that *brilliant* thoughts are proceeding from the mind.

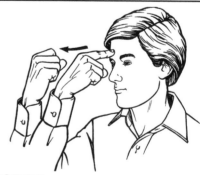

MEMORIZE
Place the right index finger on the center of the forehead; then move the right hand forward from the forehead to an *S* position, with the palm facing in.

Memory aid: Represents a firm grip on information.

CONSCIENCE, CONVICTION

Point the right index finger at the heart and shake it up and down.

Memory aid: Suggests that the right hand is scolding a guilty heart.

WISDOM, INTELLECTUAL, WISE

Move the right bent finger of the *X* hand up and down slightly just in front of the forehead. Make the movement from the wrist.

Memory aid: Measuring *intellectual* depth.

ANALYZE

Place both crooked *V* hands in front of the body with palms facing down. Pull the hands apart sideways a few times.

Memory aid: Suggests pulling something apart to examine the inner workings.

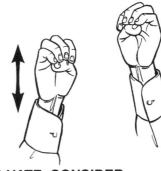

EVALUATE, CONSIDER

Move both *E* hands up and down alternately with palms facing forward.

Memory aid: The movement suggests scales and the idea of weighing first one side, then the other.

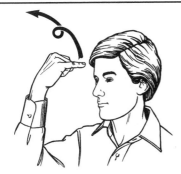

IMAGINATION, FICTION, FANTASY, THEORY

Hold right *I* hand near forehead with palm facing in. Move the *I* hand forward and upward in a few rolling circles. *Note:* To sign *fiction* or *fantasy,* use an *F* hand and to sign *theory,* use a *T* hand.

Memory aid: Suggests futuristic thoughts coming from the mind.

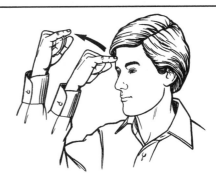

IDEA, CONCEPT, NOTION, OPINION

Place the right little finger of the *I* hand on the forehead with palm facing in. Move the right *I* forward and upward. *Note:* To sign *concept* or *opinion,* place the *C* or *O* hand respectively just before the forehead and move forward.

Memory aid: Suggests a thought coming from the mind.

DREAM, DAYDREAM

Touch the forehead with the right index finger and move it upward and forward while bending and unbending the index finger.

Memory aid: Suggests that the imagination goes on ventures of its own.

WONDER, CONCERN, CONSIDER, PONDER

Point both index fingers or *W* hands toward the forehead and rotate in small circles. Sometimes only the right hand is used.

Memory aid: Suggests the workings of a mind in motion.

CURIOUS, INQUISITIVE

Pinch a small portion of skin in the front of the neck with the right thumb and index finger. Wiggle the hand slightly from side to side.

Memory aid: The traditional apple in the Garden of Eden was eaten through *curiosity,* and the location of this sign is commonly known as the Adam's Apple.

SEEM, APPARENT, APPEAR

Hold the curved right hand up with palm facing left. Turn the hand from the wrist so that the palm faces the head. The signer often glances at the hand to emphasize the meaning.

Memory aid: Suggests that what the eyes see is usually real.

INVENT, CREATE, MAKE UP, ORIGINATE

With palm facing left, touch the forehead with the right index of the *4* hand. Beginning with the fingertips, push the length of the index upward on the forehead with a slight forward curve.

Memory aid: The *4* hand suggests lots of new ideas coming from the mind.

INFORM, INFORMATION, NOTIFY

Place the fingers of both *and* hands on each side of the forehead, then move them in a downward forward arc to an open hand position with palms facing up.

Memory aid: Suggests offering *information* from the mind.

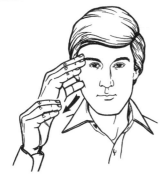

EXPERIENCE

Move the right curved open hand slightly outward from the right temple while simultaneously closing the hand to the *and* position.

Memory aid: Suggests an area of the head (sideburns) where an old and *experienced* man is still likely to have hair.

REMIND

Tap the forehead with the fingertips of the right *R* hand.

Memory aid: The initial indicates the word, and the action suggests the idea of jogging the memory.

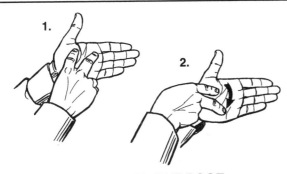

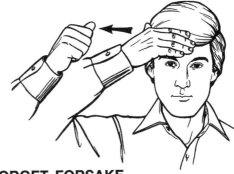

MEAN (verb), INTEND, PURPOSE

Place the fingertips of the right *V* hand in the palm of the left flat hand, which has its palm facing either to the right or upward. Draw the right hand away slightly; rotate it in a clockwise direction and rethrust the *V* fingers into the left palm.

Memory aid: Suggests the *intention* to go from one situation to another.

FORGET, FORSAKE

Wipe the palm side of the right open hand across the forehead from left to right. End with the right hand in the *A* position close to the right temple.

Memory aid: Indicates wiping information from the mind.

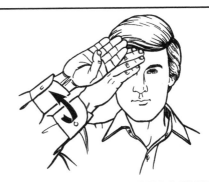

KNOW, RECOGNIZE, INTELLIGENCE, KNOWLEDGE

Tap the fingers of the right slightly curved hand on the forehead a few times.

Memory aid: The repository of *knowledge* is considered to be the brain.

DON'T KNOW, DIDN'T RECOGNIZE

Place the fingers of the right flat hand on the forehead (the sign for *know*); then move the right hand away from the forehead with the palm facing forward.

Memory aid: The turning-away action indicates the negative.

BROAD-MINDED, OPEN-MINDED

Position both flat hands forward with palms facing each other just in front of the forehead. Move the hands forward and outward with a widening *V* shape.

Memory aid: Suggests an expanding mind.

NARROW-MINDED

Hold both flat hands near the sides of the forehead with palms facing and fingers pointing forward. Move both hands forward and inward until the fingertips meet.

Memory aid: Suggests a mind that is closed.

UNDERSTAND, COMPREHEND

With the palm facing in, flick the right index finger up vertically in front of the forehead.

Memory aid: The sign suggests a figurative light of *understanding* coming on in the mind.

MISUNDERSTAND

Put the right *V* hand to the forehead, touching first with the middle finger, then twisting the hand and touching with the index finger.

Memory aid: The twisting motion and the use of two fingers suggest uncertainty in the mind.

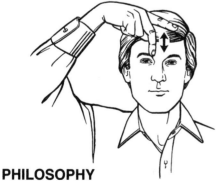

PHILOSOPHY

Move the right *P* hand up and down just in front of the forehead. Make the movement from the wrist.

Memory aid: The *P* hand searches the mind for *philosophical* understanding.

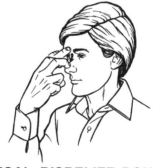

SKEPTICAL, DISBELIEF, DOUBT, UNSURE, I DOUBT IT

Crook and uncrook the right *V* fingers in front of the eyes several times. Facial expression should be appropriate.

Memory aid: The bent fingers can suggest question marks.

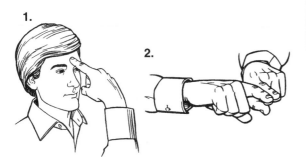

AGREE, ACCORD, COINCIDE, CONSENT, CORRESPOND

Touch the forehead with the right index finger; then move both *D* hands to chest level with palms down and sides of index fingers touching. The latter is the sign for *same.*

Memory aid: A meeting of minds in unison.

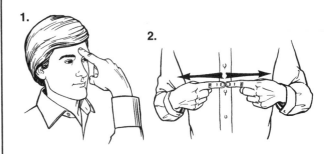

DISAGREE, CONTRADICT, CONTRARY TO

Touch the forehead with the right index finger; then bring both *D* hands to chest level with palms facing in and index fingertips touching. Move the hands outward sharply in opposite directions.

Memory aid: A separating of minds is suggested.

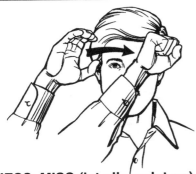

GUESS, MISS (let slip or let go)

The same basic sign is used for both words. Move the right *C* hand across the face from right to left and close to a downturned *S* position.

Memory aid: Suggests an attempt to catch something in midair.

SECRET, CONFIDENTIAL, PERSONAL, PRIVATE

Place the right *A* thumb over the pursed lips a few times.

Memory aid: Suggests that one's lips are sealed.

SUSPECT, SUSPICIOUS

With the palm facing in, bend and unbend the right index finger at the temple a few times.

Memory aid: The right index finger seems to be questioning the mind.

CARELESS, RECKLESS, THOUGHTLESS

Place the right *V* hand in front of the forehead with palm facing left. Move back and forth across the forehead a few times.

Memory aid: The *V* hand can suggest a mind void of common sense.

CONFUSE, MIX, SCRAMBLE

Place the left curved open hand in front with palm facing up. Circle the right curved open hand in a counterclockwise direction above the left.

Memory aid: The circular action suggests the meaning.

STUPID, DULL, DUMB, DUNCE

Knock the *A* (or *S*) hand against the forehead a few times with the palm facing in.

Memory aid: Knocking on the head can indicate a figuratively hollow interior.

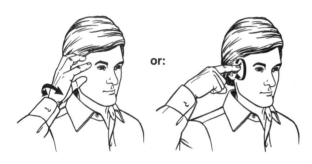

or:

CRAZY, NUTS (adjective)

Point the right curved open hand to the temple and rotate back and forth from the wrist. *Alternative:* Point the right index finger to the temple and make a small circular movement.

Memory aid: Both signs symbolize a scrambled brain.

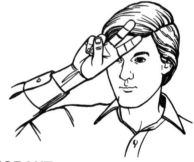

IGNORANT

Place the back of the right *V* hand on the forehead. It can tap the forehead a few times if emphasis is required.

Memory aid: The *V* hand could suggest a mind void of knowledge.

FOOL (verb), JOKE, HOAX

Place the bent index finger across the bridge of the nose and move both head and hand downward simultaneously.

Memory aid: Suggests a person being pulled in a direction they did not choose.

FOOLISH, NONSENSE, RIDICULOUS, SILLY

Pass the right *Y* hand rapidly back and forth in front of the forehead a few times. The palm faces left.

Memory aid: Suggests a young or childish mind that constantly fluctuates in opinion.

PUZZLED, PERPLEXED

With the palm facing forward, move the right index finger backward to the forehead, and then crook the finger.

Memory aid: The crooked index finger suggests a question mark, and the location of the implied question is in the mind.

BUNGLE, BOTCH, FOUL UP, MESS UP, TOPSY-TURVY, UPSIDE DOWN

Place the right downturned curved open hand over the left upturned curved hand; then reverse positions.

Memory aid: Suggests that things are unsettled.

CONFLICT

Point the left index finger to the right and the right index finger to the left at right angles. Move them forward so that they cross.

Memory aid: The action suggests two people going in different directions.

REFUSE, WON'T

Hold the right S (or A) hand in a natural position to the front; then move it sharply upward over the right shoulder while simultaneously turning the head to the left at the same time.

Memory aid: Suggests pulling back instead of proceeding in harmony.

PRESSURE

Point the left G hand forward; then push down with the right flat hand on the index side of the left G hand.

Memory aid: One hand puts *pressure* on the other.

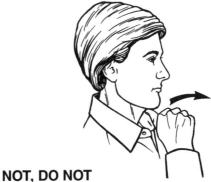

NOT, DO NOT

Place the right A thumb, palm left, under the chin and move it forward and away from the chin.

Memory aid: The thumb moving out from under the chin suggests something that cannot be swallowed.

OR, EITHER

Point the index finger of the left *L* hand forward with palm facing right. Move the right index finger from the tip of the left thumb to the top of the left index finger a few times.

Memory aid: The back-and-forth movement suggests one finger *or* the other.

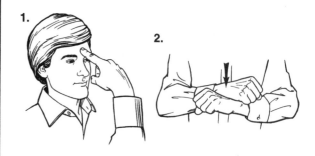

HABIT, CUSTOM, PRACTICE

Touch the forehead with the right index finger. Change the right hand to an *S* hand as it is brought down and crosses the left *S* hand at the wrist. Push both hands down slightly.

Memory aid: Suggests that the mind is bound by *habit*.

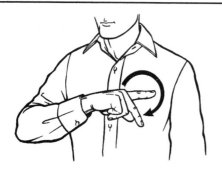

PERSONALITY, ATTITUDE, CHARACTER

Move the right *P* hand in a counterclockwise circle over the heart. To sign *attitude* and *character,* initialize the same action with an *A* and *C* hand respectively.

Memory aid: The letter signed over the heart suggests the meaning.

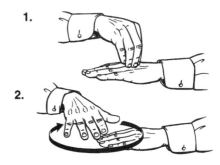

INFLUENCE

Hold the left flat or curved hand with palm down and fingers facing right. Place the fingers of the right *and* hand on the back of the left hand and move the right hand forward and to the right while opening the fingers.

Memory aid: Suggests an area of *influence*.

ATTENTION, CONCENTRATION, FOCUS, PAY ATTENTION

Hold both flat hands at the sides of the face with palms facing; then move them both forward simultaneously.

Memory aid: Suggests *concentration* in one direction without deviating.

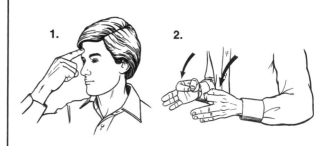

DECIDE, DECISION, DETERMINE, MAKE UP ONE'S MIND

Touch the forehead with the right index finger, then bring both *F* hands down with palms facing.

Memory aid: Suggests a mind that is free to act.

ALL RIGHT, OK
Hold the left flat hand with palm facing up. Move the little-finger edge of the right flat hand across the face of the left hand from the heel to the fingertips. *OK* is often fingerspelled.

Memory aid: The movement suggests a straight line with agreement to move ahead.

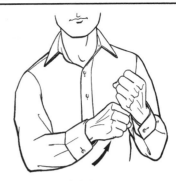

CONFIDENCE, TRUST
Begin with slightly curved open hands. Move the right *S* hand slightly under the left *S* hand in front of the left shoulder.

Memory aid: Suggests preparing to plant a flagpole into the ground.

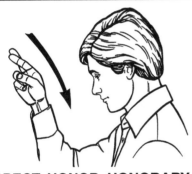

RESPECT, HONOR, HONORARY
Move the right *R* hand in a backward arc toward the face. The head is often bowed simultaneously. Use the right *H* hand for *honor* and *honorary*.

Memory aid: The initial and the bowed head symbolize the meaning.

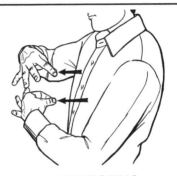

INTEREST, INTERESTING
Place the thumb and index finger of each hand on the chest, with one hand above the other. Bring the index fingers and thumbs together as the hands are moved forward. Keep the other fingers extended.

Memory aid: Suggests that a person's inner feelings are being drawn toward something.

HONEST
Move the middle finger of the right *H* hand along the left upturned flat hand from palm to fingertips.

Memory aid: The initial *H* makes a straight and *honest* line.

SATISFACTION, CONTENT
Place the right flat hand against the chest a short distance above the left hand in similar position. Simultaneously push both hands down a short distance.

Memory aid: Suggests that the inner feelings are settled.

EMOTION

Stroke the chest a few times with the palm side of both *E* hands. Move them alternately in a forward-circular motion.

Memory aid: Suggests the beating of the heart with *emotion*.

FEELING, MOTIVE, SENSATION

Move the right middle finger upward on the chest with other fingers extended.

Memory aid: Suggests the direction of inner *feelings*.

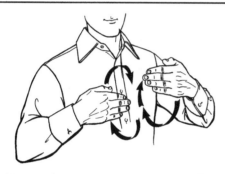

HAPPY, DELIGHT, GLAD, JOY, MERRY

Move both flat hands in forward circular movements with palms touching the chest alternately or simultaneously. One hand is often used by itself.

Memory aid: Suggests *happy* feelings springing up from within.

SAD, DEJECTED, DESPONDENT, DOWNCAST, FORLORN, SORROWFUL

With palms facing in, bend the head forward slightly while dropping the open hands down the length of the face. Assume a sad expression.

Memory aid: Suggests an expression of melancholy.

FEAR, DREAD, TERROR

Hold both open hands to the front with the palms facing forward; then draw them in and down toward the body with a trembling motion. Assume an appropriate facial expression.

Memory aid: Suggests an attempt to ward off something undesirable.

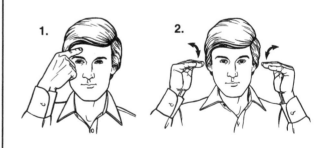

HOPE, ANTICIPATE, EXPECT

Touch the forehead with the right index finger; then bring both flat hands before the chest or head with palms facing. Bend and unbend them simultaneously a few times.

Memory aid: Suggests that the mind *anticipates* something while the hands nod in agreement.

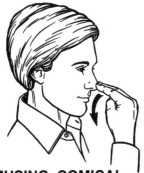

FUNNY, AMUSING, COMICAL, HILARIOUS, HUMOROUS

Brush the tip of the nose with the fingers of the right *U* hand several times.

Memory aid: Suggests that people's noses wrinkle when they laugh.

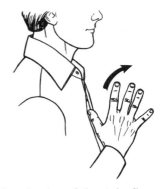

FINE

Place the thumb edge of the right flat open hand at the chest and pivot the hand forward.

Memory aid: Symbolizes an old-fashioned shirt or blouse with ruffles.

LIKE, ADMIRE

Place the right thumb and index finger against the chest, with the other fingers extended. Bring the thumb and index finger together as the hand is moved a short distance forward.

Memory aid: Symbolizes the inner feelings going out to someone or something.

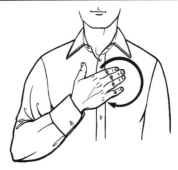

PLEASE, ENJOY, GRATIFY, LIKE, PLEASURE, WILLING

Make a circle with the right flat hand over the heart.

Memory aid: Circling the heart indicates a feeling of well-being.

EAGER, AMBITIOUS, ANXIOUS, EARNEST, ENTHUSIASTIC, ZEAL

Rub the flat hands together enthusiastically.

Memory aid: Rubbing things together produces heat.

LAZY, SLOTHFUL

Tap the palm of the right *L* hand at the left shoulder several times.

Memory aid: Suggests that a person needs to shoulder his or her load of the work.

HUMBLE, MEEK, MODEST

Point the left flat hand to the right with palm down. Touch the lips with the index finger of the right *B* hand and move it down and forward under the left hand. The head is often bowed simultaneously.

Memory aid: Suggests a willingness to take the lower position.

PROUD, ARROGANT, HAUGHTY

With palm facing down, place the thumb of the right *A* hand against the chest and move straight up. The head can be raised slightly with a disdainful facial expression.

Memory aid: Suggests the feelings rising up with *pride.*

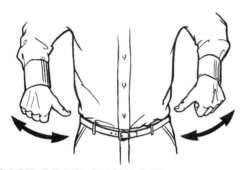

BOAST, BRAG, SHOW OFF

Move one or both *A*-hand thumbs in and out at the sides just above the waist.

Memory aid: Pointing continually to self suggests a self-centered person.

ENVY

Place the tip of the right index finger between the teeth and move slightly from side to side a few times.

Memory aid: Suggests that a person might almost bite off a finger to get something desired.

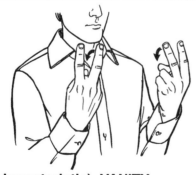

VAIN (characteristic), VANITY

With palms facing in, point the two *V* hands at the face, and bend and unbend the *V* fingers simultaneously a few times.

Memory aid: The *V* hands suggest two pairs of eyes looking at the person.

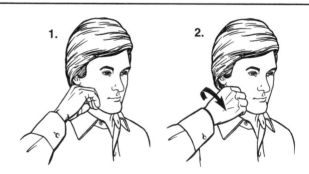

SHAME, ASHAMED

Place the back of the bent right hand against the right cheek with fingers pointing down. Twist the hand so that the fingers point backward.

Memory aid: Both signs indicate the blushing of the cheek.

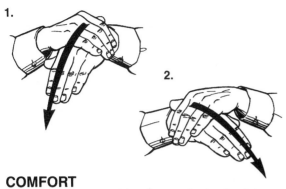

COMFORT

Rub the right curved hand over the back of the left, and vice versa.

Memory aid: The movement suggests smooth hands that lack roughness.

PITY, COMPASSION, MERCY, POOR (person or thing), SYMPATHY

Move the right middle finger upward on the chest with other fingers extended; then make forward circular motions in front of the chest with palm down and fingers still in the same position.

Memory aid: Suggests feelings of *compassion.*

CROSS, GROUCHY, GRUMPY, MAD, MOODY, SULKY

Hold the right open hand in front of the face with palm facing in. Bend and unbend the fingers a few times, and assume an appropriate expression.

Memory aid: The movement suggests tension of the face.

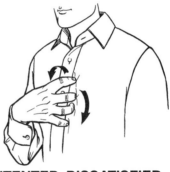

DISCONTENTED, DISSATISFIED, AGGRAVATED, DISGUSTED, DISPLEASING, REVOLTING

Place the thumb and fingertips of the right open curved hand on the chest and move the hand back and forth sideways or in a slight circular movement.

Memory aid: Suggests churning feelings.

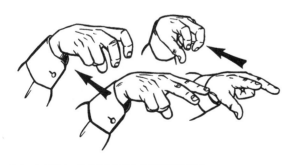

SELFISH, GREEDY, MISERLY

Point both *V* hands forward with palms facing down; then pull the hands in toward self while simultaneously bending the *V* fingers.

Memory aid: Suggests grabbing everything for oneself.

JEALOUS

Put the right little fingertip at the corner of the mouth and give it a twist.

Memory aid: The little finger suggests the *J,* which causes the mouth to open and drool with *jealousy.*

DEPRESSED, DISCOURAGED
Stroke the chest downward with both middle fingers simultaneously. Extend the remaining fingers.

Memory aid: Suggests sinking feelings.

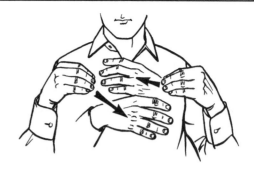

AFRAID, FRIGHTENED, SCARED, TERRIFIED
Move both *and* hands simultaneously across the chest from the sides in opposite directions. During the movement, change the hand positions to open hands.

Memory aid: Suggests reaction of self-protection.

STUBBORN, OBSTINATE, DONKEY, MULE
Place the right flat hand at the temple with the fingers pointing up and palm facing forward. Bend the hand forward. Sometimes two hands are used.

Memory aid: Suggests the downturned ear of an unwilling *donkey* or *mule*.

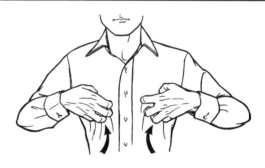

ANGER, FUME, RAGE, WRATH
Place the fingertips of both curved hands against the abdomen and draw them forcefully up to the chest with slight inward curves.

Memory aid: Suggests *angry* feelings rising from within.

UNFAIR, UNJUST
With palms facing, strike the fingertips of the left *F* hand with the fingertips of the right *F* hand in a downward movement.

Memory aid: The left hand is treated *unfairly*.

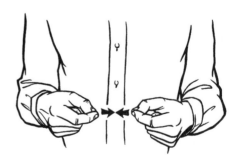

REVENGE
Position the fingertips of the index fingers and thumbs of both hands together, with the other fingers closed and palms facing each other. Strike the index fingers and thumbs together a few times.

Memory aid: Suggests two individuals striking each other.

DISAPPOINT, MISS
Place the tip of the right index finger on the chin, and assume the appropriate facial expression.

Memory aid: Suggests the expression Take it on the chin, which can indicate suffering as a result of *disappointment.*

FRUSTRATE
Bring the back of the right flat hand sharply toward the face. The head can also move back slightly.

Memory aid: Suggests a wall of opposition.

GRIEF, MOURN
Bring the palm sides of both *A* hands together in front of the heart and rotate them back and forth as though crushing something between the hands.

Memory aid: Suggests that the heart is crushed with the weight of *grief.*

SUFFER, AGONY, ENDURE
Slowly revolve right *S* hand in a forward circle around left stationary *S* hand. Assume appropriate facial expression.

Memory aid: The S hands, facial expression, and cycle action suggest continuous suffering.

SORRY, SORROW, APOLOGY, REGRET
Rotate the right *A* (or *S*) hand in a few circles over the heart.

Memory aid: Rubbing the heart suggests inner feelings of *sorrow.*

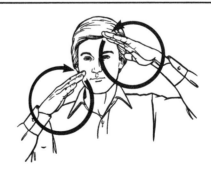

WORRY, ANXIOUS, FRET
Rotate both flat or slightly curved hands in front of the head in opposite directions.

Memory aid: Suggests problems being heaped upon the mind.

SURPRISE, AMAZE, ASTONISH, ASTOUND

Place both closed hands at the temples with index fingertips and thumb tips touching. Flick both index fingers up simultaneously.

Memory aid: Suggests wide-eyed *surprise.*

SHOCK, BEWILDER, DUMBFOUND, STUN

Circle the eyes with both *C* hands and suddenly open the hands to a wide *C* position.

Memory aid: The sign suggests the eyes opening wide with *shock.*

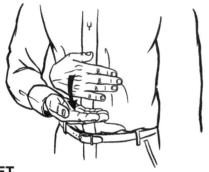

UPSET

Place the palm of the right flat hand on the stomach; then move the hand forward and face the palm up.

Memory aid: Symbolizes a stomach turning over in nausea.

CRY, BAWL, SOB, TEARDROP, TEARS, WEEP

Move one or both index fingers down the cheeks from underneath the eyes a few times.

Memory aid: Suggests falling *tears.*

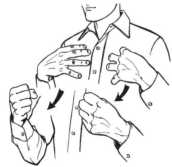

BRAVE, COURAGEOUS, FEARLESS

Touch the chest below the shoulders with the fingertips of both open hands; then move them forward forcefully into *S* positions.

Memory aid: Suggests strong shoulders prepared for a battle.

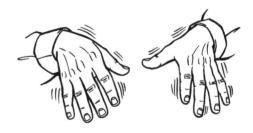

NERVOUS, JITTERY, JUMPY

Hold both open hands to the front with palms facing down and make the hands tremble.

Memory aid: Suggests the physical expression of *nervousness.*

EMBARRASS, SHY, BASHFUL

Raise and lower both open hands alternately in front of the face with palms facing in. Sometimes the hands are rotated slightly forward at the same time.

Memory aid: Suggests the desire to hide the face because of *embarrassment.*

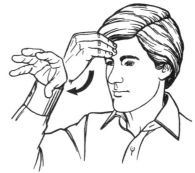

DON'T CARE

Place the fingers of the closed *and* hand on the forehead; then flick the hand forward while simultaneously opening the fingers.

Memory aid: Suggests that the concern of the mind is discarded.

WISH

With the palm facing in, draw the right *C* hand down the chest from just below the neck.

Memory aid: The *C* hand suggests a craving, such as for food.

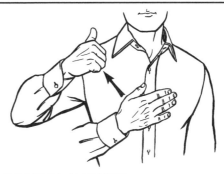

PREFER, RATHER

Place the right flat hand on the chest and move it up toward the right while simultaneously changing to an *A* hand.

Memory aid: The *A* hand seems to suggest an alternative.

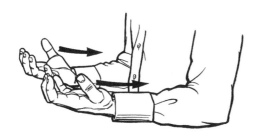

WANT, COVET, DESIRE

With palms facing up, move both open curved hands toward self a few times.

Memory aid: Suggests pulling something toward self.

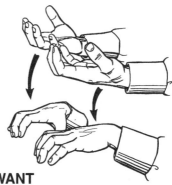

DON'T WANT

Move both open curved hands from a palm-up to a palm-down position.

Memory aid: Suggests throwing something down or away.

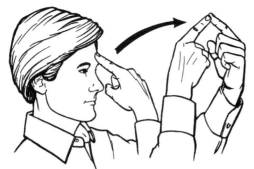 

AMBITION, AIM, GOAL, OBJECTIVE

Hold the left index finger upward to the front in a position slightly higher than the head. Touch the forehead with the right index finger and move it forward and upward until it touches the tip of the left index finger.

Memory aid: Suggests the forward and upward progression toward a *goal.*

PATIENT, PATIENCE, BEAR

Move the right *A* thumb downward over the lips.

Memory aid: Suggests a person experiencing difficulties or frustrations without talking about it.

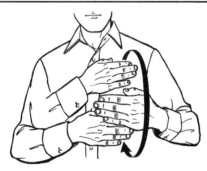 

KIND (emotion), BENEVOLENT, GENTLE, GRACIOUS

Place the right flat hand over the heart; then circle it around the left flat hand which is held a short distance from the chest with palm facing in.

Memory aid: Suggests a heart that is giving of itself unselfishly.

MEAN (adjective), CRUEL, HURTFUL

Strike the right bent *V* knuckles against the left bent *V* knuckles with a downward movement.

Memory aid: Suggests unpleasant contact.

 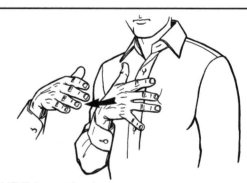

APPRECIATE

Make a circle with the right middle finger over the heart. The sign for *please* may also be used.

Memory aid: Suggests feelings of the heart.

HURT (emotion)

Place the right middle finger on the heart with other fingers extended; then twist the hand quickly forward and outward from the wrist.

Memory aid: Suggests that the feelings of the heart have been wrenched from the chest.

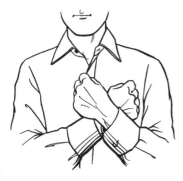

LOVE

Cross either the closed or flat hands over the heart with palms facing in.

Memory aid: Symbolizes the *love* of the heart.

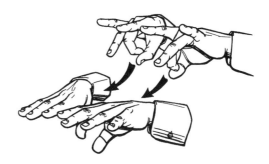

HATE, ABHOR, DESPISE, DETEST, LOATHE

Hold both open hands in front of the chest with palms facing down, and flick both middle fingers outward simultaneously.

Memory aid: Symbolizes the desire to get rid of something.

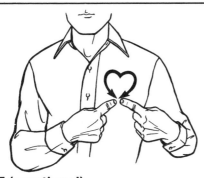

HEART (emotional)

Outline the shape of a heart on the chest with both index or middle fingers.

Memory aid: The outlined shape indicates the *heart.*

I LOVE YOU

Hold the right hand up with palm facing forward. The thumb, index, and little fingers are extended.

Memory aid: The letters *I, L,* and *Y* are combined.

VALENTINE

Outline a heart shape on the chest with the fingers of both *V* hands.

Memory aid: The *V* hands and the heart shape indicate the meaning.

LONELY, LONESOME

Hold the right index finger in front of the lips with the palm facing left. Move the index finger down across the lips a few times.

Memory aid: Suggests that persons by themselves are silent.

FAVORITE

Tap the chin a few times with the right middle finger.

Memory aid: Suggests a dimple on the chin, which is considered cute by many people.

SPECIAL, EXCEPT, EXCEPTIONAL, EXTRAORDINARY, OUTSTANDING, UNIQUE

Point the left index finger up and take hold of it with the right thumb and index finger. Raise both hands together.

Memory aid: One finger is selected for *special* treatment.

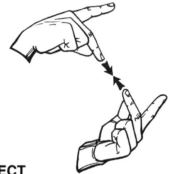

PERFECT

Move the middle fingertips of both *P* hands together so that they touch.

Memory aid: The letter *P*s meet perfectly.

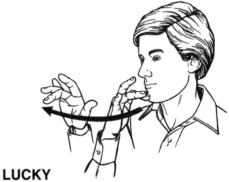

LUCKY

Touch the chin with the right middle finger; then flip the hand around so that the palm faces forward.

Memory aid: Some people consider themselves *lucky* to have a dimple on the chin.

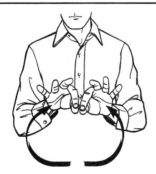

IMPORTANT, MERIT, SIGNIFICANT, PRECIOUS, USEFUL, VALUABLE, WORTHY

Bring both *F* hands up to the center of the chest beginning with palms facing up, and turn them palms down with the thumbs and index fingers touching.

Memory aid: The *F* hands can represent something that is first and, therefore, *important*.

BETTER

Touch the lips with the fingers of the right flat hand; then move it to the right side of the head while forming an *A* hand.

Memory aid: Suggests tasting something and giving a thumbs-up sign of approval.

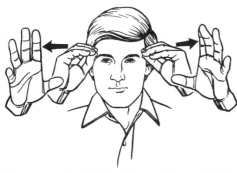

AWFUL, CATASTROPHIC, DREADFUL, FEARFUL, HORRIBLE, TERRIBLE, TRAGIC

Place both *O* hands near the temples and flick the fingers out while forming open hands with palms facing.

Memory aid: Suggests that a person's attention is riveted to something unpleasant.

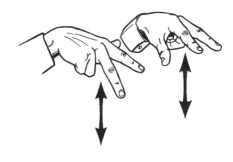

AWKWARD, BUNGLING, CLUMSY

Point both 3 hands forward with the palms facing down. Move them back and forth or up and down with an *awkward* jerking motion.

Memory aid: Suggests a person trying to walk with some toes missing.

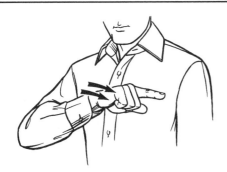

WORTHLESS, USELESS

Bring both *F* hands up from the sides to the center until the thumbs and index fingers touch. Swing the hands away to the sides while simultaneously forming open hands.

Memory aid: This is a combination of the signs for *important* and *finish*.

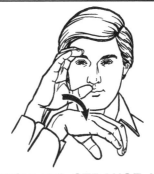

ODD, PECULIAR, STRANGE, WEIRD

Give the right *C* hand a quick downward twist in front of the eyes.

Memory aid: Suggests distorted vision.

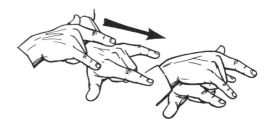

GUILTY

Tap the right *G* hand against the heart area a few times.

Memory aid: The initial indicates the word, and the action suggests that the heart is beating rapidly because of *guilt*.

CHEAT, BETRAY, FRAUD, DECEIVE

Point both modified *Y* hands forward with the index fingers also extended and palms down. Position one hand over the other (either is acceptable), and move the top one forward and backward a few times.

Memory aid: One hand seems to be trying to hide the other one from view.

PROOF, EVIDENCE, PROVE

Touch the lips with the right index finger; then bring the right flat hand down onto the palm of the left flat hand. Both hands have palms facing up in the ending position.

Memory aid: Suggests the placing of tangible *proof* in front of a person.

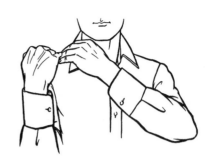

RESPONSIBILITY, BURDEN, OBLIGATION

Place the fingers of both curved hands on the right shoulder. Sometimes both *R* hands are placed on the right shoulder to sign *responsibility*.

Memory aid: Suggests the expression, Carrying a load on his shoulders.

EXPERT, SHARP, SKILLFUL, COMPETENT

Point the fingers of the left hand upward with palm facing right. Grasp the little-finger side of the left hand with the right, and move the right hand forward.

Memory aid: The action suggests that the edge of the left hand is being *sharpened.*

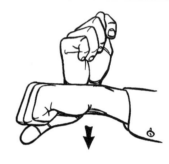

TRADITION

Bring the wrist of the right *T* hand down on the wrist of the left *S* hand; then push both hands down slightly.

Memory aid: This is similar to the basic sign for *habit,* with the initial added.

PROMISE

Touch the lips with the right index finger; then move the right flat hand down and slap it against the thumb and index-finger side of the closed left hand.

Memory aid: The sign suggests the spoken word is sealed and sure.

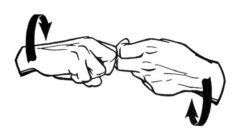

PROBLEM, DIFFICULTY

Touch the bent knuckles of the two *U* (or *V*) hands together and twist in opposite directions while moving downward slightly.

Memory aid: The rubbing knuckles suggest friction.

COOPERATE

Interlock the index fingers and thumbs of both hands, with the other fingers extended. Move as one unit in a counterclockwise circle.

Memory aid: The links of a chain are moving in harmony.

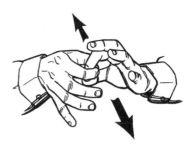

CONNECTION, BELONG, RELATIONSHIP

Interlock the index fingers and thumbs of both hands, with all the other fingers extended. Move as one unit either forward and backward or from left to right a few times.

Memory aid: Suggests the links of a chain *connected* to each other.

COMPARE, CONTRAST

With palms facing each other, hold both curved hands up near the head; then rotate the hands with an inward twist from the wrists so that both palms face the head.

Memory aid: Suggests a side-by-side *comparison*.

ANYHOW, ALTHOUGH, ANYWAY, DOESN'T MATTER, NO MATTER, REGARDLESS

Hold both slightly curved hands to the front with palms facing up and fingertips pointing toward each other. Brush the fingertips back and forth over each other a few times.

Memory aid: A vague action implying possibilities.

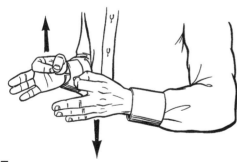

IF

Point the two *F* hands forward and move them up and down alternately with palms facing each other.

Memory aid: The movement suggests scales that may tip one way or the other.

BUT, ALTHOUGH, HOWEVER

Cross both index fingers with palms facing out; then draw them apart a short distance.

Memory aid: Indicates that an opposite or alternative suggestion may be forthcoming.

MATCHING SKILL

Look at the words at the left side of the page. Then match the signs with the words by writing the correct word next to the sign.

MATCHING
WORDS

dream

lazy

love

obedience

proof

know

happy

I love you

please

invent

respect

skeptical

stubborn

wish

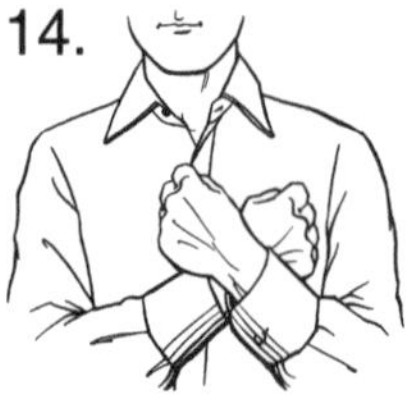

*Answers are
on page 285.*

1. _____

2. _____

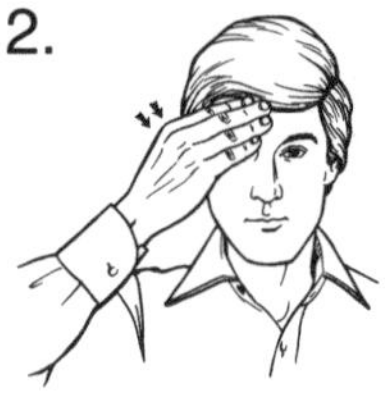

3. _____

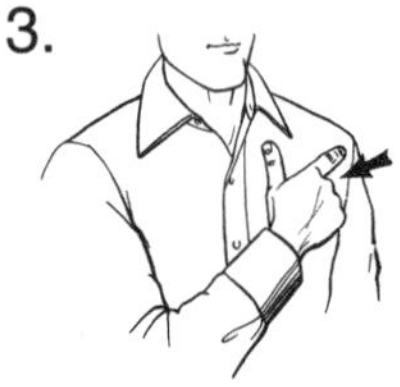

4. _____

5. _____

6. _____

7. _____

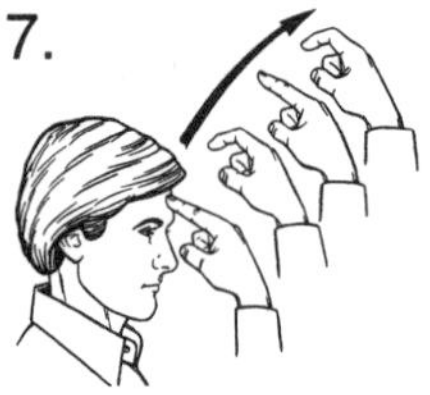

8. _____

9. _____

10. _____

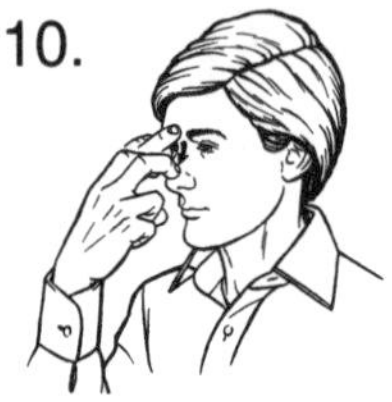

11. _____

12. _____

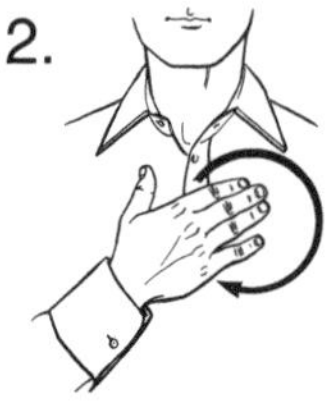

13. _____

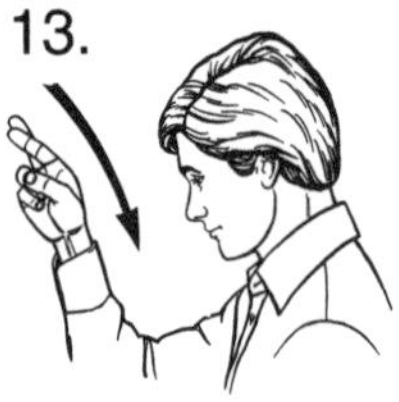

14. _____

Chapter———

9

God
and
Religion

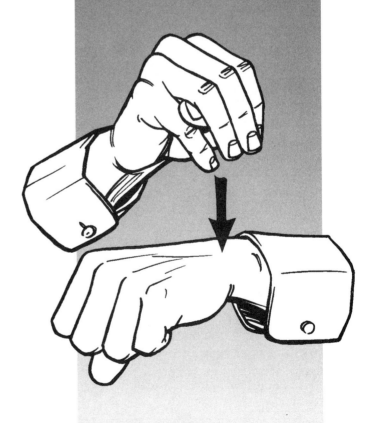

GOD

Point the right *G* finger in a forward-upward direction at head level. Some signers use the flat hand. Move the right hand in a backward-downward arc toward self, ending with a *B* hand in front of the upper chest with palm still facing left.

Memory aid: The finger or hand pointing upward suggests *God* is above all.

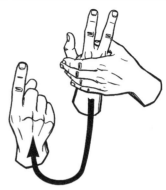

TRINITY

With palms facing in, slide the right *3* hand down through the left *C* hand. Bring the right hand from beneath the left *C* hand and point the right index finger up.

Memory aid: Symbolizes the concept that three become one.

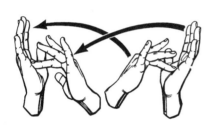

JESUS

Hold both open and slightly curved hands to the front with palms facing. Touch the left palm with the right middle finger; then touch the right palm with the left middle finger.

Memory aid: Indicates the nail scars caused by crucifixion.

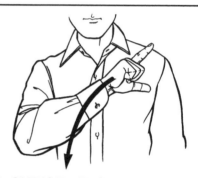

LORD, CHRIST, KING, QUEEN, ROYAL

Move the right *L* hand from the left shoulder to the right waist. Initialize the other words with the same basic movement.

Memory aid: Suggests the sash sometimes worn by *royalty.*

SAVIOR, SALVATION, SAVE, SAFE

Cross the *S* hands on the chest with palms facing in; then rotate them to the sides with palms facing forward.

Memory aid: Suggests breaking a rope tied around the wrists.

HOLY, HALLOWED, DIVINE, RIGHTEOUS, SANCTIFIED

Make a right *H* hand; then move the right flat palm across the left flat palm from heel to fingertips. *Note:* Initialize each word individually.

Memory aid: The initials indicate the words, and the movement is the same as that for *clean.*

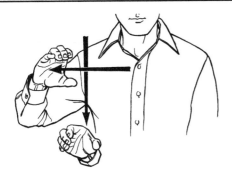

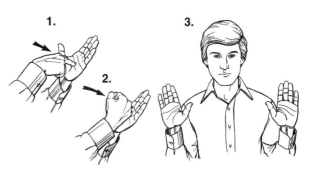

CROSS (noun)

Trace the outline of a cross with the fingers and thumb of the right *C* hand. First move down, then across from left to right.

Memory aid: The initial indicates the word, and the action portrays the shape of a *cross*.

CRUCIFY, CRUCIFIXION

Thrust the right index finger into the palm of the left open hand; then strike the left palm with the little-finger edge of the closed right hand. Hold both flat open hands up to the front with palms facing forward.

Memory aid: Symbolizes the *crucifixion.*

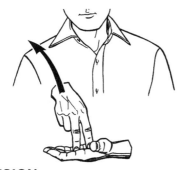

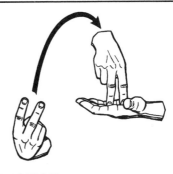

ASCENSION

Hold the left flat hand to the front with palm facing up. Place the right *V* hand fingertips on the left palm; then raise the right *V* hand upward with fingertips pointing down.

Memory aid: Someone rising to heaven.

RESURRECTION

Hold the left flat hand to the front with palm facing up. Bring the right *V* hand up from a palm-up position until the *V* fingers stand on the left palm.

Memory aid: The meaning is pictured by the idea of a person rising from a lying position to a standing one.

GLORY, GLORIOUS

Holding the hands in the horizontal position with the right hand above the left, clap once. Raise the open right hand to head level while moving it in an arc to the right side with a wavy movement.

Memory aid: Suggests something or someone that is shining or shimmering and worthy of applause.

WORSHIP, ADORE, AMEN

Close the left hand over the right closed hand and move them slowly toward self.

Memory aid: A common position of reverence.

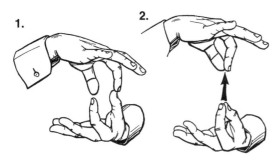

SPIRIT, GHOST

Bring the right open hand down toward the left open hand with palms facing. Create *F* hands as the right hand is drawn upward.

Memory aid: The rising of a hand suggests the rising of a *spirit.*

SOUL

Place the left *O* hand close to the body with the palm facing self. Bring the right open hand down over the *O* hand and raise it to shoulder level while simultaneously forming the *F* hand.

Memory aid: Suggests that the *soul* is to be found deep within a person.

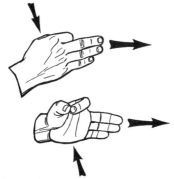

FAITHFUL

Point both *F* hands forward with the right hand over the left. Move both hands forward while simultaneously striking the lower side of the right hand on the upper side of the left a few times.

Memory aid: The repeated striking action indicates *faithfulness.*

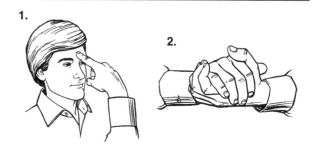

BELIEVE

Touch the forehead with the right index finger; then bring the right hand down until it clasps left hand in front of chest.

Memory aid: Suggests that belief is something to be held onto.

FAITH

Touch the forehead with the right index finger; then move both hands to the center of the chest, or slightly to the left, while closing them to the *S* position. Position left hand above the right, and a slight downward movement can be made.

Memory aid: Symbolizes the planting of a flag to show *faith* in one's country.

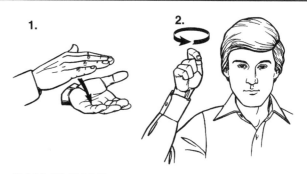

HALLELUJAH

Clap the hands; then hold up one or both closed hands with the thumb tips and index fingertips touching. Make small circular movements.

Memory aid: The initial action expresses appreciation which is then followed by an action symbolizing the waving of small flags.

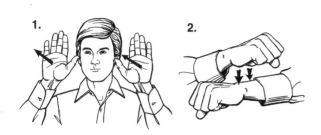

MIRACLE, MARVEL

Move the open hands up and forward a few times with palms facing out. Tap the wrist of the right *S* hand on the wrist of the left *S* hand a few times. This sign is a combination of the signs for *wonderful* and *work.*

Memory aid: Suggests an attitude of awe while beholding the work of a *miracle.*

INNOCENT

Place the fingers of both *H* hands at the mouth and move both hands out and down until the palms face up. *Alternative:* Sign *not* and *blame.*

Memory aid: Suggests that the lips have spoken honestly and *innocently.*

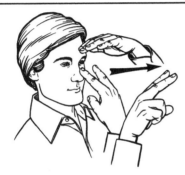

VISION, FORECAST, FORESEE, PROPHECY

With the palm facing in, point to the eyes with the right *V* fingers. Move the right hand forward, turning the palm outward as it passes under the left flat palm.

Memory aid: The movement of the right hand suggests it can go beyond normal *vision.*

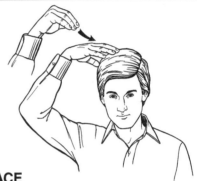

GRACE

Move the right *and* hand down over the head while changing it to a slightly curved open hand.

Memory aid: Symbolizes showers of blessings coming from above.

ANGEL, WINGS

Touch the shoulders with the fingertips of both hands (sometimes only one hand is used). Point the fingers of both downturned hands outward to the sides; then flap the hands up and down a few times.

Memory aid: Suggests the general location and action of *wings.*

BLESS

Place the thumbs of both *A* hands at the lips. Move both hands in a forward-downward movement while changing them to palm-down flat hands.

Memory aid: Suggests the *blessing* of a kiss and the laying on of hands.

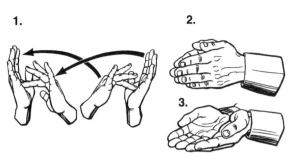

BIBLE, GOD'S BOOK

Hold both open hands to the front with palms facing. Touch left palm with right middle finger; then touch right palm with left middle finger. This is the sign for *Jesus*. Last, point both hands forward with palms touching; then open them.

Memory aid: The signs for *Jesus* and *book*.

COMMANDMENTS

Place the index and thumb side of the right *C* hand on the front of the palm-forward left hand near the top; then move it downward in an arc until it rests at the base of the left hand.

Memory aid: The right hand seems to be pointing out written rules on the left hand.

HEAVEN, CELESTIAL

Hold both flat hands out in front and make a circle with both hands toward self; then pass the right hand under the left palm and up as the hands are crossed at forehead level.

Memory aid: The circle suggests that *heaven* is a perfect place, and the upward movement indicates that *heaven* is above.

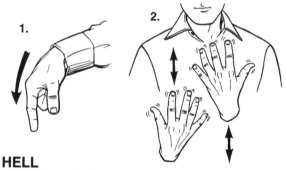

HELL

The right index finger points down, then with palms facing the body, move both slightly curved open hands up and down alternately in front of the body while wiggling the fingers.

Memory aid: Symbolizes leaping flames.

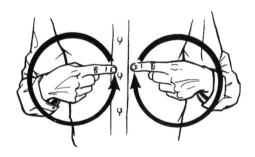

EVIL, CRIME, SIN, WICKED

Point both index fingers toward each other with palms facing self. Move them simultaneously in up-out-down-in circles.

Memory aid: The direction of the circles oppose each other, and likewise, that which is considered *evil* generates opposition.

DEVIL, DEMON, DEVILMENT, MISCHIEF, SATAN

Touch the temple with the thumb of the right palm-forward *3* hand. Bend and unbend the index and middle fingers a few times.

Memory aid: Suggests the medieval conception of a horned *devil*.

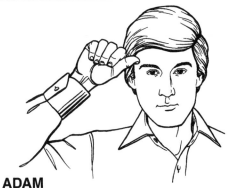

ADAM

Touch the right temple with the thumb tip of the right *A* hand.

Memory aid: The initial indicates the word, and the location is the basic area for *male.*

EVE

Swing the right *E* hand up to the right side of the chin.

Memory aid: The initial indicates the word, and the location conveys the meaning of *female.*

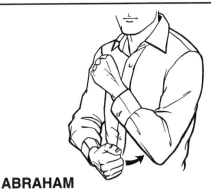

ABRAHAM

Hold the closed left hand near the right shoulder. Strike close to the left elbow with the palm side of the right *A* hand.

Memory aid: The initial indicates the word, and the action locates the same place used for the sign *Passover,* which is a Jewish celebration.

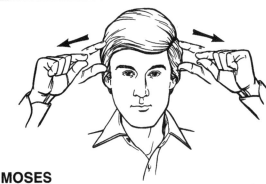

MOSES

Place the *Q* fingers of both hands at the temples with the palms facing each other. Close the fingers as the hands are moved to the sides.

Memory aid: Suggests the pulling of the veil over *Moses'* face after his conversation with God. The Bible records that *Moses'* face shone to the extent that people could not look at him.

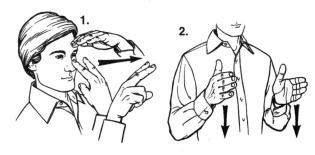

PROPHET

With the right palm facing in, point to the eyes with the right *V* fingers. Move the right hand forward, turning the palm outward as it passes under the left flat palm. Add the *person (personalizing word ending)* sign.

Memory aid: This sign is a combination of *vision* and *person (personalizing word ending).*

ANOINT

Place the right *C* hand slightly above head level with palm facing forward. Tilt the *C* hand toward the head.

Memory aid: Symbolizes pouring onto the head.

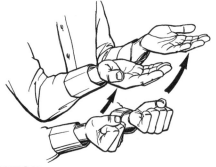

SACRIFICE

Place both *S* hands to the front with palms facing up, and move them in a forward-upward direction while simultaneously opening into palm-up flat hands.

Memory aid: The initial indicates the word, and the movement is similar to that of the sign for *offer.* A *sacrifice* is an offering.

PASSOVER

Tap the left elbow with the right *P* fingers a few times.

Memory aid: The initial indicates the word, and the action (the same basic movement as for *cracker*) suggests the Jewish use of unleavened bread during the Passover holiday.

CHRISTIAN

Hold both open slightly curved hands to the front, palms facing each other. Touch the left palm with the right middle finger; then touch the right palm with the left middle finger. Add the *person (personalizing word ending)* sign.

Memory aid: This is a combination of the signs for *Jesus* and *person (personalizing word ending).*

BAPTIZE, CHRISTEN (sprinkling)

Place the closed *S* (or *and*) hand above the head and thrust downward toward the head simultaneously opening the hand.

Memory aid: Symbolizes water falling on the head.

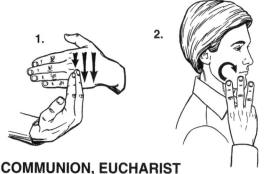

COMMUNION, EUCHARIST

Draw the little-finger edge of the right hand downward over the back of the left flat hand which has palm facing self. Make a forward circular movement with the right *W* hand on the right cheek.

Memory aid: Symbolizes the cutting of bread slices and the redness of cheeks caused by wine.

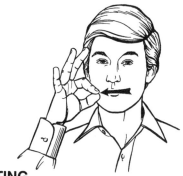

FASTING

Move the right thumb and index side of the *F* hand across the mouth from left to right.

Memory aid: The initial indicates the word, and the action suggests dryness of the mouth.

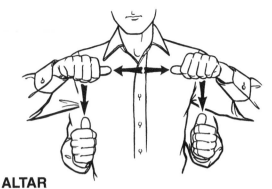

ALTAR

Touch the *A* thumbs in front with the palms facing down. Move them apart sideways a short distance, then down a short distance with the palms now facing.

Memory aid: The initials indicate the word, and the movement outlines the tablelike shape of an *altar*.

KNEEL, PROTESTANT

Imitate kneeling legs with the fingers of the right *V* hand on the left flat palm.

Memory aid: Symbolizes a person *kneeling*.

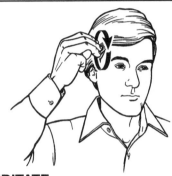

MEDITATE

Make forward circles with the right *M* hand near the right temple.

Memory aid: The *M* hand indicates the word, and the movement suggests action taking place in the mind.

PRAY, PRAYER

Place both flat hands to the front with palms touching; then move them toward self while simultaneously inclining the head slightly forward.

Memory aid: A traditional position of the head and hands during *prayer*.

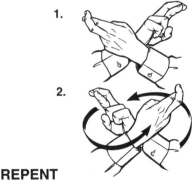

REPENT

Cross the right *R* wrist over the left *R* wrist with palms facing. Reverse the position by twisting the hands at the wrist.

Memory aid: The initials indicate the word, and the movement suggests a change of heart.

FORGIVE, PARDON

Stroke the lower part of the left flat hand with the right fingertips several times.

Memory aid: Suggests a wiping movement and the expression A clean slate.

CONFESS, ACKNOWLEDGE, ADMIT

Begin with the fingertips of both hands pointing down and touching the chest. Simultaneously move the hands in an upward-forward arc until they are pointing forward with palms facing up.

Memory aid: Symbolizes the expression Getting something off his chest.

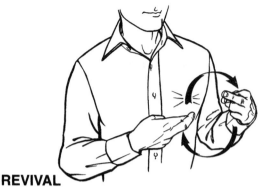

REVIVAL

Brush the *R* fingers alternately upward over the heart with circular motions.

Memory aid: Suggests an excitement of the heart.

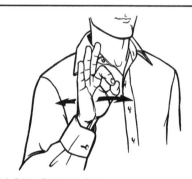

PREACH, SERMON

Place the right *F* hand in front of the right shoulder with palm facing forward. Move it forward and backward a few times.

Memory aid: The *F* hand can suggest that the preacher encourages people to have faith in God. The action suggests repeated emphasis.

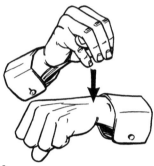

MINISTRY

Tap the wrist of the left downturned closed hand with the wrist of the right downturned *M* hand a few times.

Memory aid: The initial indicates the word, and the action suggests the sign for *work*.

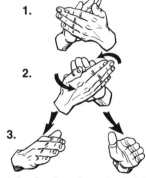

PEACE

Place the right flat hand on the left flat hand at chest level; then place the left on the right. Now move both flat hands down and to the sides with palms down. Pass from one position to another smoothly and continuously.

Memory aid: Symbolizes hands grasping in agreement.

GOSPEL

Slide the little-finger edge of the right *G* hand across the flat left hand from fingertips to heel a few times.

Memory aid: The initial indicates the word, and the action is similar to the sign for *new*. Thus something new is "news," and the meaning of *gospel* is "good news."

MISSION

Make a circle with the right *M* hand over the heart.

Memory aid: The initial indicates the word, and the action suggests that one's heart must be in it to be successful.

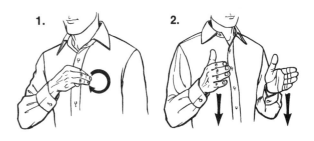

MISSIONARY

Make a circle with the right M hand over the heart. Add the *person (personalizing word ending)* sign.

Memory aid: The initial indicates the word, and the action suggests that one's heart must be in it to be successful.

NUN

Outline a semi-circle with the right *N* hand by going up the left side, across the forehead, then down the right side of the face.

Memory aid: The outline resembles a veil.

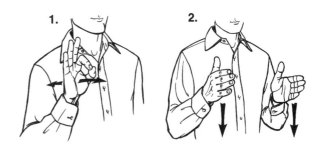

MINISTER, PASTOR

Place the right *F* hand in front of the right shoulder with palm facing forward. Move it forward and backward a few times. Add the *person (personalizing word ending)* sign.

Memory aid: The F hand can suggest that the preacher encourages people to have faith in God. The action suggests repeated emphasis.

PRIEST, CHAPLAIN, CLERGYMAN, MINISTER

Draw the right *Q* fingertips backward around the right side of the neck.

Memory aid: Suggests the clerical collar.

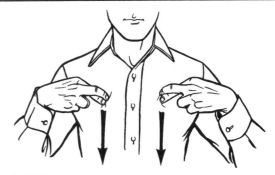

RABBI

With the palms facing in, place the fingertips of the *R* hands on the chest. Move both hands downward simultaneously to the abdomen.

Memory aid: Suggests the rabbinical prayer shawl *(tallit)* that is worn around the neck and covers the shoulders and chest.

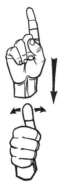

TITHE

Point the right index finger up; then lower the hand to an *A* position and pivot the hand slightly back and forth sideways.

Memory aid: The signs for *1* and *10* indicate the fraction ¹⁄₁₀.

CHURCH, CHAPEL, DENOMINATION

Tap the thumb of the right *C* hand on the back of the closed left hand.

Memory aid: The initial indicates the word (except for *denomination*), and the position suggests that the *church* is built on a solid foundation.

TEMPLE (building)

Place the heel of the right *T* hand on the back of the closed left hand.

Memory aid: The initial indicates the word, and the position suggests that a *temple* has a solid foundation.

RELIGION, RELIGIOUS

Place the right *R* fingers on the heart and move the hand in a forward-upward arc, leaving the palm facing forward.

Memory aid: The initial indicates the word, and the action suggests that *religion* concerns the heart's relationship with God.

BAPTIST, BAPTISM, IMMERSION

Hold both *A* hands to the front with palms facing. Move both hands to the right and down slightly, while at the same time turning the hands so that the thumbs point to the right.

Memory aid: Symbolizes water *baptism* by *immersion*.

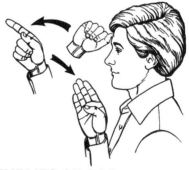

ASSEMBLIES OF GOD

Put thumb of right *A* hand on forehead; then point right *G* finger forward and upward at head level. (Some use the flat hand with palm facing left.) Move right hand in a downward arc toward self, ending with a *B* hand in front of the chest.

Memory aid: The *A* hand indicates the name; the pointing finger suggests God is above all.

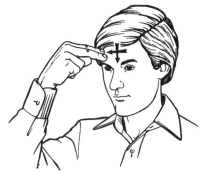

CATHOLIC

Outline a cross in front of the forehead with the right *U* fingers. Move down first, then from left to right.

Memory aid: Symbolizes the cross of Christ, which is central to *Catholic* belief.

JEWISH

Place the right open fingers and thumb on the chin with the palm facing self. Draw the hand down below the chin and form an *and* hand.

Memory aid: Symbolizes the beards worn by Hasidic *Jews.*

METHODIST

Rub the flat hands together enthusiastically.

Memory aid: The early *Methodists* were particularly noted for their enthusiastic worship.

LUTHERAN

Hold the left flat hand up with the palm facing right. Place the thumb of the right *L* in the center of the left palm.

Memory aid: The initialized sign indicates the word.

EPISCOPAL

Hold the left arm in front of the chest with the palm down and the hand closed. Touch the underside of the left forearm with the right index finger at the wrist; then dip the right index hand before touching the left elbow.

Memory aid: Suggests the enlarged sleeve of a priest's robe.

PRESBYTERIAN

Place (or tap) the right middle finger of the *P* hand on the flat left palm.

Memory aid: The initial indicates the word, and the standing position can suggest the *Presbyterian* stand for church government by the presbyters (ministers and elders).

MATCHING SKILL

Look at the words at the left side of the page. Then match the signs with the words by writing the correct word next to the sign.

1.

MATCHING
WORDS

faith

believe

God

spirit

communion

worship

kneel

resurrection

Jesus

bless

Gospel

tithe

angel

evil

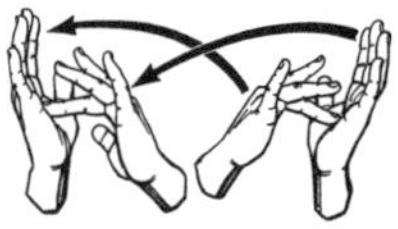

2.

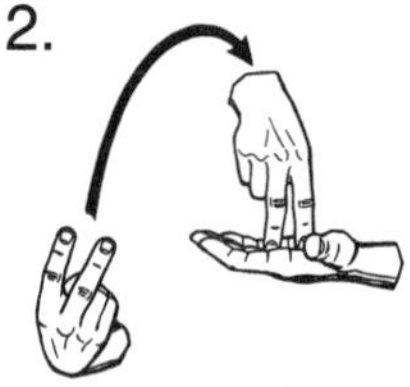

3.

4.

5.

6.

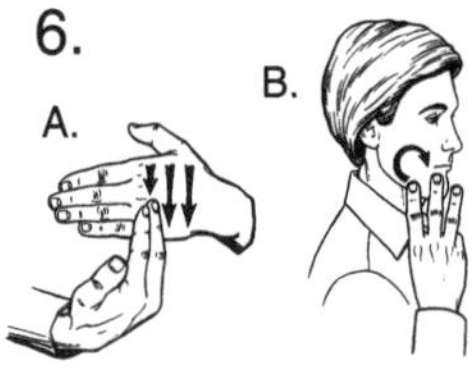

7.

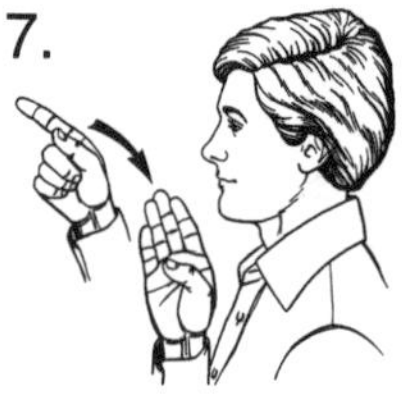

8.

9.

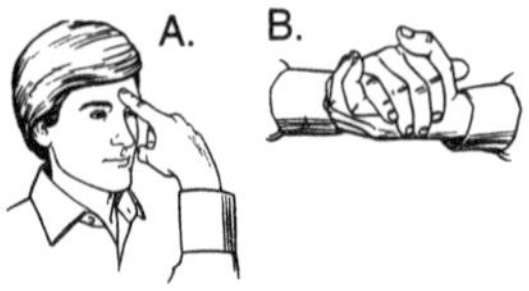

10.

11.

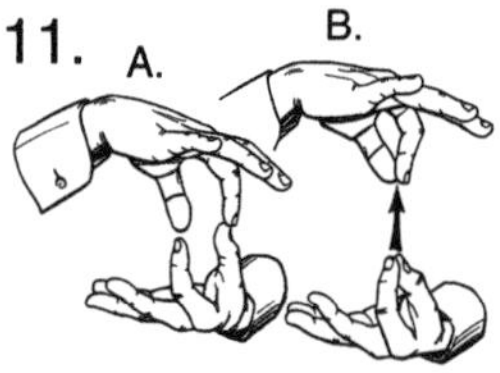

12.

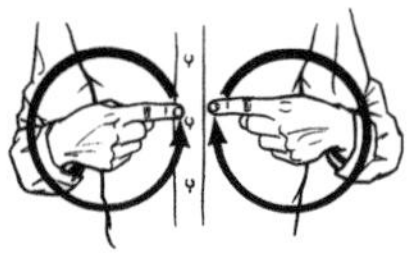

13.

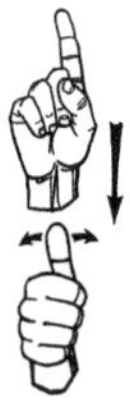

14.

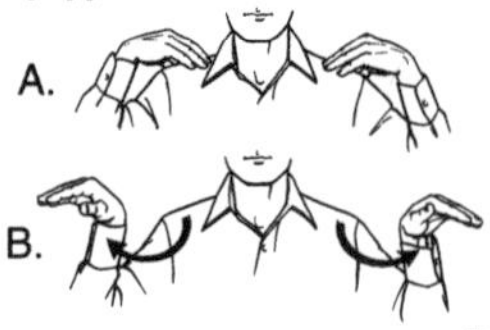

*Answers are
on page 285.*

Chapter ———————————————

10

Education, Careers, and Communication

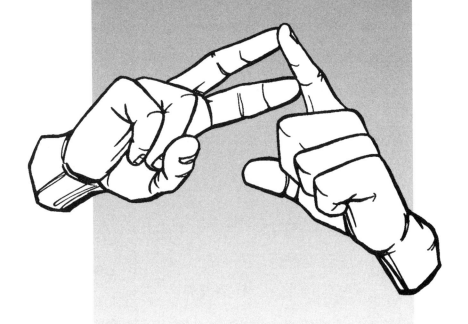

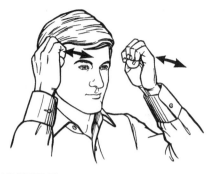

EDUCATION

With palms facing each other, move both *E* hands forward from the forehead a few times.

Memory aid: Suggests the mind's involvement in giving and receiving information.

SCHOOL

Clap the hands two or three times.

Memory aid: Symbolizes a teacher clapping for attention.

COLLEGE

Place the right flat palm on the left upturned flat palm, then make a counterclockwise circle with the right hand above the left.

Memory aid: The first part of the sign is similar to the clapping sign for *school*. The second part shows that this is something above and superior to a school.

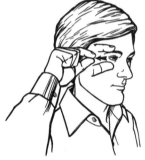

GALLAUDET (college), GLASSES

Place the fingers and thumb of the right *G* hand above and below the right eye at the side. Move the fingers back to the ear while closing them.

Memory aid: Suggests a person who wears *glasses*. Thomas Hopkins Gallaudet, founder of *Gallaudet College* for the deaf, wore *glasses*.

HISTORY

Shake the right *H* hand up and down a short distance.

Memory aid: The initial indicates the word, and the action can suggest the up-and-down experiences of *history*.

LIBRARY

Make a small clockwise circle with the right *L* hand.

Memory aid: The initial indicates the word, which requires context and simultaneous lipreading for full comprehension.

CURRICULUM

Hold the thumb and index-finger side of the right hand against the fingers of the left flat hand. Move the right *C* hand down to the base of the left hand while forming an *M* hand.

Memory aid: The first and last letters of the word.

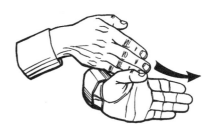

MAJOR, AREA, FIELD, SPECIALTY

Point the fingers of the left hand forward with the palm facing right. Move the little-finger edge of the right flat hand foward along the left index finger.

Memory aid: Suggests the idea of going in a definite direction.

PROGRAM

Move the middle finger of the right *P* hand down the left flat palm; then down the back of the left hand. Twist the left hand slightly between the two phases of this sign so that the observer can see clearly.

Memory aid: Suggests a sheet of paper that is printed on both sides.

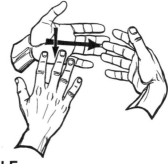

SCHEDULE

Hold the left open hand to the front with palm facing right. Move the right open hand down across the left hand with palms facing; then move the back of the right hand across the left hand from left to right.

Memory aid: Suggests the vertical and horizontal lines printed on a *schedule* sheet.

COURSE

Place the little-finger edge of the right *C* hand against the fingers of the left flat hand. The left palm can face up or toward self. Move the *C* hand down to the base of the left hand.

Memory aid: The initial indicates the word, and the action is similar to the sign for *lesson*.

PROJECT

Move the middle finger of the right *P* hand down the left flat palm; then move the little finger of the right *J* hand down the back of the left flat hand. Twist the left hand slightly between the two phases of this sign so that the observer can see clearly.

Memory aid: The initial suggests the word.

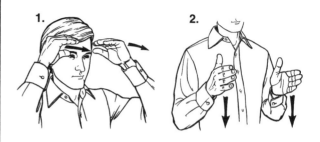

TEACH, EDUCATE, INDOCTRINATE, INSTRUCT

Position both open *and* hands at the front and sides of the head, then move them forward while simultaneously forming closed *and* hands.

Memory aid: Suggests pulling out knowledge from the mind and presenting it to others.

TEACHER

Position both open *and* hands at the front and sides of the head; then move them forward while simultaneously forming closed *and* hands. Add the sign for *person (personalizing word ending)*.

Memory aid: Symbolizes a person who pulls out knowledge from the mind and presents it to others.

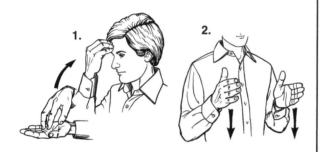

STUDENT

Place the fingers of the right open hand on the upturned left palm. Close the right fingers as the hand is moved to the forehead. The fingertips are then placed on the forehead. Add the sign for *person (personalizing word ending)*.

Memory aid: Right hand seems to be taking information from left hand and putting it into the mind.

STUDY

Point the right open fingers toward the left flat hand. Move the right hand back and forth a short distance from the left while simultaneously wiggling the right fingers.

Memory aid: The right hand seems to be *studying* the left hand intently. The left hand can represent a book.

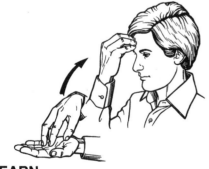

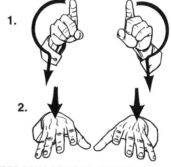

LEARN

Place the fingers of the right open hand on the upturned left palm. Close the right fingers as the hand is moved to the forehead. The fingertips are then placed on the forehead.

Memory aid: The right hand seems to be taking information from the left hand and putting it into the mind. The left hand can represent a book.

TEST, EXAMINATION, QUIZ

Hold both index fingers up and draw the shape of question marks in opposite directions, then open both hands and move them forward.

Memory aid: Suggests that questions are sent out.

FRESHMAN
Touch the fourth finger of the open left hand with the right index finger.

Memory aid: Counting from the thumb, a *freshman* still has four years of study to complete.

SOPHOMORE
Touch the middle finger of the open left hand with the right index finger.

Memory aid: Counting from the thumb, a *sophomore* still has three years of study to complete.

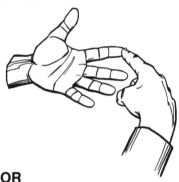

JUNIOR
Touch the index finger of the left open hand with the right index finger.

Memory aid: Counting from the thumb, a *junior* still has two years of study to complete.

SENIOR
Touch the thumb of the open left hand with the right index finger.

Memory aid: Counting from the thumb, a *senior* has only one year of study to complete.

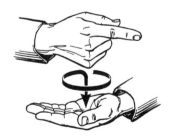

GRADUATE
Make a small clockwise circle with the right *G* hand and bring it down onto the left flat palm.

Memory aid: The initial indicates the word, and the action is similar to that for *seal.* Therefore, a *graduate's* education is sealed.

DIPLOMA, DEGREE
Place the thumb and index-finger sides of both *O* hands together, then move them horizontally away from each other to the sides.

Memory aid: Symbolizes the cylindrical shape of a *diploma.*

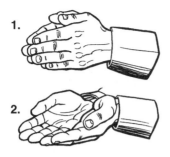

BOOK, TEXTBOOK, VOLUME

Place the hands palm to palm, with fingers pointing forward. Open both hands to the palm-up position while maintaining contact with the little fingers.

Memory aid: Pictures the opening of a *book*.

WORD

Hold the left index finger up with palm facing right; then place the thumb and index finger of the right *Q* hand against it.

Memory aid: Symbolizes that a *word* is just a small section of a sentence.

LINE

Trace a line down the center of the left flat hand with the right little finger.

Memory aid: Illustrates a straight *line*.

PARAGRAPH

Place the thumb and fingertips of the right *C* hand against the left flat palm.

Memory aid: The space between the right thumb and fingers can indicate the depth of a *paragraph* on a page.

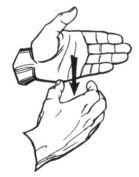

CHAPTER

Move the thumb and fingertips of the right *C* hand downward across the left flat palm.

Memory aid: The initial position of this sign is similar to that for *paragraph*, but the action suggests something of greater length than a paragraph.

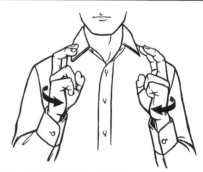

QUOTE, CAPTION, CITE, SUBJECT, THEME, TITLE, TOPIC

Hold both curved V hands to the front with palms facing forward. Twist them simultaneously so that the palms face each other.

Memory aid: Symbolizes quotation marks.

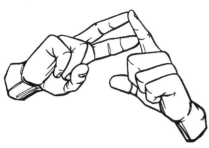

VOCABULARY

Place the tips of the right *V* fingers against the upright left index finger. The right palm faces forward and the left palm faces right.

Memory aid: The initial suggests the word, and the position is related to the sign for *word*.

LESSON, EXERCISE (mental)

Place the little-finger edge of the right flat hand across the fingers of the left flat hand. Move the right hand in a small arc so that it rests at the base of the left hand.

Memory aid: Suggests a section of a page to be studied.

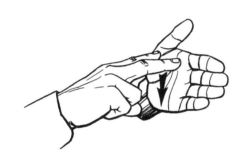

READ

Point the right *V* fingers at the left flat palm and move them downward.

Memory aid: The *V* fingers symbolize two eyes *reading* a book.

WRITE

Touch the right index finger and thumb with the other fingers closed; then move the right hand horizontally across the flat left palm with a slight wavy motion.

Memory aid: Symbolizes *writing* on paper.

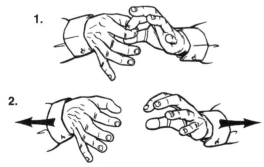

STORY, TALE

Link the thumbs and index fingers of both *F* hands and pull them apart several times.

Memory aid: Suggests many sentences linked together to make a *story*.

PAPER

Strike the heel of the left upturned palm two glancing blows with the heel of the right downturned palm. The right hand moves from right to left to perform the movement.

Memory aid: Can suggest the pressing of pulp to make *paper*.

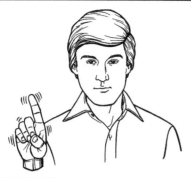

DICTIONARY

Hold the right *D* hand up and shake it.

Memory aid: The initial indicates the word, which requires context and simultaneous lipreading for full comprehension.

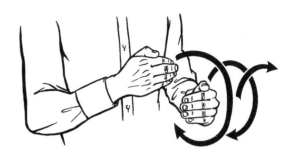

PROCESS, PROCEDURE, PROGRESS

With the palms facing in, roll both bent hands over each other a few times with a forward motion.

Memory aid: Suggests that action continues while forward *progress* is made.

PRACTICE, DISCIPLINE, TRAINING

Rub the knuckles of the right *A* hand back and forth across the left index finger. A *T* hand can be used for *training*.

Memory aid: The right hand seems to be polishing the left index finger to improve the shine, just as *practice* will improve quality.

OPPORTUNITY

Hold both *O* hands to the front with palms down. Move both hands forward and up while forming *P* hands.

Memory aid: The first two letters of *opportunity* are signed.

BUSY

Tap the wrist of the left closed palm-down hand with the wrist of the right *B* hand, which has palm facing forward. The right hand moves from right to left as it taps the left wrist.

Memory aid: The initial indicates the word, and the action suggests the sign for *work*.

SIGNATURE, REGISTER

Slap the right *H* fingers down onto the left upturned palm.

Memory aid: The right hand identifies the place for *signing*.

COMPUTER

Move the right *C* hand, palm left, across the forehead in two arcs from right to left. *Note: Computer* can be signed several ways. See *alternative* on page 274.

Memory aid: The initial indicates the word, and the location in front of the brain suggests *computers* contain knowledge.

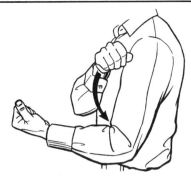

AUTHORITY, ENERGY

Make a downward arc with the right *A* hand (or curved hand) from the left shoulder to the inside of the left elbow. Use the *E* hand for *energy*.

Memory aid: Suggests the power of a biceps muscle.

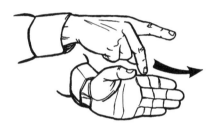

PROFESSION, PROFESSIONAL

Point the fingers of the left hand forward with the palm facing right. Move the initial *P* sign of the right hand forward along the left index fingers.

Memory aid: Suggests the idea of moving forward in a profession.

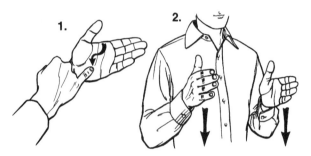

ARTIST

Hold the left flat hand to the front with the palm facing left; then trace a wavy line over the left palm with the right *I* finger. End with the sign for *person (personalizing word ending)*.

Memory aid: Symbolizes a person using a pencil or brush.

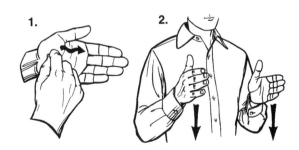

WRITER, REPORTER

Touch the right index finger and thumb with the other fingers closed; then move the right hand across the left flat hand from the base of the palm to fingertips, and repeat. Add the sign for *person (personalizing word ending)*.

Memory aid: Suggests a person who is *writing*.

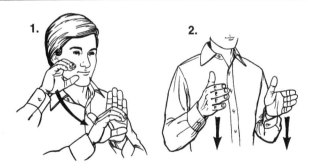

PHOTOGRAPHER

Move the right C hand down and forward from the right side of the face until the thumb side of the right C hand is placed against the left flat palm. Add the sign for *person (personalizing word ending)*.

Memory aid: A combination of the signs for *picture* and *person*.

PSYCHOLOGY

Place the little-finger edge of the right flat hand on the palm-forward left hand between the thumb and index finger. The movement is often repeated.

Memory aid: The right hand suggests a dividing line between the left thumb and index finger. *Psychologists* attempt to divide and analyze the mind.

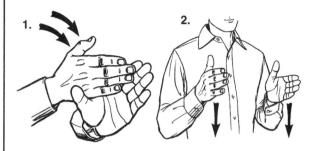

PSYCHOLOGIST

Strike the little-finger edge of the right flat hand on the palm-forward left hand between the thumb and index finger, and repeat. Add the sign for *person (personalizing word ending)*.

Memory aid: The first action of the right hand suggests a division, which can in turn suggest a person who divides and analyzes the mind.

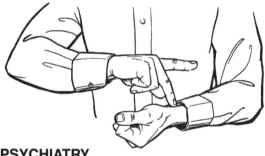

PSYCHIATRY

Place the right *P* hand on the upturned left wrist.

Memory aid: As a doctor takes a person's pulse rate, *psychiatry* studies the working of the mind.

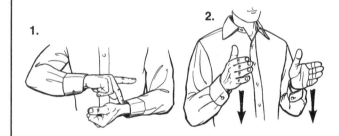

PSYCHIATRIST

Place the right *P* hand on the upturned left wrist. Then sign *person (personalizing word ending)* by holding both flat open hands to the front with palms facing; then move them down simultaneously.

Memory aid: A *psychiatrist* attempts to put his finger on the workings of the mind.

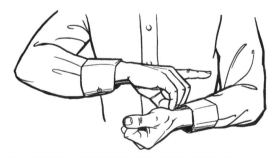

DOCTOR, PHYSICIAN, SURGEON

Place the right *D* hand or *M* fingers on the upturned left wrist.

Memory aid: Suggests taking a person's pulse rate.

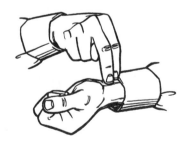

NURSE

Place the right extended *N* fingertips on the upturned left wrist.

Memory aid: The initial indicates the word, and the action suggests the taking of a person's pulse rate.

FARMER
Place the thumb of the right open hand on the left side of the chin with the palm facing in. Rub the right thumb across the chin to the right. Add the sign for *person (personalizing word ending)*.

Memory aid: Suggests an unshaven *farmer*.

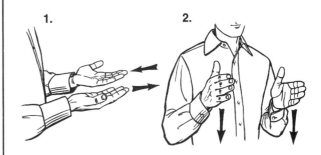

WAITER, SERVANT, WAITRESS
Move both upturned flat hands back and forth alternately. Add the sign for *person (personalizing word ending)*.

Memory aid: The movement suggests someone who offers something to another.

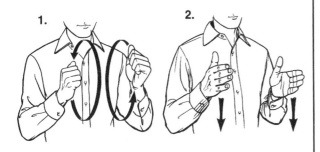

ACTOR, ACTRESS
Rotate both *A* hands inward toward the body with the palms facing each other; then add the sign for *person (personalizing word ending)*.

Memory aid: The initialized hands indicate the words, and the movement suggests the action that accompanies drama.

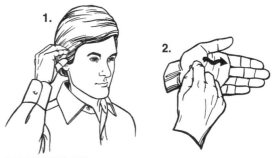

SECRETARY
Remove an imaginary pencil from above the right ear, and mimic handwriting action on the left flat hand.

Memory aid: Suggests a *secretary* taking notes on a pad.

DENTIST
Touch the teeth with the thumb of the right *D* hand.

Memory aid: The initial and location combined suggest the meaning.

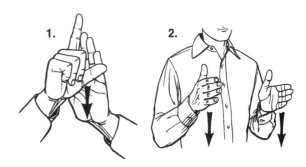

LAWYER, ATTORNEY
Place the index and thumb side of the right *L* hand on the front of the palm-forward left hand. Begin near the top; then move the right hand downward in a small arc to the base of the left hand. Add the sign for *person (personalizing word ending)*.

Memory aid: The right hand seems to be pointing out written *laws* on a printed page.

ASSISTANT

Bring the right *L* hand up under the closed left hand and touch the little-finger edge of the left hand with the right thumb. Sometimes the left hand remains open.

Memory aid: Suggests support from underneath.

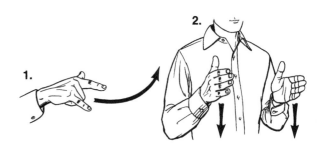

PILOT

Make a forward-upward sweeping motion with the right *Y* hand which also has its index finger extended. Add the sign for *person (personalizing word ending)*.

Memory aid: Suggests a person involved with a plane taking off.

PRINCIPAL

Circle the right palm-down *P* hand in a counter-clockwise direction over the back of the left flat hand.

Memory aid: This is the basic movement of the sign for *over,* which indicates authority over others.

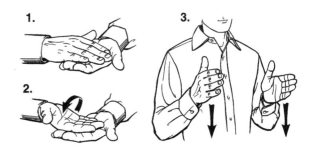

CHEF, COOK (noun)

Place first the palm side and then the back of the right flat hand on the upturned palm of the left flat hand. Add the sign for *person (personalizing word ending)*.

Memory aid: Suggests a *chef* turning over food in a frying pan.

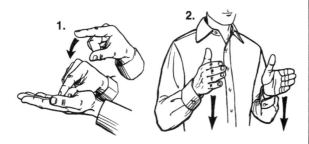

PRINTER

Move the right index finger and thumb together as though picking something up; then place them on the left flat palm. Add the sign for *person (personalizing word ending)*.

Memory aid: Symbolizes a person who uses the old-fashioned method of hand-setting type.

BOSS, CHAIRMAN, OFFICER, CAPTAIN, GENERAL

Touch the right shoulder with the fingertips of the curved right open hand. This is sometimes done with both hands on both shoulders.

Memory aid: Suggests the location of military shoulder bars, thus indicating authority.

BUSINESS

Strike the wrist of the right *B* hand on the down-turned wrist of the closed left hand a few times. The right *B* hand faces foward.

Memory aid: The initial indicates the word, and the action suggests the sign for *work*.

WORK, JOB, LABOR, TASK

With the palms facing down, tap the wrist of the right *S* hand on the wrist of the left *S* hand a few times.

Memory aid: Suggests the action of a hammer.

SELL, SALE, STORE

Point both *and* hands down with bent wrists and pivot them in and out from the body a few times.

Memory aid: Suggests holding up a cloth item for *sale*.

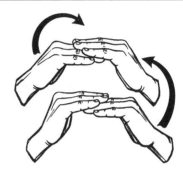

BUILD, CONSTRUCT, ERECT

Place both bent hands to the front with palms down. Position the fingers of the hands one above the other alternately a few times.

Memory aid: Suggests building blocks going up.

BUILDING

Place both bent hands in front with palms down. Position the fingers one above the other alternately a few times. Form a triangle point at head level with both flat hands; move them apart and down simultaneously with fingers pointing up.

Memory aid: Suggests the action of *building* and the shape of a house.

ELEVATOR

Raise and lower the right *E* hand.

Memory aid: The initial and movement of the sign suggest the meaning.

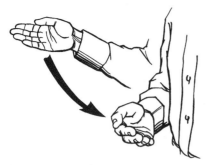

HIRE, EMPLOY, INVITE

Swing the right *H* or flat hand in toward the right side with palm facing up.

Memory aid: Suggests the idea of pulling someone in to oneself and supporting the person.

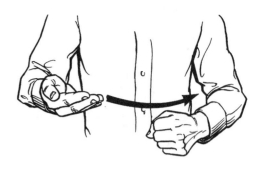

FIRED, EXPELLED, DISCHARGED

Sweep the upturned right flat hand across the top of the left closed hand from right to left.

Memory aid: Suggests someone's head being cut off.

PASS

Pass the right *A* hand forward from behind the left *A* hand.

Memory aid: Represents the action of *passing*.

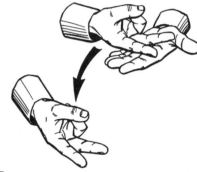

FAIL

Slide the back of the right *V* hand across the upturned left hand and go beyond and below the left fingertips.

Memory aid: The downward movement can suggest *failure*. Or, victory has fallen.

MEMBER, BOARD, CONGRESS, SENATE, LEGISLATURE

Place the right extended *M* fingers at the left shoulder and move them across to the right shoulder. Initialize each word.

Memory aid: The initial suggests the word, and the shoulders symbolize authority.

PROMINENT, CHIEF, MAIN

Raise the right *A* hand above head level with the palm facing left.

Memory aid: Points to a high elevation.

SUCCESS, ACCOMPLISH, PROSPER, SUCCEED

Point both index fingers toward each other or toward the head; then move them upward while simultaneously making little forward circles. End with both index fingers pointing up and palms facing forward.

Memory aid: Suggests increasingly higher stages.

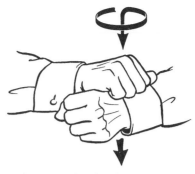

APPOINTMENT, ENGAGEMENT, RESERVATION

Circle the palm-down right *A* hand above the palm-in left *S* hand in a counterclockwise direction. Bring the right wrist down onto the left and move both hands down together a short distance.

Memory aid: Indicates a binding together of the hands in commitment.

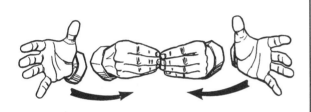

MEETING, ASSEMBLE

Bring both open hands in from the sides while forming *and* hands, and let the fingertips touch.

Memory aid: The fingers symbolize individuals coming together.

TALK, COMMUNICATE, CONVERSATION, DIALOGUE, INTERVIEW

Move both index fingers back and forth from the lips alternately. Use initialized hands for *communicate, conversation, dialogue,* and *interview.*

Memory aid: Suggests the words coming and going in a *conversation.*

SAY, MENTION, REMARK, SPEAK, SPEECH, STATE, TELL

Make a small forward circular movement in front of the mouth with the right index finger.

Memory aid: Suggests a flow of words from the mouth.

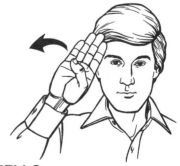

HI, HELLO

Move the right *B* hand in a small arc to the right from the forehead.

Memory aid: Similar to a salute.

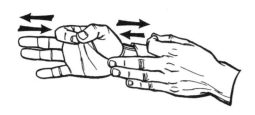

EXPLAIN, DEFINE, DESCRIBE

Point the extended fingers of both *F* hands forward with palms facing; then move the hands back and forth alternately. For added clarity the *D* hands may be used for *define* and *describe*.

Memory aid: The action seems to suggest that the hands are not sure which way to go until further *explanation* is given.

ANNOUNCE, DECLARE, PROCLAIM

Touch the lips with both index fingers and swing them forward and to the sides.

Memory aid: Something is *proclaimed* from the mouth that expands to a wide group of hearers.

DISCUSS

Sign *discuss* by striking the left palm with the right index finger several times.

Memory aid: The movement is a common gesture used when one wishes to emphasize a point.

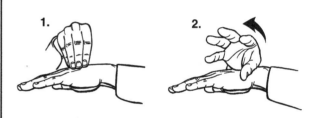

ADVICE, ADVISE, COUNSEL

Touch the back of the left flat hand with the fingertips of the right *and* hand. Form an open right hand while moving it forward across the left hand.

Memory aid: Suggests giving out information in many directions.

EXPRESSION

Move both *X* (or modified *A*) hands up and down alternately at the sides of the face.

Memory aid: Suggests facial movements.

EXAGGERATE

Hold the left *S* hand in front of the chest with palm facing right. Place the right *S* hand in front of the left *S* hand and move it forward while pivoting it several times from the wrist.

Memory aid: The right hand seems to be stretching something held by the left hand.

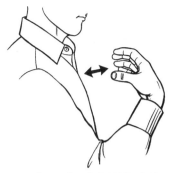

COMPLAIN, GRIPE, GRUMBLE, OBJECT, PROTEST

Strike the fingertips of the curved right hand sharply against the chest. Repeat a few times.

Memory aid: Suggests the expression Something on his chest.

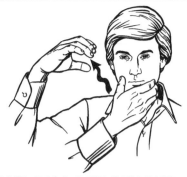

SHOUT, CALL OUT, CRY OUT, ROAR, SCREAM

Place either the right *C* or curved open hand in front of the mouth and move it forward and upward with a wavy motion.

Memory aid: Suggests strong vibrations coming from the mouth.

SCOLD, REPRIMAND, TELL OFF

Point the right index finger forward and shake it up and down.

Memory aid: A common gesture for *reprimanding* someone.

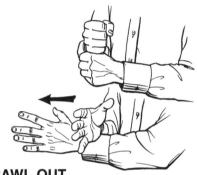

BAWL OUT

Place the little-finger edge of the right *S* hand over the thumb edge of the left *S* hand. Move both hands forward while quickly forming open hands that are crossed at the wrists.

Memory aid: The fingers are thrust vigorously toward another person, representing a barrage of words.

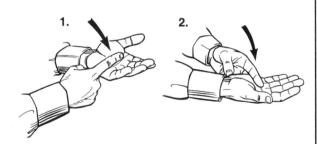

ARGUE, DISPUTE, DEBATE, CONTROVERSY

First strike the left palm with the right index finger and then the right palm with the left index finger. Repeat several times.

Memory aid: The movement suggests two sides or opposing opinions.

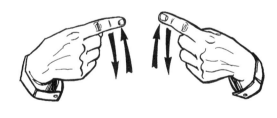

QUARREL, ROW, SQUABBLE

Point both index fingers toward each other in front of the chest and shake them up and down from the wrists. The hands are often moved parallel to one another, but some move them up and down alternately.

Memory aid: The hands seem to be shooting at each other.

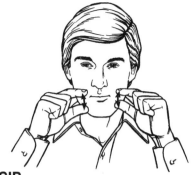

GOSSIP

Open and close the Q fingers and thumbs several times in front of the mouth.

Memory aid: The fingers seem to be talking rapidly to each other.

LIE, FALSEHOOD

Point the right index finger to the left and move it horizontally across the lips from right to left.

Memory aid: Symbolizes the idea that spoken truth is diverted from its normally straight course.

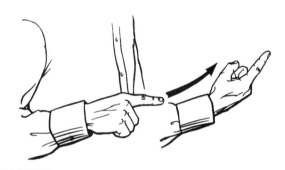

INSULT

Move the right index finger forward and up with a slight twist.

Memory aid: The hand symbolizes a sword that is used to injure an opponent.

COMMAND, ORDER

Point the right index finger to the mouth and then move it forward and slightly down with considerable emphasis. The index finger ends pointing forward.

Memory aid: Suggests strong words coming from the mouth.

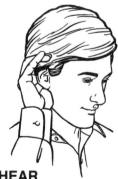

LISTEN, HEAR

Place the cupped right hand behind the right ear and turn the head a little to the left.

Memory aid: The sign is a natural gesture.

THANKS, THANK YOU, YOU'RE WELCOME

Touch the lips with the fingertips of one or both flat hands, then move the hands forward until the palms are facing up. It is natural to smile and nod the head while making this sign.

Memory aid: A natural expression of affection used when one is grateful.

WHISPER
Hold the slightly curved right hand over the right side of the mouth, and lean slightly forward or to the side.

Memory aid: The slightly cupped hand projects the *whisper* to its intended receiver.

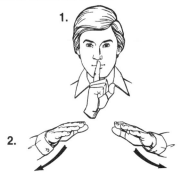

QUIET, CALM, PEACEFUL, SERENE, SILENT, STILL, TRANQUIL
Touch the lips with the right index finger and move both flat hands down and to the sides with palm facing down.

Memory aid: These are gestures that indicate *silence* and *peace*.

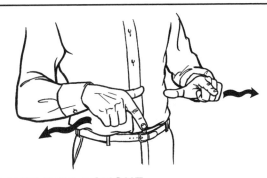

LANGUAGE, TONGUE
Point both *L* hands toward each other (sometimes the index fingers point up), and move them to the sides with a twisting motion from the wrists.

Memory aid: The *L* hands indicate the word, and the action is similar to that of the sign for *sentence*.

VOICE, VOCAL
Draw the back of the right *V* fingers up the neck and forward under the chin.

Memory aid: The initial indicates the word, and the action shows the location.

AUDIOLOGY
Circle the right *A* hand in a forward circle at the right ear.

Memory aid: The initial indicates the word, and the action suggests a continuing emphasis on the ear.

SPEECH, ADDRESS, LECTURE, TESTIMONY
Pivot the slightly curved right hand forward and backward several times from an upright position at the front and right of the head.

Memory aid: A speaker's common gesture.

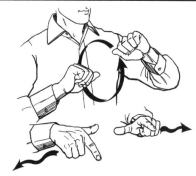

SIGN (language)

Hold both index fingers to the front with the fingers pointing toward each other and the palms facing out. Rotate both index fingers alternately toward the body.

Memory aid: Symbolizes the necessary moving of the hands to engage in *sign* language.

AMESLAN (American Sign Language)

Rotate both *A* hands alternately toward the body with palms facing forward. Then point both *L* hands toward each other and move them to the sides with a twisting motion from the wrists.

Memory aid: The first part of the movement is the sign for *signs,* and the second part is the sign for *language.*

FINGERSPELLING, ALPHABET, SPELL, DACTYLOLOGY, MANUAL ALPHABET

With palm facing down, wiggle the fingers of the right flat open hand as the hand moves along a horizontal line to the right.

Memory aid: Emphasizes the use of fingers in *fingerspelling.*

LIPREADING, ORAL, SPEECHREADING

Hold the right curved *V* fingers at the mouth. Move around the mouth in a counterclockwise direction.

Memory aid: The initial and location indicate the voice.

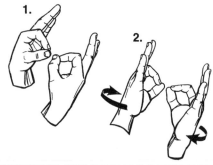

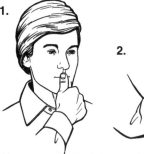

INTERPRET, REVERSE INTERPRET, TRANSLATE

Make *F* hands, palms facing, and left palm forward; then reverse hands. *Reverse interpret:* Use *R* hands with reverse action of *interpret,* and follow with the sign for *interpret. Translate:* Use *T* hands and the same movement for *interpret.*

Memory aid: Changing positions suggests changing languages.

LETTER, MAIL

Place the right *A* thumb on the mouth and then on the palm of the upturned left hand.

Memory aid: Suggests moistening a stamp and placing it on an envelope.

MAGAZINE, BOOKLET, BROCHURE, CATALOG, LEAFLET, MANUAL, PAMPHLET

Move the right thumb and index finger along the little-finger edge of the left hand. The direction of this movement varies in different locations.

Memory aid: Suggests the thinness of a *magazine*.

POSTER, SIGN

Hold both index fingers up with palms facing forward and outline a square.

Memory aid: Suggests the shape of a *poster*.

NEWSPAPER, PRINTING, PUBLISHING

Move the right index finger and thumb together as though picking something up; then place them on the left flat palm.

Memory aid: Symbolizes the old-fashioned method of hand-setting type.

VIDEOTAPE

Rotate the thumb side of the right *V* hand in a clockwise circle on the left flat palm which is facing right. Make the same movement with the right *T* hand on the left flat palm.

Memory aid: The initialized movement suggests the sign.

RADIO

Cup both hands over the ears.

Memory aid: Suggests the use of *radio* headphones.

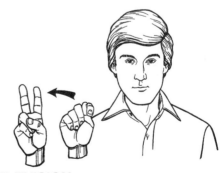

TELEVISION

Fingerspell T-V.

Memory aid: The initials indicate the word.

NAME THE SIGN

To reinforce the vocabulary you have already learned, identify the following signs from this chapter by writing the names underneath the signs.

  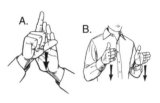

1. _____ 2. _____ 3. _____ 4. _____

5. _____ 6. _____ 7. _____ 8. _____

9. _____ 10. _____ 11. _____ 12. _____

13. _____ 14. _____ 15. _____ 16. _____

17. _____ 18. _____ 19. _____ 20. _____

21. _____ 22. _____ 23. _____ 24. _____

Answers are on page 285.

Chapter

11

Cities, States, Countries, and Governments

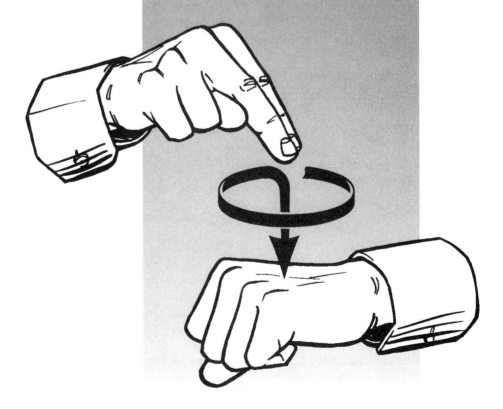

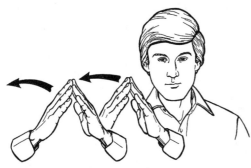

CITY, COMMUNITY, TOWN, VILLAGE

Make the point of a triangle with both flat hands in front of the chest. Repeat a few times while moving the hands to the right.

Memory aid: Symbolizes the roofs of many houses.

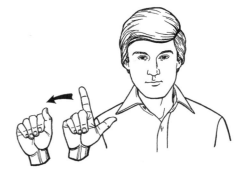

LOS ANGELES

Fingerspell L-A.

Memory aid: The initials combined with the context and simultaneous lipreading indicate the meaning.

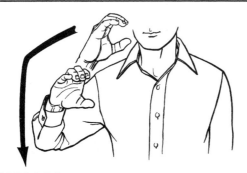

CHICAGO

Move the right *C* hand to the right from just above shoulder level; then move it downward a short distance. Some use a slight wavy motion for the downward movement.

Memory aid: The downward movement can symbolize the changing directions of wind. *Chicago* is known as the "windy city."

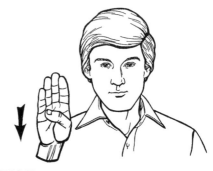

BOSTON

Place the *B* hand near the right shoulder with the palm facing forward, and then make a few short downward movements.

Memory aid: The initial indicates the word, which requires context and simultaneous lipreading for full comprehension.

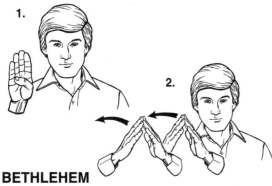

BETHLEHEM

Fingerspell the word, or sign *B* followed by the sign for *city*. *City* is signed by making the point of a triangle with both flat hands in front of the chest. This is repeated a few times while moving the hands to the right.

Memory aid: The initial followed by the sign for *city* indicates the meaning.

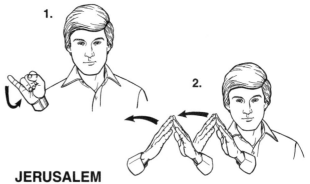

JERUSALEM

Fingerspell the word, or sign *J* followed by the sign for *city*. *City* is signed by making the point of a triangle with both flat hands in front of the chest. This is repeated a few times while moving the hands to the right.

Memory aid: The initial followed by the sign for *city* indicates the meaning.

STATE (geographical)

Place the index-finger side of the right *S* hand near the top of the left flat hand, which has its palm facing forward. Move the right *S* hand in a downward arc to the base of the left hand.

Memory aid: The initial combined with context indicates the word.

CALIFORNIA

Touch the right ear with the right index finger, or grasp the right earlobe between the right index finger and thumb. Shake the right *Y* hand as it moves down and forward.

Memory aid: Suggests both the idea of earrings and the color of *gold.*

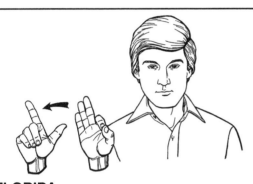

FLORIDA

Fingerspell F-L.

Memory aid: The first two letters of the word are initialized. Context and simultaneous lipreading are required for full comprehension.

HAWAII

Make a counterclockwise circle with the right *H* hand in front of the face with the palm facing self.

Memory aid: The initial suggests the word, which requires context and simultaneous lipreading for full comprehension.

NEW YORK

Place the right *Y* hand on the left flat hand and slide it back and forth.

Memory aid: The initial combined with the context indicates the name, and the movement suggests the busy atmosphere of a large city.

ARIZONA

Slide the right *A* hand thumb from right to left across the chin with palm facing left.

Memory aid: The word *"Arizona"* means "little spring place." The movement and location of this sign are similar to those for *dry.*

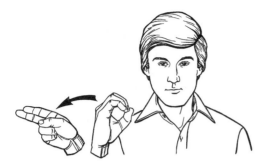

OHIO
Fingerspell O-H.

Memory aid: The initials indicate the first two letters of the word, which requires context and simultaneous lipreading for full comprehension.

COUNTRY (national territory)
Rub the palm side of the right *Y* hand in a counterclockwise direction on the underside of the left forearm near the elbow.

Memory aid: Can suggest a patriotic willingness to wear out one's elbow for one's *country*.

NATION, NATIONAL, NATURE, NATURAL
Make a clockwise circle above the back of the left *S* hand with the right extended *N* fingers; then bring the *N* fingers down on the back of the left hand.

Memory aid: The initial indicates the word, and the action suggests something that is established on a solid foundation.

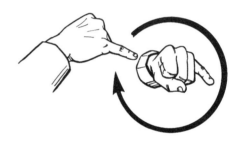

INTERNATIONAL
Point the little finger of the left *I* hand forward with the palm facing down. With the palm facing down, rotate the right *I* hand forward around the left *I* hand.

Memory aid: The initial indicates the word, and the action suggests the idea of something that goes around the world.

FOREIGN
Rub the index finger and thumb side of the right *F* hand in a few counterclockwise circles on the underside of the left forearm near the elbow.

Memory aid: The initial indicates the word, and the action is the same as that for *country*.

EUROPE, EUROPEAN
The right *E* hand moves in a small clockwise circle, with palm out, at the right side of the head. Add the sign for *person (personalizing word ending)* when signing *European* with reference to a person.

Memory aid: The initial indicates the word, and the movement suggests many countries.

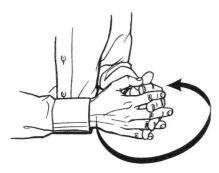

AMERICA, AMERICAN

Interlock the fingers of both slightly curved open hands and move them from right to left in an outward circle. For *American* add the sign for *person (personalized word ending)* in reference to a person.

Memory aid: The interlocked fingers suggest the log fences made by *America's* early settlers.

UNITED STATES

With one flowing movement make a three-quarter counterclockwise circle with the right *U* hand, repeating the movement with the right *S* hand as the hand moves to the right.

Memory aid: The initials indicate the words, which require context and simultaneous lipreading for full comprehension.

CANADA, CANADIAN

Grasp the right jacket or coat lapel (or an imaginary one) and shake it. Add *person (personalized word ending)* when signing *Canadian* with reference to a person.

Memory aid: Suggests shaking snow from one's coat.

MEXICO, MEXICAN

Draw the right extended *M* fingertips downward over the right cheek a few times. Add *person (personalized word ending)* when signing *Mexican* with reference to a person.

Memory aid: The initial of the sign indicates the word, and the actions of the sign suggest *Pancho Villa's* whiskers.

ENGLAND, ENGLISH

Grasp the outer edge of the left closed hand at the wrist with the curved right hand, and move both hands back and forth. Add *person (personalized word ending)* when signing *English* with reference to a person.

Memory aid: Symbolizes that *England* once ruled much of the world with a firm hand.

ISRAEL, ISRAELI

Using the palm side of the right *I* finger, stroke downward at each side of the chin. Add the sign for *person (personalizing word ending)* when signing *Israeli* with reference to a person.

Memory aid: The initial indicates the word, and the action suggests the stroking of the beard traditionally worn by Hasidic Jews.

GERMANY, GERMAN

Cross the hands at the wrists with palms facing the body and wiggle the fingers. Add the sign for *person (personalizing word ending)* when signing *German* with reference to a person.

Memory aid: Reminds one of the double eagle emblem of the old German empire.

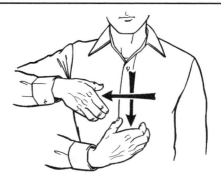

SWITZERLAND

Draw a cross on the chest with the right *C* hand.

Memory aid: Reminds one of the cross on a Swiss flag.

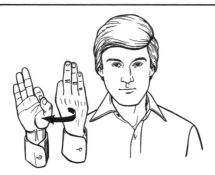

FRANCE, FRENCH

With the right palm facing the right shoulder, flick or twist the *F* hand until the palm faces forward. Add the sign for *person (personalizing word ending)* when signing *French* with reference to a person.

Memory aid: A French chef's sign of approval of a meal well prepared.

EGYPT, EGYPTIAN

With the right palm forward, form a *C* shape with the index finger and thumb and place it on the forehead. Add the sign for *person (personalizing word ending)* when signing *Egyptian* with reference to a person.

Memory aid: The *C* shape resembles the crescent on a Moslem flag.

AFRICA, AFRICAN

Make a counterclockwise circle in front of the face with the right *A* hand. The palm faces left. Add the sign for *person (personalizing word ending)* when signing *African* with reference to a person.

Memory aid: The initial indicates the word, which requires context and simultaneous lipreading for full comprehension.

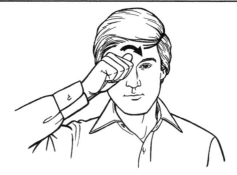

INDIA, INDIAN

With palm facing left, place the tip of the *A* thumb on the center of the forehead and twist slightly. Add the sign for *person (personalizing word ending)* when signing *Indian* with reference to a person.

Memory aid: Touching the forehead reminds one of the red dot some *Indian* women wear.

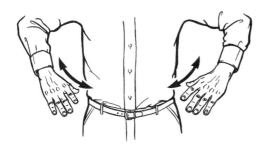

RUSSIA, RUSSIAN

Tap the flat open hands, palms down, on the sides of the waist a few times. Add the sign for *person (personalizing word ending)* when signing *Russian* with reference to a person.

Memory aid: The sign reminds one of a Russian dance.

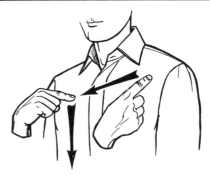

CHINA, CHINESE

Touch the left side of chest then right side of chest with the extended right index finger, palm facing body, then move index finger straight down. Add the sign for *person (personalizing word ending)* when signing *Chinese* with reference to a person.

Memory aid: Suggests the shape of *Chinese* military uniforms.

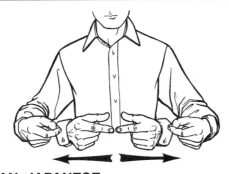

JAPAN, JAPANESE

Point the extended fingers of both *G* hands toward each other and pull them to the sides of the body while closing *G* hands. Add the sign for *person (personalizing word ending)* when signing *Japanese* with reference to a person.

Memory aid: Suggests the shape of the *Japanese* islands.

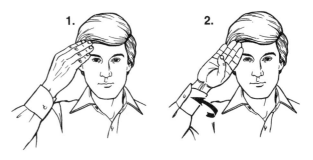

AUSTRALIA, AUSTRALIAN

Touch right side of forehead with the fingertips of the right flat hand, palm in; twist hand, palm out, with the fingertips again touching the forehead. Add *person (personalizing word ending)* when signing *Australian* with reference to a person.

Memory aid: Suggests the wide upturned brim of the traditional *Australian* bush hat.

GOVERNMENT, CAPITAL, FEDERAL, POLITICS

With the right index finger at the right temple, make a small forward circle; then place the index finger on the temple. An initialized hand may be used for *capital, federal,* and *politics.*

Memory aid: Pointing to the head symbolizes the authority of *government.*

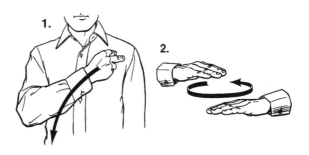

KINGDOM

Move the right *K* hand from the left shoulder to the right waist; then circle the right flat hand over the left flat hand in a counterclockwise direction.

Memory aid: A combination of the signs for *king* and *over.*

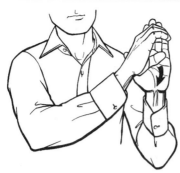

CONSTITUTION, PARLIAMENTARY, PRINCIPLES

Place the right *C* hand on the palm-forward left hand near the top; then move it downward in an arc until it rests at the base of the left hand. *Note:* Initialize each word individually.

Memory aid: The right hand seems to be pointing out written *rules* on a printed page.

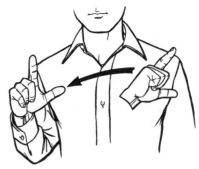

LEGISLATION

Place the thumb of the right *L* hand first on the left shoulder and then on the right.

Memory aid: Can suggest the idea that when *legislation* is passed, the weight of government's shoulders is behind it.

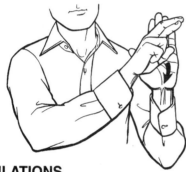

REGULATIONS

Place the index and thumb side of the right *R* hand on the front of the palm-forward left hand near the top; then move it downward in an arc until it rests at the base of the left hand.

Memory aid: The right hand seems to be pointing out written *rules* on the left hand, which can represent the printed page.

LAW

Place the index and thumb side of the right *L* hand on the front of the palm-forward left hand. Begin near the top; then move the right hand downward in a small arc to the base of the left hand.

Memory aid: The right hand seems to be pointing out written *laws* on a printed page.

RULES

Move the right *R* fingers in a downward arc from the fingertips to the base of the palm of the left flat hand.

Memory aid: The left hand can represent a printed page upon which rules are written.

TESTAMENT, WILL (legal statement)

Place the index side of the right *T* hand on the front of the palm-forward left hand near the top, then move it downward in a small arc to the base of the left hand. Use the right *W* hand for *will*.

Memory aid: The right hand seems to be drawing attention to a written statement.

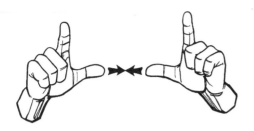

LICENSE, CERTIFICATE
Touch the thumb tips of both *L* hands together a few times with palms facing forward. The *C* hands may be used for *certificate*.

Memory aid: Uses both the initial and the shape.

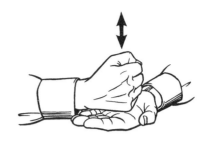

SEAL, STAMP
Drop the right *S* hand sharply into the left flat palm and raise it again.

Memory aid: Suggests the use of a rubber *stamp*.

FLAG, BANNER
Place the right elbow in the left hand and wave the right hand back and forth.

Memory aid: Suggests a *flag* waving on a pole.

STAMP (postal)
With the palm facing in, touch the lips with the right *U* fingers; then place them with palm facing down on the left palm.

Memory aid: Symbolizes moistening a *stamp* and sticking it on an envelope.

PRESIDENT, SUPERINTENDENT
Hold both *C* hands at the temples with palms facing forward. Change to the *S* position as the hands are moved upward and outward.

Memory aid: Suggests the outline of horns symbolizing authority.

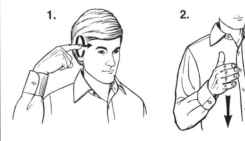

GOVERNOR
With the right index finger at the right temple, make a small forward circle; then place the index finger on the temple. Add the sign for *person (personalizing word ending)*.

Memory aid: Pointing to the head symbolizes the authority of *government*.

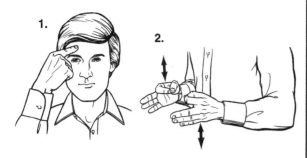

JUDGE, COURT, JUDGMENT, JUSTICE, TRIAL

Touch the forehead with the right index finger and form two *F* hands with palms facing. Move the hands up and down alternately.

Memory aid: Suggests that the mind is weighing the evidence.

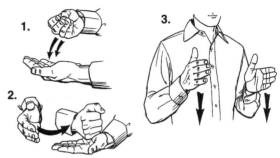

TREASURER

Bring the back of the *and* hand down onto the palm of the left flat hand a few times. Scoop the right hand from the fingertips to the heel of the left flat hand. Bring both flat hands down simultaneously with palms facing.

Memory aid: A combination of *money, collection,* and *person (personalizing word ending).*

REPUBLICAN

Hold up the right *R* hand and shake it.

Memory aid: The initial suggests the word, which requires context and simultaneous lipreading for full comprehension.

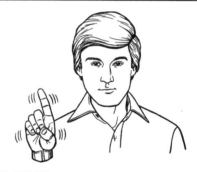

DEMOCRAT

Hold up the right *D* hand and shake it.

Memory aid: The initial suggests the word, which requires context and simultaneous lipreading for full comprehension.

VOTE, ELECT, ELECTION

Place the thumb and index finger of the down-turned right *F* hand into the left *O* hand.

Memory aid: Suggests placing a ballot in a box.

DUTY

Strike the wrist of the downturned left *S* hand with the right *D* hand a few times.

Memory aid: The position can suggest binding the hands and thus the idea of being bound by *duty.*

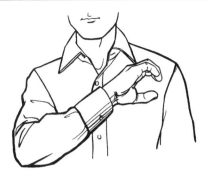

POLICE, COP, SHERIFF
Place the thumb side of the right *C* hand at the left shoulder.

Memory aid: The position at the shoulder indicates those who bear responsibility and authority.

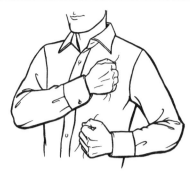

SOLDIER, ARMS
Place the palm side of the right *A* hand just below the left shoulder and the palm side of the left *A* hand several inches below the right hand.

Memory aid: Symbolizes a *soldier* holding a rifle at the left shoulder.

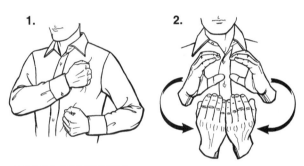

ARMY, MILITARY
Place palm side of right *A* hand just below left shoulder and palm side of left *A* hand several inches below right hand. Then hold both *C* hands upright before the chest with palms facing. Move hands outward in a circle until little fingers touch.

Memory aid: A combination of the signs for *soldier* and *group.*

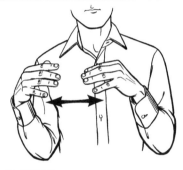

BATTLE, WAR
Hold both open bent hands at chest level with fingertips pointing toward each other. Move both hands simultaneously to the left and then to the right a few times.

Memory aid: Suggests the advance and retreat of military forces.

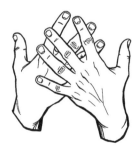

PRISON, BARS, PENITENTIARY
With palms facing in, cross the four fingers of the right *B* hand across the four fingers of the left *B* hand.

Memory aid: Symbolizes the *bars* of a *prison.*

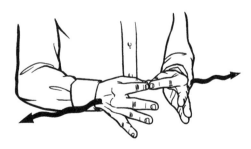

SENTENCE
Touch the thumb and index fingers of each *F* hand in front of the chest. Pull the hands apart to the sides, either with a straight or wavy motion.

Memory aid: Suggests that words linked together stretch out to form a *sentence.*

NAME THE SIGN

To reinforce the vocabulary you have already learned, identify the following signs from this chapter by writing the names underneath the signs.

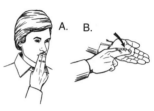 

1. _____ 2. _____ 3. _____ 4. _____

5. _____ 6. _____ 7. _____ 8. _____

  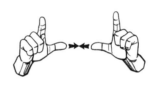  

9. _____ 10. _____ 11. _____ 12. _____

   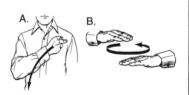

13. _____ 14. _____ 15. _____ 16. _____

17. _____ 18. _____ 19. _____ 20. _____

21. _____ 22. _____ 23. _____ 24. _____

Answers are on page 285.

Chapter

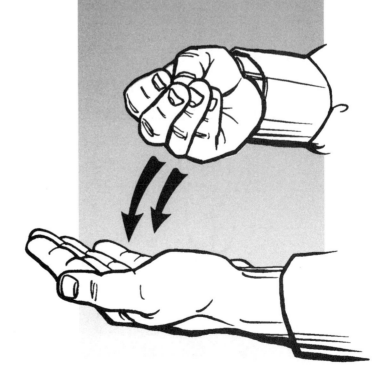

12

Numbers, Money, and Quantity

ZERO
Hold up the right *O* hand with palm facing left.

ONE
Hold up the right index finger with palm facing forward.

TWO
Hold up the separated right index and middle finger with palm facing forward.

THREE
Hold up the separated right index, middle finger, and thumb with palm facing forward.

FOUR
Hold up the separated right four fingers with thumb bent over palm and palm facing forward.

FIVE
Hold up the right open hand with palm facing forward.

SIX
Hold up the right separated index, middle, and ring fingers, palm forward, while touching the tips of the thumb and little finger.

SEVEN
Hold up the right separated index, middle, and little fingers, palm forward, while touching the tips of the thumb and ring finger.

EIGHT
Hold up the right separated index, ring, and little fingers, palm forward, while touching the tips of the thumb and middle finger.

NINE
Hold up the right separated middle, ring, and little fingers, palm forward, while touching the tips of the thumb and index finger.

TEN
Shake the *A* hand back and forth at the wrist with palm facing left and thumb extended upward.

ELEVEN
Hold up the right *S* hand, palm facing self, and flick the index finger up.

TWELVE
Hold up the right *S* hand, palm facing self, and flick the index and middle fingers up.

THIRTEEN
Hold up the right 3 hand, palm facing self, and move the index and middle fingers up and down a few times.

FOURTEEN
Hold up the right *4* hand, palm facing self, and move all four fingers up and down a few times.

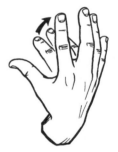

FIFTEEN
Hold up the right 5 hand, palm facing self, and move all four fingers up and down a few times.

SIXTEEN
Hold up the right *A* hand, palm left and thumb extended, then quickly twist the wrist forward while changing to a 6 hand (touching the tips of the thumb and little finger).

SEVENTEEN
Hold up the right *A* hand, palm left and thumb extended, then quickly twist the wrist forward while changing to a 7 hand (touching the tips of the thumb and ring finger).

EIGHTEEN
Hold up the right *A* hand, palm left and thumb extended, then quickly twist the wrist forward while changing to an *8* hand (touching the tips of the thumb and middle finger).

NINETEEN
Hold up the right *A* hand, palm left and thumb extended, then quickly twist the wrist forward while changing to a *9* hand (touching the tips of the thumb and index finger).

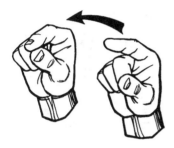

TWENTY
Point the extended right index and thumb forward, palm down with other fingers closed, then bring the thumb and index finger together.

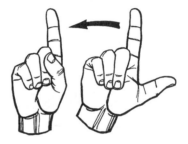

TWENTY-ONE
Hold up the extended right index and thumb with palm forward and other fingers closed. Move the hand slightly to the right as it changes to a *1* hand (the thumb closes).

TWENTY-TWO
Hold up the *2* hand, palm down and fingers at an upward angle, then move the hand to the right in a small arc from the wrist.

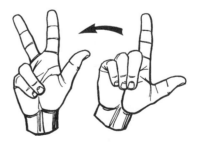

TWENTY-THREE
Hold up the extended right index and thumb with palm forward and other fingers closed. Move the hand slightly to the right as it changes to a *3* hand.

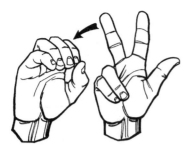

THIRTY

Hold up the right *3* hand (thumb, index, and middle finger extended, other fingers closed) and change it to an *0* hand as it moves slightly to the right.

ONE HUNDRED

Hold up the right index finger with palm forward; move the hand slightly to the right as it changes to a palm-forward *C* hand.

THOUSAND

Bring the right *M* fingertips down into the left flat hand. To sign a specific number of thousand(s), preceed *thousand* with the desired quantity. *Example:* Sign *five* then *thousand* for *five thousand.*

MILLION

Bring the right *M* fingertips down into the left flat palm twice. To sign a specific number of million(s), preceed *million* with the desired quantity. *Example:* Sign *seven* then *million* for *seven million.*

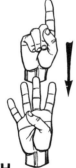

ONE-FOURTH

Hold up the right *1* hand, palm forward, and move it down a short distance as it changes to a *4* hand.

ONE-HALF

Hold up the right *1* hand, palm forward, and move it down a short distance as it changes to a *2* hand.

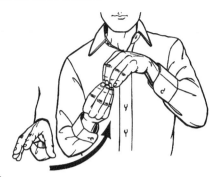

ADD

Hold the left *and* hand to the front at chest level, and the right open hand at chest level to the right with palm facing down. Move the right hand toward the left while simultaneously changing it to an *and* hand. End with all fingertips touching.

Memory aid: Suggests that the right hand grasps something and *adds* it to the left hand.

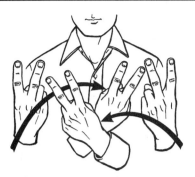

MULTIPLY, ARITHMETIC, CALCULATE, ESTIMATE, FIGURE, WORSE

Make an upward and inward motion with both *V* hands so that the right *V* crosses inside the left.

Memory aid: The X-shaped movement suggests the *multiplication* symbol.

SUBTRACT, DEDUCT, DELETE, ELIMINATE, REMOVE, ABORTION

Move the bent fingers of the right hand downward across the left flat palm.

Memory aid: The right hand seems to be *removing* something from the left.

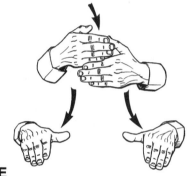

DIVIDE

Cross the little-finger edge of the right flat hand over the index-finger edge of the left flat hand. Move both hands down and to the sides with the palms facing down.

Memory aid: Suggests separating into two sides.

COUNT

Hold up the left flat hand with the palm facing right. Move the thumb and index finger of the right *F* hand upward over the left hand from wrist to fingertips.

Memory aid: Can symbolize the moving of beads on an abacus or old-fashioned *counting* board.

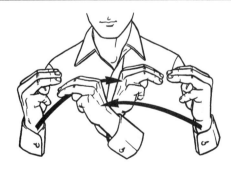

MATHEMATICS, ALGEBRA, CALCULUS, GEOMETRY, STATISTICS, TRIGONOMETRY

Make an upward and inward motion with both *M* hands so that the right *M* hand crosses inside the left. Initialize all signs.

Memory aid: The X-shaped movement suggests the multiplication symbol.

FIRST

Hold the left hand forward in the traditional "thumbs up" position with palm facing right. Touch the left thumb with the right index finger.

Memory aid: The typical gesture of a speaker making his or her *first* point.

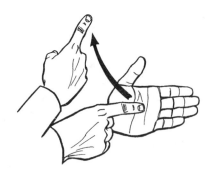

ONCE

Hold the left flat hand at chest level with the palm facing right. Touch the left palm with the right index (or *L* hand), which is then moved sharply upward to a vertical position.

Memory aid: The single finger indicates the meaning.

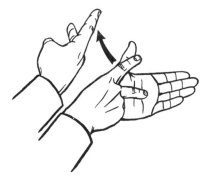

TWICE

Hold the left flat hand at chest level with the palm facing right. Touch the left palm with the second finger of the right *2* hand. Move the right hand upward to a vertical position.

Memory aid: The use of two fingers indicates the meaning.

SAVE, ECONOMIZE, STORE

Place the right *V* fingers on the back of the closed left hand with both palms facing in.

Memory aid: The *V* can symbolize the bars of the bank window, and the closed left hand can represent *savings* held safely behind the bank bars.

MONEY, CAPITAL, FINANCES, FUNDS

Strike the back of the right *and* hand into the left upturned palm a few times.

Memory aid: Suggests a person showing another how much *money* is in the hand.

COINS

Make a small circle on the left flat palm with the right index finger.

Memory aid: Suggests the size and shape of a *coin.*

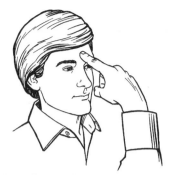

CENT, CENTS, PENNY
Touch the forehead with the right index finger and then sign the appropriate number.

Memory aid: Suggests the heads on coins.

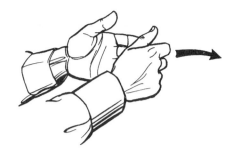

DOLLARS, BILLS
Point the fingers of the left flat hand to the right. Grasp the left fingers between the right palm and fingers (or thumb and fingers), then pull the right hand away from the left a few times.

Memory aid: Suggests counting out individual paper *bills.*

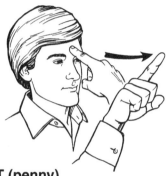

ONE CENT (penny)
Touch the forehead with the right index finger, palm towards self, then twist the hand forward with the index finger pointing at an upward angle.

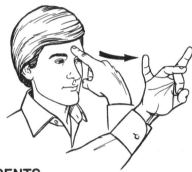

EIGHT CENTS
Touch the forehead with the right index finger, palm towards self, then twist the hand forward as it changes to an *8* hand.

ONE DOLLAR
Hold up the right *1* hand, palm forward, then twist the wrist until the palm faces self.

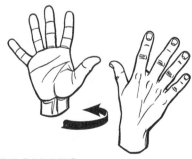

FIVE DOLLARS
Hold up the right *5* hand, palm forward, then twist the wrist until the palm faces self.

PROFIT, BENEFIT, GAIN
Place the touching thumb and index finger of the right *F* hand into an imaginary shirt pocket.

Memory aid: Suggests the idea of pocketing the *profit.*

EARN, SALARY, WAGES, COLLECT, ACCUMULATE
Slide the little-finger edge of the right curved hand inward across the left flat hand. Some end with the right hand closed.

Memory aid: Suggests gathering coins into the hand from the edge of the table.

DEPOSIT
Form *A* hands with palms facing the body and thumbs pointing at each other. Twist the wrists so that both hands move down and apart.

Memory aid: The action implies putting something aside.

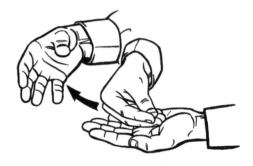

SPEND, SQUANDER, WASTE
Bring the back of the right *and* hand down into the left upturned palm. Open the right hand as it slides off the fingertips of the left hand.

Memory aid: Suggests money slipping away.

BUY, PURCHASE
Move the back of the right *and* hand down into the upturned palm of the left hand, then up and straight out or slightly to the right.

Memory aid: Symbolizes laying down and giving out money for a *purchase.*

COST, CHARGE, EXPENSE, FEE, FINE, PRICE, TAX
Strike the right crooked index finger against the left flat palm with a downward movement.

Memory aid: Suggests the idea of making a dent in one's finances.

CHEAP, INEXPENSIVE

Hold the left flat hand with fingers pointing forward and palm facing right. Brush the index-finger side of the slightly curved right hand downward across the palm of the left hand.

Memory aid: Something brushed off easily cannot be of great consequence.

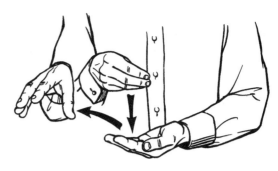

EXPENSIVE, COSTLY

Slap the back of the right *and* hand in the upturned palm of the left hand (the sign for *money*); then lift the right hand and open it while simultaneously pivoting it to the right.

Memory aid: Symbolizes throwing money away.

CREDIT CARD

Slide the right palm-down *A* hand back and forth across the palm of the flat upturned left hand.

Memory aid: The action suggests the movement of impressing a *credit card* in a credit card machine.

CHECK (bank)

Draw the fingertips of the right *C* hand, palm down, across the flat open palm and fingers of the left upturned hand.

Memory aid: The initial indicates the word, and the movement indicates the size of the *check.*

OWE, DEBT, DUE

Tap the left palm with the right index finger several times.

Memory aid: Symbolizes a request to put money in the palm.

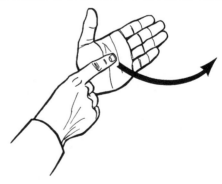

PAY

Hold the left flat hand to the front with palm facing up. Place the tip of the right index finger into the left palm and swing it forward until the index finger points away from the body.

Memory aid: Suggests that the money held in the left hand is being *paid* out for something.

BORROW

Cross the *V* hands at the wrists (the sign for *keep*) and move them toward the body.

Memory aid: The inward action suggests the keeping of something to oneself for a while.

LEND, LOAN

Cross the *V* hands (the sign for *keep*) at the wrists and move them away from the body.

Memory aid: The outward action suggests that something is being offered to another.

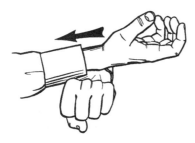

BEG, ENTREAT, PLEAD

Pull the right upturned curved hand backward across the back of the left downturned closed hand.

Memory aid: The upturned hand suggests a desire to grasp something.

ALL, ENTIRE, WHOLE

Hold the left flat hand to the front with palm facing the body. Move the right flat hand, with palm facing out, over-down-in-up, ending with the back of the right hand in the palm of the left hand.

Memory aid: The circular action suggests an encompassing and a completeness.

NONE, NO

Hold both *O* hands in front of the chest and move them to the side in opposite directions.

Memory aid: A double zero emphasizes the meaning.

TOO, ALSO

Bring both index fingers together with the palms facing down. Repeat slightly to the left.

Memory aid: The repeated action indicates something extra.

FULL, FILLED
Move the right flat hand to the left over the thumb edge of the left closed hand.

Memory aid: Indicates that a container is *full* by leveling it off at the brim.

EMPTY, BARE, NAKED, VACANT
Place the right middle finger on the back of the downturned left hand and move it from the wrist to beyond the knuckles.

Memory aid: Symbolizes the idea that the back of a hand is *empty* and *bare*.

FULL (physical and emotional), FED UP
Bring the back of the right flat hand up under the chin. Assume the appropriate facial expression.

Memory aid: The gesture symbolizes *fullness.*

NOTHING
Hold both *O* hands in front of the chest with palms forward and move them to the sides in opposite directions while simultaneously opening both hands.

Memory aid: A double zero emphasizes the meaning.

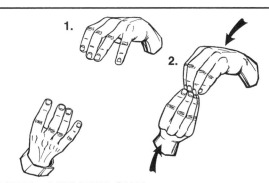

TOTAL, AMOUNT, SUM
Hold the left open curved hand over the right open curved hand with palms facing. Bring the hands together while simultaneously forming *and* hands until the fingertips touch.

Memory aid: The fingers can represent several individual *amounts* that are brought together.

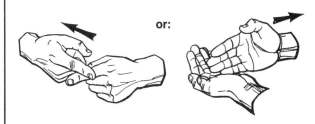

HALF
Cross the right index finger over the left index finger and pull it back toward self. *Alternative:* Pull the little-finger edge of the right flat hand toward self across the left flat hand.

Memory aid: Suggests *half* of a finger or *half* of a hand.

INCREASE, ADD, GAIN WEIGHT, LOSE WEIGHT

Move the right *H* fingers from a palm-up position to a palm-down position and place them on the left palm-down *H* fingers. Repeat a few times. To sign *lose weight,* reverse the action.

Memory aid: Weight is either added to or removed from the left *H* fingers.

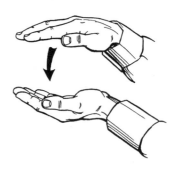

DECREASE, DIMINISH, LESS, LESSEN, REDUCE, SHRINK

Hold both slightly curved open hands to the front with palms facing and hands several inches apart. Reduce the distance between the hands.

Memory aid: The distance between the two hands becomes *less.*

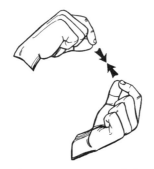

EXACT, ACCURATE, PRECISE, SPECIFIC

Place the thumb tips and index fingertips of each hand together. Position the right hand with palm facing forward and the left hand with palm facing the right hand. Move the hands together until the thumb and index fingers touch.

Memory aid: Meeting at an *exact* point.

LIST

Place the little-finger edge of the bent right hand on the fingers of the left flat hand. Move the right hand down the left hand in several short arcs.

Memory aid: The right hand seems to be pointing out items on a *list* in the left hand.

LITTLE (quantity, amount)

Rub the tip of the right thumb and index finger together.

Memory aid: The slight movement indicates the meaning.

WEIGH

Cross the middle finger of the right *H* hand over the index finger of the left *H* hand. Rock the right *H* hand back and forth over the left *H* hand.

Memory aid: Symbolizes scales.

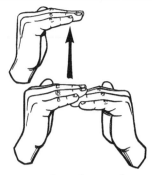

ABOVE (comparative degree), EXCEED, MORE THAN, OVER

Hold both bent hands to the front of the body with the right fingers on top of the left fingers. Raise the bent right hand a short distance.

Memory aid: The right hand moves *above* the left hand.

BELOW (comparative degree), LESS THAN, UNDER

Hold both bent hands to the front with the left fingers on top of the right fingers. Lower the right hand a short distance.

Memory aid: The right hand moves *below* the left hand.

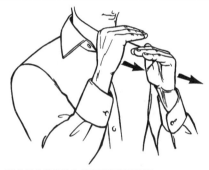

LIMIT, CAPACITY, RESTRICT

Place both bent hands in front with the thumb sides closest to the chest and the right hand a short distance above the left. Move both hands forward a short distance.

Memory aid: The space between the hands can suggest a *limited* area.

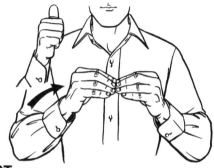

MOST

Touch the fingertips of both *and* hands together before the chest with palms facing down (the sign for *more*). Move the right hand up while forming the *A* hand.

Memory aid: Raising the right hand higher suggests the meaning.

THAN

Hold the left flat or curved hand to the front with palm facing down. Brush the index-finger edge of the right flat hand down off the fingertips of the left hand.

Memory aid: The right hand is both above and below the left hand, thus showing a comparison.

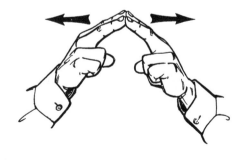

VERY

With the palms facing in, touch the fingertips of both *V* hands; then draw both hands apart to the sides.

Memory aid: The initial plus the same movement as is used for *much* indicate the meaning.

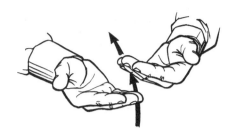

ALMOST, NEARLY
Brush the little-finger edge of the right hand upward over the fingertips of the curved left hand. Both palms face up.

Memory aid: The left hand *almost* stops the upward movement of the right hand.

ENOUGH, ADEQUATE, AMPLE, PLENTY, SUBSTANTIAL, SUFFICIENT
Hold the left *S* hand forward with palm facing right. Move the right flat open hand across the top of the left hand from left to right a few times.

Memory aid: Suggests that a container is filled to the brim.

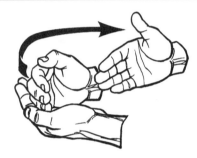

SOME, PART, PORTION, SECTION
Place the little-finger edge of the slightly curved right hand onto the left flat palm. Pull the right hand toward self while forming a flat right hand.

Memory aid: Suggests the action of separating a *portion* for oneself.

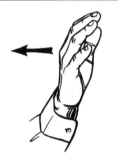

MUCH, LOT
Place both open and slightly curved hands to the front with palms facing; then draw them apart to the sides.

Memory aid: The hands seem to be holding something that is expanding.

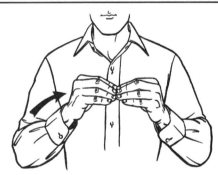

MORE
Touch the fingertips of both *and* hands before the chest with palms facing down. The right hand can be brought up to meet the left from a slightly lower position.

Memory aid: Adding one *and* to another suggests the meaning.

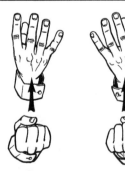

MANY, LOTS, NUMEROUS, PLURAL, SCORES
Hold both *S* hands to the front with palms facing up. Flick the fingers and thumbs open several times.

Memory aid: The use of all the fingers represents the meaning.

BOTH, PAIR

Hold the left *C* hand to the front with palm facing in. With the right palm facing in, draw the right open *V* fingers down through the left *C* hand and close the *V* fingers.

Memory aid: Suggests two becoming one.

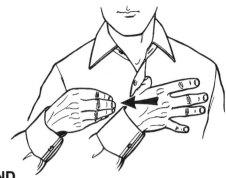

AND

Place the right open hand in front with palm facing in and fingers pointing to the left. Move the hand to the right while bringing the fingertips and thumb together.

Memory aid: Symbolizes a stretching action. The conjunction *and* stretches sentences.

AS

Point both index fingers forward together with a short distance between them and the palms facing down. Maintain this position as both hands are moved to the left.

Memory aid: The repeated action indicates something extra or added.

BROKE, BANKRUPT

Strike the neck with the little-finger edge of the right bent hand.

Memory aid: Symbolizes the head being cut off.

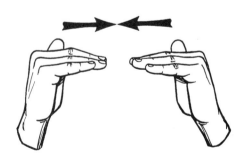

EQUAL, EVEN, FAIR

Bring the fingertips of both bent hands together a few times in front of the chest.

Memory aid: Neither hand has an advantage over the other.

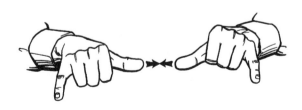

MEASURE

Touch the thumb tips of both *Y* hands together a few times.

Memory aid: Indicates *measuring* by using the extended thumbs and little fingers.

MULTIPLE CHOICE

Draw a circle around or place a check mark beside the word that matches the sign at left.

1.

A. One thousand
B. Money
C. One hundred

2.

A. Expensive
B. Limit
C. Five

3.

A. Weigh
B. Coins
C. Count

4.

A. Divide
B. None
C. Exact

5.

A. Save
B. Lend
C. Profit

6.

A. Expensive
B. Multiply
C. Enough

7.

A. Money
B. Empty
C. Owe

8.

A. Empty
B. And
C. Spend

9.

A. Measure
B. Empty
C. Much

10.

A. More
B. Both
C. Lend

11.

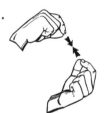

A. Exact
B. Some
C. Too

12.

A. Almost
B. All
C. Enough

13.

A. Weigh
B. Beg
C. Half

14.

A. Twice
B. Pay
C. Some

Answers are on page 285.

Chapter

13

Health, Medical, and the Body

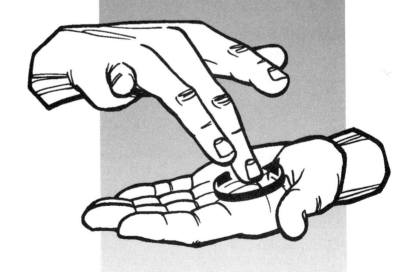

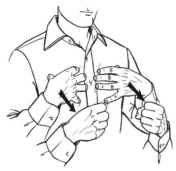

HEALTHY, ROBUST, WELL, WHOLESOME
Place the fingertips and thumbs of both curved open hands on the chest, then move them forward while forming *S* hands.

Memory aid: Suggests that the body has strength.

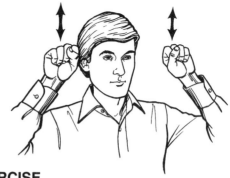

EXERCISE
Hold both *S* hands up to the front with palms facing forward. Move both hands up and down (or forward and backward) simultaneously.

Memory aid: Suggests using dumbbells for *exercise*.

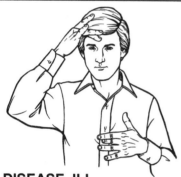

SICK, DISEASE, ILL
Place the right middle finger on the forehead and the left middle finger on the stomach. Assume an appropriate facial expression.

Memory aid: The right hand seems to be feeling the temperature of the forehead, while the left hand indicates an area of discomfort.

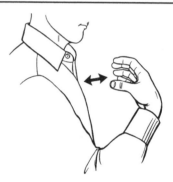

COUGH
Strike the chest sharply a few times with the fingertips of the right curved open hand. The signer may also open the mouth and simulate a coughing action while signing.

Memory aid: Suggests violent action in the chest.

COLD (sickness)
Place the thumb and bent index finger on either side of the nose and draw down a few times.

Memory aid: Symbolizes wiping the nose.

VOMIT, THROW UP
Move both open hands forward and down from the mouth. Sometimes one hand is used and the mouth is opened while the head tilts forward.

Memory aid: Symbolizes the action and direction of *vomiting*.

CIGARETTE
Point the left index finger in a forward direction. Extend the right index and little finger with other fingers closed. Place the right index finger on the left index knuckle and the right little finger on the left index tip.

Memory aid: Suggests the length of a *cigarette*.

SMOKING
Hold the right *V* fingers in front of the lips with palm facing in.

Memory aid: The position for holding a cigarette.

DANGER, PERIL
Hold the left closed hand to the front with the palm facing the body and the arm pointing right. Move the back of the right *A* thumb up across the back of the left hand a few times.

Memory aid: The left arm seems to be protecting the body from an attack by the right hand.

POISON
Make small circles on the left palm with the middle finger of the right *P* hand.

Memory aid: Suggests grinding *poisonous* herbs.

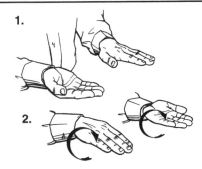

DEATH, DEAD, DIE, EXPIRE, PERISH
Hold both flat hands to the front with the right palm facing up and the left palm facing down. Move both hands in an arc to the left while changing the hand positions so that the palms reverse direction.

Memory aid: Symbolizes a body rolling over at the moment of *death*.

FUNERAL, PARADE, PROCESSION
With palms facing forward, hold the right *V* hand up behind the left *V* hand, and move the hands forward with a few short movements.

Memory aid: Suggests people moving in line, as for a *funeral* or *parade*.

MEASLES
Tap the right side of the face in several places with the fingertips of the right curved open hand.

Memory aid: Suggests the spots produced by *measles*.

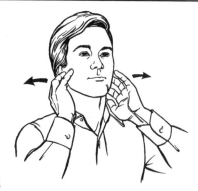

MUMPS
Place the curved fingertips of both hands at the neck and move outward slightly.

Memory aid: Suggests the swollen neck glands evident in a person with *mumps*.

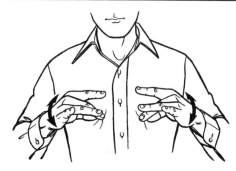

PNEUMONIA
Place the middle fingers of both *P* hands against the chest. Rock them up and down while maintaining contact with the chest.

Memory aid: The initial indicates the word, and the action symbolizes the breathing movement of the lungs.

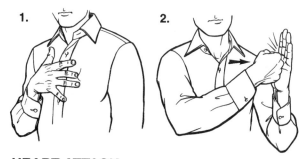

HEART ATTACK
Place the right middle finger over the heart with the other fingers extended. Close the right hand and strike the left palm sharply.

Memory aid: Suggests that the heart has suffered a blow.

SORE, SORENESS
Put the tip of the *A* hand thumb on the chin and twist it from side to side.

Memory aid: The action suggests an irritant to the body making one *sore*.

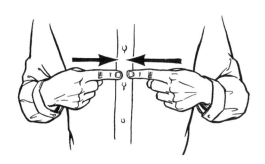

PAIN, ACHE, HURT, INJURY, WOUND
Thrust the index fingers toward each other several times. This may be done adjacent to the particular area of the body that is suffering from *pain*.

Memory aid: Suggests the throbbing of *pain*.

DIZZY

Hold the palm side of the right curved open hand in front of the face and move it in a few slow counterclockwise circles.

Memory aid: Suggests that things seem to be going around in circles.

BLIND

Place the fingertips of the right curved *V* fingers in front of the eyes and lower slightly. Sometimes the eyes are closed momentarily.

Memory aid: Suggests that the eyes are closed.

 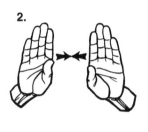

DEAF

Touch or point to the right ear with the right index finger. Place both downturned flat hands to the front and draw them together until the index fingers and thumbs touch. This last movement is the sign for *closed.*

Memory aid: Suggests that the ears are closed.

HARD-OF-HEARING

Point the right *H* hand forward and move it in a short arc to the right.

Memory aid: The use of two *H* positions suggests the phrase.

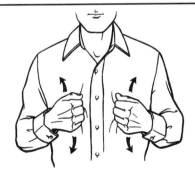

BATH, BATHE

Rub both *A* hands up and down on the chest several times.

Memory aid: Symbolizes washing the body.

SHOWER

Place the closed *S* (or *and*) hand above the head and thrust downward toward the head while simultaneously opening the hand.

Memory aid: Symbolizes water falling on the head.

TOOTHBRUSH, BRUSH TEETH
Shake the right horizontal index finger up and down in front of the teeth.

Memory aid: The action for cleaning teeth.

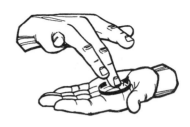

MEDICINE, DRUG, PRESCRIPTION
Make small circles on the left palm with the right middle finger.

Memory aid: Suggests the grinding of herbs or elements used in making *medicine*.

HOSPITAL
Use the right *H* fingers and draw a cross on the upper left arm.

Memory aid: Symbolizes the Red Cross emblem for the relief of suffering.

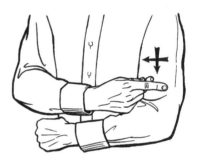

PATIENT (noun)
Use the right *P* fingers and draw a cross on the upper left arm.

Memory aid: The initial *P* combined with the sign for *hospital* indicate the word.

PILL, CAPSULE, TAKE A PILL
Hold the right closed index finger and thumb in front of the mouth and open them quickly as the hand moves toward the mouth.

Memory aid: Symbolizes putting a *pill* into the mouth.

INJECTION, SHOT, SYRINGE, VACCINATION
Place the curved thumb, index, and middle fingers of the right hand at the upper left arm and move the thumb toward the curved fingers.

Memory aid: Symbolizes the use of a hypodermic *syringe* or needle.

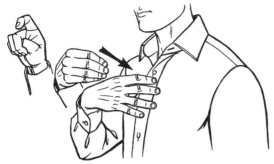

X RAY

Hold the right *X* hand up with palm facing forward; then form an *O* position and twist the hand until the palm faces self. Open the hand as it is moved toward the chest.

Memory aid: The initial indicates the word, and the action suggests *X rays* penetrating the body.

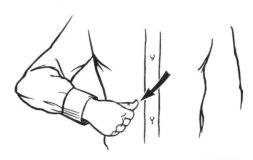

OPERATION, INCISION, SURGERY

Move the right *A* thumbnail down (or across) the chest or abdomen.

Memory aid: Symbolizes the use of a *surgical* knife.

HEARING AID

Place the curved fingers of the right *V* hand at the right ear. Twist a few times.

Memory aid: Suggests placing a *hearing aid* in the ear.

INSURANCE

Hold up the right *I* hand and shake it.

Memory aid: The initial indicates the word, which requires context and simultaneous lipreading for full comprehension.

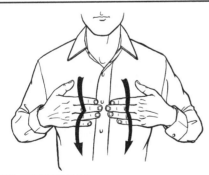

BODY, PHYSICAL

Place the palms of both flat hands against the chest and repeat a little lower. Sometimes one hand is used.

Memory aid: The hands feel the *body*.

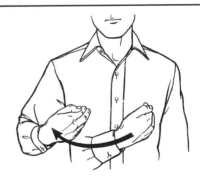

BREAST

Place the fingertips of the right curved hand at the left breast and then at the right.

Memory aid: The location suggests the meaning.

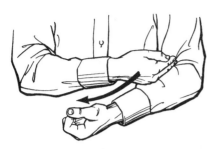

ARM

Move the fingertips of the upturned curved right hand down the left arm.

Memory aid: The length of the *arm* is pointed out.

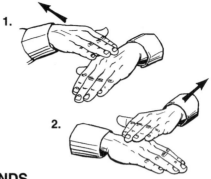

HANDS

Place the downturned right hand over the back of the downturned left hand. Move the right hand toward self, and repeat the action with the left hand over the right.

Memory aid: Each *hand* is referred to individually without reference to the arm.

FEET

Point first to one foot and then the other.

Memory aid: Both *feet* are identified by pointing to them.

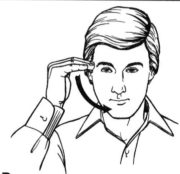

HEAD

Place the fingertips of the right bent hand against the right temple and move the right hand downward in an arc until the fingertips touch the jaw.

Memory aid: The fingers feel the side of the *head.*

FACE

Move the right index finger in a counterclockwise direction around the face.

Memory aid: The action points to the *face.*

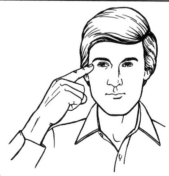

EYE

Point to the eye with the right index finger.

Memory aid: The *eye* is identified by pointing.

EAR, HEAR, NOISE, SOUND
Touch or point to the right ear with the right index finger.

Memory aid: The *ear* is identified by pointing.

NOSE
Touch the tip of the nose with the right index finger.

Memory aid: The *nose* is identified by pointing to it.

MOUTH
Point to the mouth with the right index finger.

Memory aid: The *mouth* is identified by pointing to it.

LIPS
Outline the lips with the right index finger.

Memory aid: The *lips* are emphasized.

TEETH
Move the tip of the right index finger sideways across the front teeth.

Memory aid: The *teeth* are indicated by pointing to them.

TONGUE
Touch the tongue with the tip of the right index finger.

Memory aid: The *tongue* is pointed to and touched.

SMELL, FRAGRANCE, FUMES, ODOR, SCENT

Pass the slightly curved palm of the right hand upward in front of the nose a few times.

Memory aid: Suggests passing something in front of the nose in order to *smell* it.

TASTE

Touch the tip of the tongue with the right middle finger. The other fingers of the right open hand are extended.

Memory aid: The finger is giving the tongue a sample *taste*.

SEE, PERCEIVE, SIGHT, VISION

With the palm facing in, place the fingertips of the right *V* hand near eyes and move the right hand forward.

Memory aid: The *V* fingers suggest eyes that are actively *seeing*.

TOUCH, CONTACT

Touch the back of the left downturned curved hand with the right middle finger. The other fingers of the right open hand are extended.

Memory aid: A gesture of *touching*.

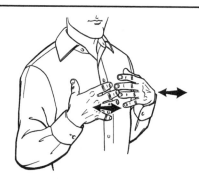

BREATH, BREATHE

Place both open hands, palms in and left hand above right, on the chest and move them simultaneously on and off the chest several times.

Memory aid: Indicates the expansion and contraction of the chest when *breathing*.

SWALLOW

With the palm facing left, trace a line downward with the right index finger from under the chin to near the base of the neck.

Memory aid: Suggests the direction that liquid flows when *swallowed*.

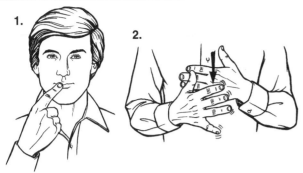

BLOOD, BLEED, HEMORRHAGE

Wiggle the fingers of the right open hand as they move down the back of the left open hand. Sometimes the lips are touched first with the right index finger, which is the sign for *red*.

Memory aid: Symbolizes a *bleeding* left hand with *blood* trickling down.

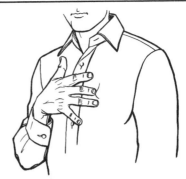

HEART (physical)

Place the right middle finger over the heart with the other fingers extended.

Memory aid: The right hand feels for a heartbeat.

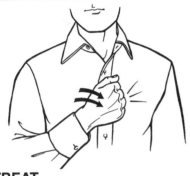

HEARTBEAT

Strike the chest with the right *A* hand several times. The palm faces self.

Memory aid: The action represents the *heartbeat*.

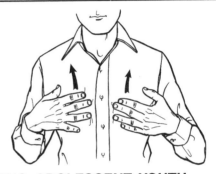

YOUNG, ADOLESCENT, YOUTH

Place the fingertips of both curved hands on the upper chest and quickly pivot them upward from the wrists several times.

Memory aid: Symbolizes a fast pace of life and *youthful* exuberance.

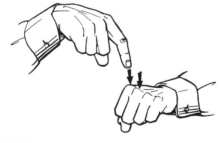

BONES

Close the downturned left hand and tap the knuckles with the right *X* finger.

Memory aid: An obviously bony part of the hand is indicated.

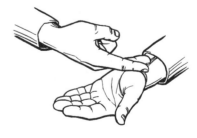

VEIN

Place the fingertip of the right middle-finger *V* hand on the upturned left wrist.

Memory aid: The initial and location combined indicate the meaning.

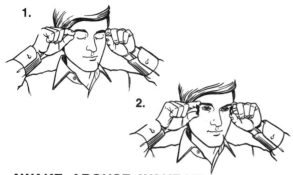

AWAKE, AROUSE, WAKE UP

Place the closed thumbs and index fingers of both *Q* hands at the corners of the eyes; then open eyes and fingers simultaneously.

Memory aid: Symbolizes the eyes opening.

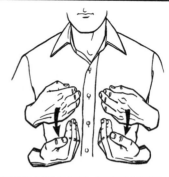

TIRED, EXHAUSTED, FATIGUED, WEARY

Place the fingertips of both bent hands on the upper chest, then pivot the hands downward while maintaining contact with the chest. The fingertips point upward in the final position.

Memory aid: Suggests that the body is ready to drop in *exhaustion.*

LIE DOWN, RECLINE

Place the back of the right *V* fingers on the left flat palm.

Memory aid: Symbolizes a person in the *reclining* position.

SLEEP, DOZE, NAP, SIESTA, SLUMBER

Place the palm side of the right open hand in front of the face and move it down to chin level while forming an *and* hand.

Memory aid: Suggests closing the eyes.

SWEAT, PERSPIRE

With the palm facing down, rub the index-finger side of the right hand across the forehead from left to right while simultaneously wiggling the fingers.

Memory aid: A common action for wiping off *perspiration.*

BEARD

Cradle the chin with the fingertips and thumb of the right open curved hand; then draw the hand down until it forms the *and* position below the chin.

Memory aid: Suggests the position and shape of a *beard.*

MENSTRUATION, PERIOD

Tap the right cheek twice with the palm side of the right *A* hand.

Memory aid: The cheek can suggest the cavity of the uterus.

SEX, INTERCOURSE

Hold the left *V* hand to the front with palm facing up. With the palm of the right *V* hand facing down, move it down onto the left *V* hand a few times.

Memory aid: Symbolizes the uniting of two bodies.

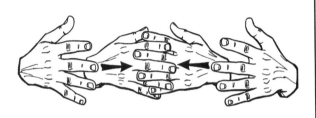

PREGNANT

Interlock the fingers of both hands in front of the abdomen.

Memory aid: Suggests the shape of a *pregnant* woman.

BIRTH, BORN

Place the back of the right flat hand into the upturned left palm (right hand may start from a position near stomach). Move both hands forward and upward together.

Memory aid: The right hand can symbolize a baby which is presented to the left hand, and then to all.

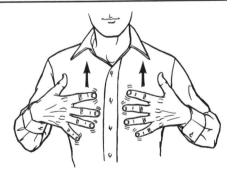

LIFE, EXISTENCE

Put palm sides of both flat open hands on abdomen and raise them up to the chest while wiggling fingers. Existence may be signed with *E* hands.

Memory aid: The first sign suggests that where there is movement there is *life,* and the second suggests the same with the additional indication of initials.

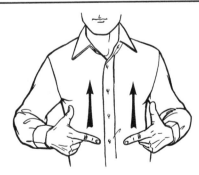

LIVE, ADDRESS, DWELL, RESIDE

Move the palm sides of both *L* (or *A*) hands up from the abdomen to the chest.

Memory aid: The initials indicate the word, and the action suggests that just as life *lives* within the body, so the body *resides* at a particular address.

MULTIPLE CHOICE

Draw a circle around or place a check mark beside the word that matches the sign at left.

1.

A. Pain
B. Touch
C. Medicine

2.

A. Hands
B. Birth
C. Bones

3.

A. Nose
B. Smell
C. Pill

4.

A. Pill
B. Cough
C. Tongue

5.

A. Healthy
B. Head
C. Shower

6.
A. Lips
B. Sore
C. Cough

7.

A. Injection
B. Mumps
C. Hospital

8.

A. Young
B. Healthy
C. Body

9.
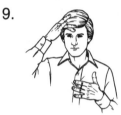
A. Sick
B. Tired
C. Touch

10.

A. Dizzy
B. Face
C. Head

11.
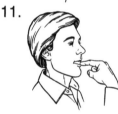
A. Taste
B. Poison
C. Tongue

12.
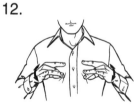
A. Body
B. Pneumonia
C. Tired

13.
A. Life
B. Live
C. Operation

14.

A. Vein
B. Bones
C. Hands

Answers are on page 285.

Chapter

14

Time, Seasons, and Weather

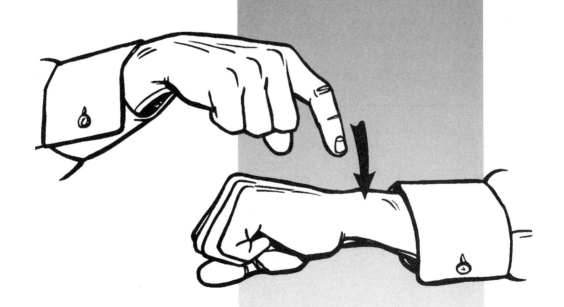

TIME, CLOCK, WATCH
The right curved index fingertip is made to tap the back of the left wrist a few times.

Memory aid: An obvious reference to a *wristwatch*.

TIME (abstract), TIMES, AGE, EPOCH, ERA
Rotate the thumb (or knuckle side) of the right *T* hand in a clockwise circle on the left flat palm.

Memory aid: The initial indicates the word, and the action symbolizes the truth that the clock stops for no one.

SECOND (time), MOMENT
Move the right index finger a short distance across the flat palm of the left flat hand, but do not go beyond the little-finger edge of the left hand.

Memory aid: The small movement suggests the action of a clock hand.

MINUTE
Hold the flat left hand vertically with palm facing right. Let the index finger of the right *D* hand touch the left palm with the index finger pointing up. Move the right index finger past the little-finger edge of the left hand.

Memory aid: Follows the movement of a *minute* hand on a clock.

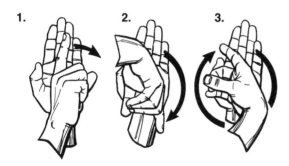

HOUR
Point the fingers of the left flat hand either up or forward with palm facing right. Move the index finger of the right *D* hand in a complete clockwise circle by rotating the wrist. Keep the right index finger in constant contact with the left hand.

Memory aid: Follows the movement of a minute hand on a clock.

DAY, ALL DAY
Point left index to the right, palm down. Rest right elbow on left index with right index pointing upward. Move right index and arm in a partial arc across the body from right to left. To sign *all day,* hold right index as far to the right as possible before making arc.

Memory aid: Suggests the sun's movement.

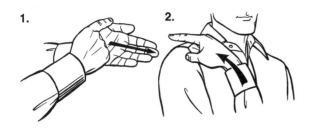

LAST WEEK
Move the right index-finger hand across the left flat palm in a forward movement. Continue the right hand in an upward-backward direction over the right shoulder.

Memory aid: The sign for *week* and pointing to the past.

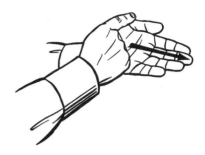

WEEK, NEXT WEEK
Move the right index-finger hand across the left flat palm in a forward movement. For *next week,* let the right hand continue beyond the left hand and point forward.

Memory aid: The five fingers of the left hand plus the thumb and index finger of the right make seven, thus symbolizing a *week.*

MONTH, MONTHLY
Point the left index finger up with palm facing right. Move the right index finger from the top to the base of the left index finger. Repeat a few times to sign *monthly.*

Memory aid: The left index finger's three joints and tip represent the four weeks of a *month.*

YEAR
Move the right *S* hand in a complete forward circle around the left *S* hand and come to rest with the right *S* hand on top of the left. Repeat the sign for the plural.

Memory aid: The movement of the right hand suggests the earth's revolution around the sun.

LAST YEAR
Move the right *S* hand in a complete forward circle around the left *S* hand and come to rest with the right *S* hand on top of the left. Then point the right index finger backward over the right shoulder.

Memory aid: The sign for *year* and pointing to the past.

NEXT YEAR
Move the right *S* hand in a complete forward circle around the left *S* hand and come to rest with the right *S* hand on top of the left. Then point the right index finger forward.

Memory aid: The sign for *year* and pointing to the future.

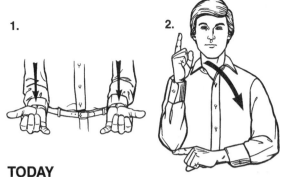

1.   **2.**

TODAY
Drop both *Y* (or flat) hands together in front of the chest. Point the left index to the right with palm down. Rest the right elbow on the left index and point the right index upward. Move the right arm in a partial arc across the body from right to left.

Memory aid: Symbolizes the sun's movement.

YESTERDAY
With the palm facing forward, place the thumb of the right *A* (or *Y*) hand on the right side of the chin. Move in a backward arc toward the ear.

Memory aid: The backward movement indicates the past.

STILL, YET
With the palm facing down, move the right *Y* hand in a downward-forward movement from in front of the right shoulder to waist level.

Memory aid: Indicates continuing from past experience.

NEXT
Hold both flat hands to the front with palms facing in and the right hand behind the left. Move the right hand over to the front of the left hand.

Memory aid: Suggests overcoming an obstacle and proceeding to whatever is *next*.

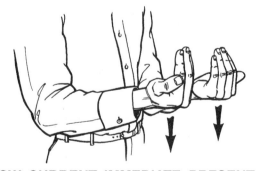

NOW, CURRENT, IMMEDIATE, PRESENT
Hold both bent (or *Y*) hands to the front at waist level with palms facing up. Drop both hands sharply a short distance.

Memory aid: Suggests that the hands feel the weight of something *now*.

FUTURE, LATER ON, BY AND BY, SOMEDAY
Hold the right flat hand with palm facing left in an upright position close to the right temple. Move it in a forward-upward arc. The greater the arc, the more distant the future that is indicated.

Memory aid: Suggests moving onward into the *future*.

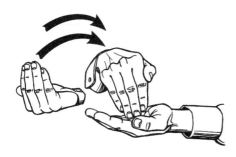

OFTEN, FREQUENT

Place the fingertips of the right bent hand into the left palm and repeat.

Memory aid: Similar to a clapping action, indicating the desire for *repetition.*

SOMETIMES, OCCASIONALLY, ONCE IN A WHILE, SELDOM

Hold the left flat hand at chest level with palm facing right. Touch the left palm with the right index fingertip; then move the right index finger upward to a vertical position. Repeat after a slight pause.

Memory aid: The slow movement indicates *irregularity.*

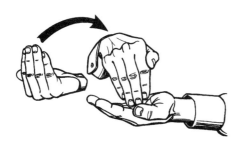

AGAIN, ENCORE, REPEAT

Hold the left flat hand pointing forward with palm up and the bent right hand palm up and parallel to the left hand. Move the bent right hand upward and turn it over until the fingertips are placed in the left palm.

Memory aid: Similar to a clapping action, indicating the desire for *repetition.*

RECENTLY, A WHILE AGO, JUST NOW, LATELY, A SHORT TIME AGO

Place the right curved index finger against the right cheek with the palm and index finger facing back. Move the index finger up and down a few times.

Memory aid: The movement suggests the meaning.

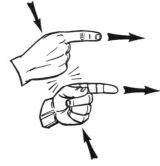

REGULAR, REGULARLY, CONSISTENT

Point both *G* (or *D*) hands forward with the right hand over the left. Move both hands forward while at the same time striking the lower side of the right hand on the upper side of the left a few times.

Memory aid: The repeated striking action indicates *regularity.*

USUALLY, USED TO

Point the fingers of the right *U* hand upward. Place the right wrist on the wrist of the left down-turned closed hand; then push both hands down slightly.

Memory aid: This is similar to the basic sign for *habit,* with the initial added.

EARLY

Hold the left closed hand palm down and pointing right. Touch the right middle fingertip on the back of the left hand beginning at the thumb side; then move it across the hand to the little-finger side.

Memory aid: Suggests the beak of a bird searching for the *early* worm.

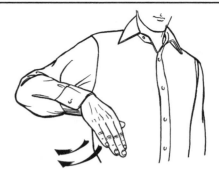

LATE, TARDY, BEHIND TIME, NOT YET, NOT DONE

Let the right hand hang loosely in the area between the armpit and waist. Move the hand back and forth from the wrist several times.

Memory aid: Suggests that the action is hanging back.

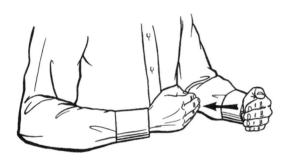

BEFORE (time)

Hold the slightly curved left hand out to the front with palm facing in. Hold the right curved hand near the palm of the left and then draw the right hand in toward the body.

Memory aid: The right hand is *before* the palm of the left.

AFTER (time)

Hold the slightly curved left hand out to the front with palm facing in. Place the curved right palm on the back of the left hand and move forward and away from the left hand.

Memory aid: The right hand moves forward *after* touching the left.

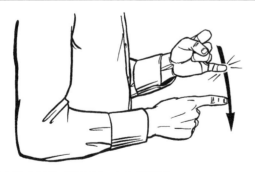

LAST, END, FINAL, LASTLY

Hold the left hand to the front with palm facing self and little finger extended. Strike the left little finger with the right index finger as the right hand moves down. Sometimes this sign is made with both little fingers.

Memory aid: The little finger is considered the *last* finger.

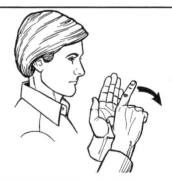

LATER, SUBSEQUENTLY, AFTER A WHILE, AFTERWARD

Hold the left flat hand up with the palm facing right. Place the thumb of the right *L* in the center of the left palm, and pivot the right index finger forward and down.

Memory aid: Suggests the hand of a clock moving an undesignated distance.

DAILY, EVERYDAY

Place the right *A* hand on the right cheek with the palm facing the cheek. Rub it forward several times.

Memory aid: Indicates a constant continuation by the repeated rubbing action.

THEN

Point the left *L* hand forward with palm facing right; then touch the left thumb and index finger with the right index finger.

Memory aid: First one location, and *then* another.

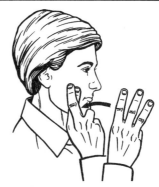

WAS

Hold the right *W* hand in front with palm facing left. Move it backward to a position by the side of the neck or cheek, and at the same time change from a *W* to an *S* hand.

Memory aid: Backward movement indicates the past.

WERE

Hold the right *W* hand slightly to the front with the palm facing left. Move it backward to a position at the side of the neck or cheek while simultaneously changing from a *W* to an *R* hand.

Memory aid: Backward movement indicates the past.

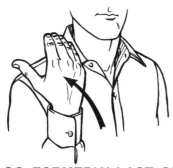

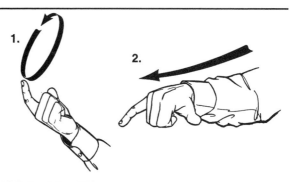

PAST, AGO, FORMERLY, LAST, ONCE UPON A TIME, USED TO, PREVIOUSLY, WAS, WERE

Move the right upraised flat hand backward over the right shoulder with palm facing the body. The amount of emphasis with which sign is made can vary depending on the length of time involved.

Memory aid: Indicates that which is behind.

FOREVER, ETERNAL, EVER, EVERLASTING

Circle the right index finger in a clockwise direction with palm facing up; then move the downturned *Y* hand forward. This is a combination of the sign for *always* and *still*.

Memory aid: Symbolizes the continuous progression of clock and time.

WOULD

With the palm facing left, place the right *W* hand in an upright position close to the side of the right cheek. Move the hand straight forward while simultaneously changing from a *W* to a *D* hand.

Memory aid: Forward movement indicates positive intention.

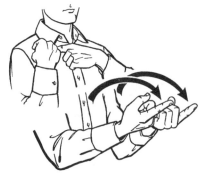

SINCE, ALL ALONG, SO FAR

Place both index-finger hands before the right shoulder with palms facing in, and index fingers pointing toward the shoulder. Bring both hands down and forward simultaneously until the index fingers are pointing forward with the palms facing up.

Memory aid: Suggests a continuation from a past time to the present.

AM, ARE

Place the right *A*-hand thumb on the lips and move the right hand straight forward. Use *R* for *are*.

Memory aid: The initial suggests the sound of the word, and the action indicates a breathing person and thus a symbolic connection with the verb *to be*.

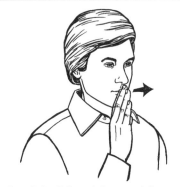

BE

Move the right *B* hand forward from the mouth.

Memory aid: The initial suggests the word, and the action indicates a breathing person and thus a symbolic connection with the verb *to be*.

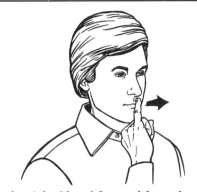

IS

Move the right *I* hand forward from the mouth.

Memory aid: The initial suggests the word, and the action indicates a breathing person and thus a symbolic connection with the verb *to be*.

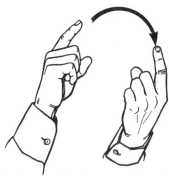

UNTIL

Hold the left index finger up with palm facing inward. Move the right index finger in a slow forward arc until it touches the tip of the left index finger.

Memory aid: Wait *until* contact is made.

DURING, IN THE MEANTIME, WHILE

Point both index-finger hands forward with palms down and a small distance between them. Move them forward simultaneously in a slight down-forward-up curve.

Memory aid: The simultaneous movement suggests parallel activities or time.

SUNRISE, SUNSET

The flat left hand points to the right across the chest with palm facing down. The right *O* hand makes an upward *(sunrise)* or downward *(sunset)* arc in front of the left arm.

Memory aid: The left arm represents the horizon, and the right *O* hand represents the sun rising or setting.

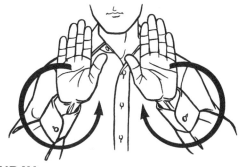

SUNDAY

Place both flat hands to the front with palms facing forward; then move them simultaneously in opposite-direction circles. The circles may be made in either direction.

Memory aid: The hand movements suggest reverential worship.

MONDAY

Make a small clockwise circle with the right *M* hand.

Memory aid: The initial suggests the word, and the circular motion suggests the passing of time.

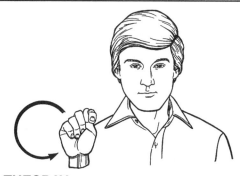

TUESDAY

Make a small clockwise circle with the right *T* hand.

Memory aid: The initial suggests the word, and the circular motion suggests the passing of time.

WEDNESDAY

Make a small clockwise circle with the right *W* hand.

Memory aid: The initial suggests the word, and the circular motion suggests the passing of time.

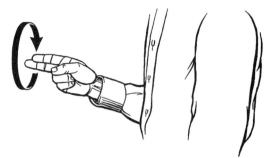

THURSDAY
Make a small clockwise circle with the right *H* hand. *Note:* This is sometimes signed with the manual *T* and *H*, with or without rotation.

Memory aid: The initial suggests the word, and the circular motion suggests the passing of time.

FRIDAY
Make a small clockwise circle with the right *F* hand.

Memory aid: The initial suggests the word, and the circular motion suggests the passing of time.

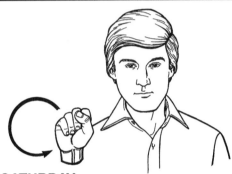

SATURDAY
Make a small clockwise circle with the right *S* hand.

Memory aid: The initial suggests the word, and the circular motion suggests the passing of time.

NOON, MIDDAY
Point the left flat hand to the right with palm facing down. Rest the right elbow on the back of the left hand with the right arm in a vertical position and the palm facing left.

Memory aid: The left arm indicates the horizon, and the right hand symbolizes the position of the sun at *midday*.

TOMORROW
Touch the right *A* thumb on the right cheek or chin area; then make a forward arc.

Memory aid: The forward movement indicates the future.

AFTERNOON
Hold the left arm in a horizontal position pointing to the right. The left hand is flat with palm facing down. Place the right forearm on the back of the left hand at a 45-degree angle.

Memory aid: Symbolizes the sun making its descent.

MORNING
Place the left flat hand with palm facing the body in the bend of the right elbow. Bring the right flat hand toward self until the arm is upright with the palm facing the body.

Memory aid: The left arm indicates the horizon, while the right hand symbolizes the rising of the sun.

NIGHT, EVENING
Hold the left arm in a horizontal position with the fingers of the left downturned flat hand pointing right. Place the right forearm on the back of the left hand and point the right curved hand downward.

Memory aid: The right hand symbolizes the sun going below the horizon.

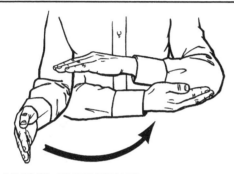

ALL NIGHT, OVERNIGHT
Hold the left arm in a horizontal position with the fingers of the left downturned flat hand pointing right. Place the right forearm on the back of the left hand and point the right curved hand downward. Make a downward sweeping motion from right to left with the right hand.

Memory aid: Symbolizes the setting sun.

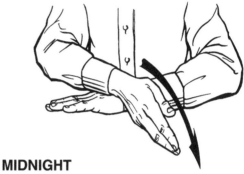

MIDNIGHT
Hold the left arm in a horizontal position pointing right with flat or curved hand facing down. Move the right hand over and below the wrist of the left with fingers pointing down.

Memory aid: Symbolizes the sun being below the horizon on the opposite side of the earth.

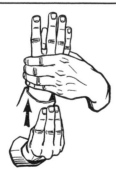

SPRING, GROW, MATURE
Open the fingers of the right *and* hand as they pass up through the left *C* hand.

Memory aid: Suggests young shoots coming up out of the ground.

SUMMER
Draw the curved right index finger across the forehead from left to right.

Memory aid: Symbolizes the wiping of perspiration.

FALL, AUTUMN
Hold the left arm upright with a slight lean to the right. Move the right index-finger side of the right flat hand downward along the left forearm.

Memory aid: Symbolizes the falling of leaves.

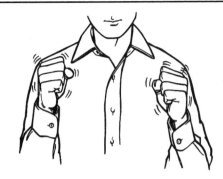

WINTER
Hold up both *S* hands in front of the chest and shake them.

Memory aid: Suggests a person shivering in the cold.

SEASON
Rotate the thumb side of the right *S* hand in a circle on the left flat palm.

Memory aid: The initial indicates the word, and the action symbolizes the fact that the cycle of *seasons* is continuous.

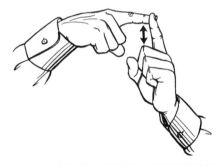

TEMPERATURE, FEVER, THERMOMETER
Rub the right index finger up and down over the central part of the left upright index finger.

Memory aid: Symbolizes the rising and falling of the mercury in a *thermometer*.

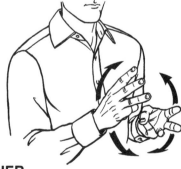

WEATHER
Hold both *W* hands to the front with palms facing; then pivot them up and down from the wrists.

Memory aid: The initials indicate the word, and the action indicates the changeable nature of *weather*.

WIND, BLOW, BREEZE
Hold both open hands up at head level with palms facing. Sweep them back and forth from left to right a few times.

Memory aid: Symbolizes the changing direction of the *wind*.

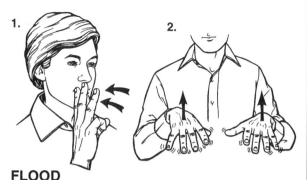

FLOOD

Touch the mouth with the index finger of the right *W* hand a few times (the sign for *water*). Point both palm-down open hands forward and raise them simultaneously while wiggling the fingers.

Memory aid: Suggests rising water.

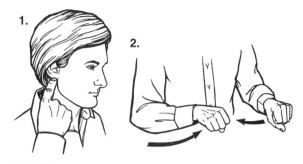

THUNDER

Point to the right ear with the right index finger; then move both palm-down closed hands alternately forward and backward with forceful action.

Memory aid: Symbolizes the sound and vibrating effect of *thunder.*

LIGHTNING

Make quick jagged downward movements with the right index finger.

Memory aid: Symbolizes the action of *lightning.*

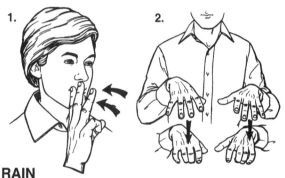

RAIN

Touch the mouth with the index finger of the right *W* hand a few times (the sign for *water*). Move both hands down in short stages with wiggling fingers. *Note:* The first part of this sign—the sign for *water*—is not always included.

Memory aid: Suggests water descending.

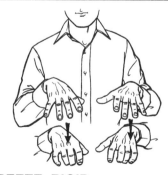

ICE, FREEZE, RIGID

Hold both open hands to the front with palms facing down. Curve the fingers and make them *rigid* while simultaneously moving the hands down a short distance.

Memory aid: The fingers become stiff and contract with cold.

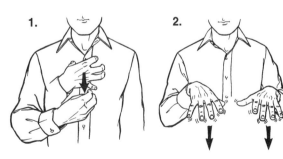

SNOW

Place the fingers and thumb of the right curved hand on the chest; then move it forward while simultaneously forming the *and* hand. Next move both palm-down open hands downward while simultaneously wiggling the fingers.

Memory aid: This is a combination of the signs for *white* and *rain.*

NAME THE SIGN

To reinforce the vocabulary you have already learned, identify the following signs from this chapter by writing the names underneath the signs.

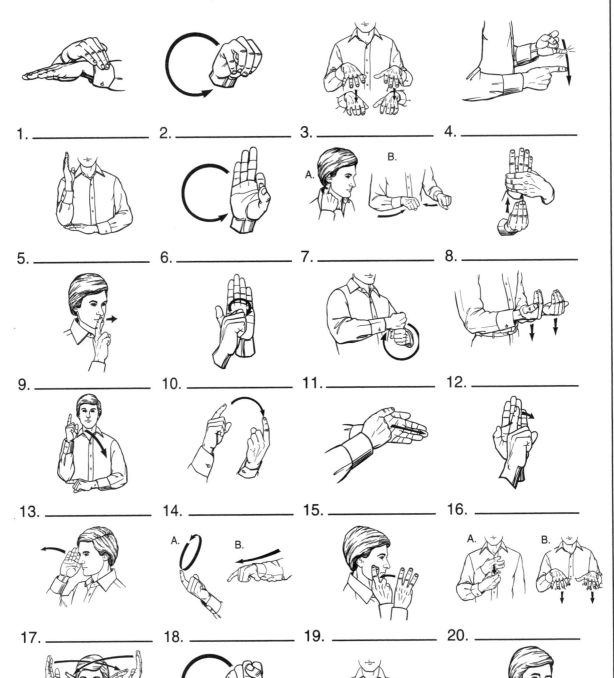

1. _____

2. _____

3. _____

4. _____

5. _____

6. _____

7. _____

8. _____

9. _____

10. _____

11. _____

12. _____

13. _____

14. _____

15. _____

16. _____

17. _____

18. _____

19. _____

20. _____

21. _____

22. _____

23. _____

24. _____

Answers are on page 285.

Chapter

15

Opposites and Questions

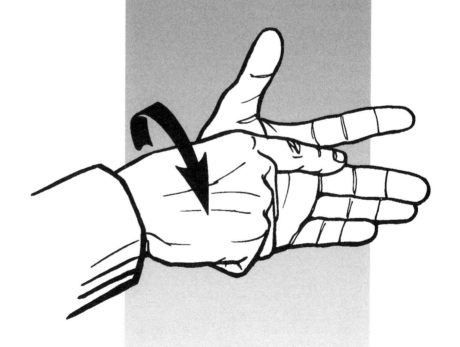

YES

Nod the right *S* hand up and down with palm facing forward.

Memory aid: Suggests a nodding head.

NO

Bring the right thumb, index, and middle fingers together.

Memory aid: Suggests a combination of the signs for *N* and *O*.

GOOD, WELL

Place the fingers of the right flat hand at the lips; then move the hand down into the palm of the left hand with both palms facing up.

Memory aid: Suggests something that has been tasted, approved, and offered to another.

BAD

Place the fingertips of the right flat hand at the lips; then move the right hand down and turn it so that the palm faces down.

Memory aid: Suggests something that has been tasted and disapproved of.

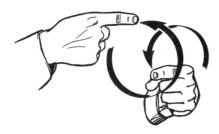

COME

Point both index fingers toward each other and rotate them around each other while simultaneously moving them toward the body. *Alternative* (not illustrated): The common action of beckoning with the hand or index finger.

Memory aid: Both signs symbolize the idea of *coming* closer to self.

GO

Point both index fingers toward each other and rotate them around each other as they are moved away from the body.

Memory aid: Symbolizes moving away from the present location.

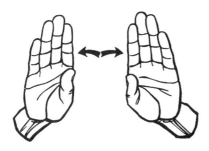

OPEN

Place the thumbs and index fingers of both flat hands together with the palms facing forward. (Some prefer the palms facing down.) Move both hands sideways in opposite directions.

Memory aid: Suggests *opening* drapes.

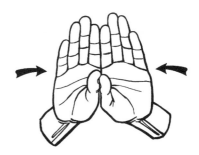

CLOSE, SHUT

Bring both flat hands together from the sides with palms facing forward.

Memory aid: Suggests the *closing* of window drapes.

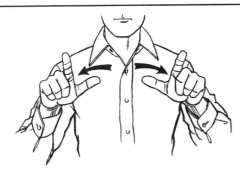

LARGE, BIG, ENORMOUS, GREAT, HUGE, IMMENSE

Hold both *L* hands to the front with palms facing. Move them outward to the sides beyond the width of the body.

Memory aid: The initial and the distance placed between the hands indicate the meaning.

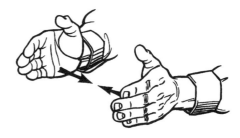

SMALL, LITTLE (measure, size), TINY

Hold both flat hands to the front with palms facing; then move them closer to each other in short stages.

Memory aid: The movement suggests a decreasing space.

START, BEGIN, COMMENCE, INITIATE

Hold the left flat hand forward with the palm facing right. Place the tip of the right index finger between the left index and middle fingers, then twist in a clockwise direction once or twice.

Memory aid: Can symbolize turning the ignition key to *start* a car.

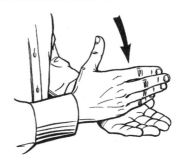

STOP, CEASE, HALT

Bring the little-finger side of the right flat hand down sharply at right angles on the left palm.

Memory aid: Suggests a barrier to *stop* progress.

NEW
Pass the back of the slightly curved right hand across the left flat palm from fingers to heel. Continue the movement of the right hand in a slight upward direction.

Memory aid: The right hand seems to be suggesting a *new* direction to the left hand.

OLD, AGE, ANCIENT, ANTIQUE
Close the right hand just below the chin and move it downward.

Memory aid: Suggests the beard of an *old* man.

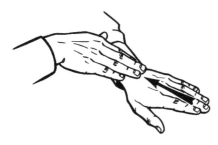

SLOW
Draw the right hand slowly upward over the back of the left hand. Begin near the fingertips and move up to the wrist.

Memory aid: The movement suggests a crawling speed.

FAST, IMMEDIATELY, QUICK, RAPID, SPEEDY, SUDDENLY, SWIFT
Flick the right thumb from the crooked index finger.

Memory aid: Suggests the *rapid* flicking of a marble from the hand.

DRY, DROUGHT, PARCHED
Move the right curved index finger across the lips from left to right.

Memory aid: Suggests wiping *dry* lips.

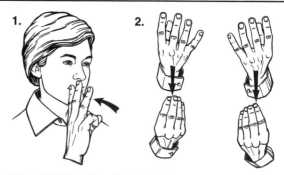

WET, DRENCH, SATURATE, SOAK
Tap the right side of the mouth with the index finger of the right *W* hand a few times. Hold both curved open hands to the front with palms facing up; then move the hands slowly down while simultaneously forming *and* hands.

Memory aid: Suggests the feeling of *wet* fingers.

CLEAN, NICE, PURE

Move the palm of the right flat hand across the palm of the left flat hand from wrist to fingertips.

Memory aid: Symbolizes the washing of the hands.

DIRTY, FILTHY, FOUL, NASTY

Place the back of the right hand under the chin and wiggle the fingers.

Memory aid: Like the sign for *pig*.

ALWAYS, CONSTANTLY, EVER

Point the right index finger forward-upward with palm up, then move it in a clockwise circle.

Memory aid: The circle suggests continuance.

NEVER

Trace a half circle in the air to the right with the right flat hand; then drop the hand away to the right.

Memory aid: Suggests a circle that can *never* be completed because the hand has dropped away.

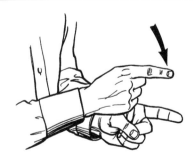

RIGHT, ACCURATE, APPROPRIATE, CORRECT, SUITABLE

Point both index fingers forward and bring the little-finger edge of the right hand down onto the thumb edge of the left hand.

Memory aid: The double-handed action can symbolize a person, thing, or circumstance as being doubly *right*.

WRONG, ERROR, FAULT, MISTAKE

Place the *Y* hand on the chin with the palm facing in.

Memory aid: The *Y* hand is normally shown with palm facing out, so this position suggests a *mistake*.

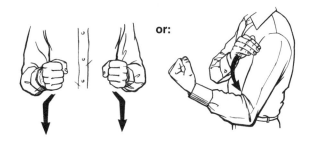

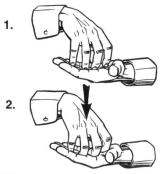

STRONG, MIGHTY, POWERFUL

Move both *S* hands firmly forward and downward. *Alternative:* Make an arc with the right curved hand from the left shoulder to the inside of the left elbow.

Memory aid: The clenched fists of the first sign suggest *strength,* and the action for the alternative sign suggests a *powerful* biceps muscle.

WEAK, FEEBLE, FRAIL

Place the right curved fingers in a standing position in the palm of the left flat hand. Cause the fingers to bend and unbend.

Memory aid: Suggests the buckling of *weak* knees.

WARM, HEAT

Hold the right *A* hand in front of the mouth with palm facing in; then move it slowly upward and forward as the hand simultaneously opens.

Memory aid: Suggests the use of breath to *warm* the hand.

COOL, REFRESH

Place both flat or open hands to the front and sides of the face with palms facing in. Simultaneously flap the fingers of both hands up and down.

Memory aid: Suggests fanning the face.

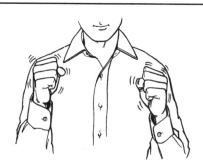

HOT, HEAT

Place the fingers and thumb of the right *C* hand at the sides of the mouth, then quickly pivot the hand forward to the right.

Memory aid: Suggests removing *hot* food from the mouth.

COLD, CHILLY, FRIGID, WINTER

Hold up both *S* hands in front of the chest and shake them.

Memory aid: Suggests a person shivering in the *cold.*

TRUE, AUTHENTIC, GENUINE, REAL, REALLY, SINCERE, SURE, TRUTH, VALID

With palm facing left, move the right index finger in a forward arc from the lips.

Memory aid: Symbolizes *true* and straightforward communication.

FALSE, ARTIFICIAL, COUNTERFEIT, FAKE, PSEUDO, SHAM

Point the right index finger up and move it across the lips from right to left.

Memory aid: Symbolizes the idea that spoken truth is diverted from its normally straight course.

POSITIVE

Cross the right index finger horizontally over the left vertical index finger.

Memory aid: A plus sign.

NEGATIVE

Place the right index finger horizontally across the left palm, which is facing out.

Memory aid: Symbolizes a minus sign.

UP

Hold up the right index finger with palm facing forward and move it up slightly. This word is sometimes fingerspelled.

Memory aid: Pointing *upward.*

DOWN

Point the right index finger *down* with palm facing in, and move it *down* slightly.

Memory aid: Pointing *downward.*

BEST

Touch the lips with the fingers of the right flat hand; then, while closing it into an *A*-hand shape, move it to the right side of the head above head level.

Memory aid: Suggests tasting something and giving a thumbs-up sign of approval.

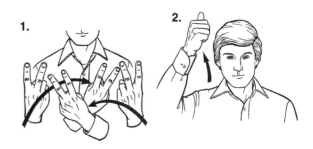

WORST

Hold both *V* hands in a vertical position with palms facing the body and cross both hands, left hand in front of right hand. Then bring the right *A* hand up quickly, just above the right side of the head.

Memory aid: The *A* hand indicates the degree.

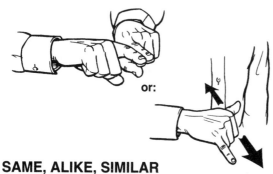

SAME, ALIKE, SIMILAR

Bring index fingers together with palms facing down. *Alternative:* Move right *Y* hand back and forth if referring to self or sideways between two similar persons or things.

Memory aid: Two *similar* index fingers indicate the meaning. The second sign uses the *same* hand to point out two persons or two similar things.

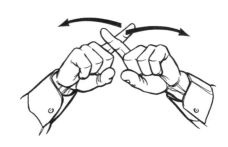

DIFFERENT, DIFFER, DIVERSE, UNLIKE, VARIED

Cross both index fingers with palms facing out; then draw them apart beyond the width of the body.

Memory aid: The movement in opposite directions indicates the meaning.

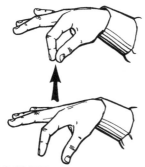

FIND, DISCOVER

Hold the right open hand in front with the palm facing down. Bring the index and thumb together as the hand is raised.

Memory aid: Symbolizes picking something up.

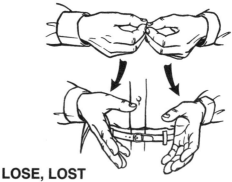

LOSE, LOST

Hold the fingertips of both palm-up *and* hands together; then separate the hands by dropping them down and opening them.

Memory aid: Suggests that something has dropped out of the hands.

EASY, SIMPLE
Hold the left curved hand to the front with the palm up. Brush the little-finger edge of the right curved hand upward over the fingertips of the left hand several times.

Memory aid: The left fingers are moved *easily*.

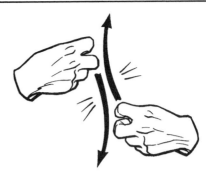

DIFFICULT, HARD
Strike the knuckles of both bent *V* hands as they are moved up and down.

Memory aid: The striking action makes it more *difficult* for the up-and-down movement.

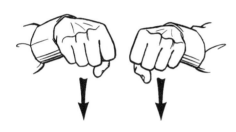

CAN, ABILITY, ABLE, CAPABLE, COMPETENT, COULD, POSSIBLE
Hold both *S* (or *A*) hands to the front and move them down firmly together.

Memory aid: The firmness of the action indicates assurance of *ability*.

CANNOT, IMPOSSIBLE, UNABLE, INCAPABLE
Strike the left index finger with the right index finger as it makes a downward movement. The left index maintains its position.

Memory aid: The left index *cannot* be moved.

WITH
Bring the two *A* hands together with palms facing.

Memory aid: The two hands are *with* each other.

WITHOUT
Make the sign for *with*, then separate the hands and move them outward while simultaneously forming open hands.

Memory aid: The hands end up *without* each other.

THIN, GAUNT, LEAN, SKINNY

Draw the right thumb and index finger down the cheeks. The remaining fingers are closed.

Memory aid: Symbolizes skin drawn tightly over the face.

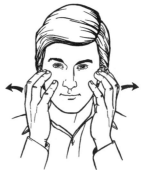

FAT, CHUBBY, OBESE, PLUMP, STOUT

Place both curved open hands by the cheeks and move outward.

Memory aid: Suggests the large round cheeks of a *fat* person.

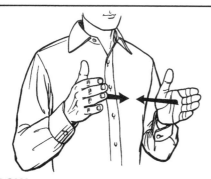

NARROW

Place both flat hands to the front with palms facing and move them closer together.

Memory aid: The decreasing distance indicates the meaning.

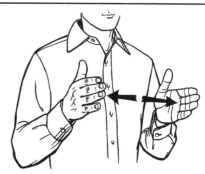

WIDE, BROAD

Place both flat hands to the front with palms facing and draw them apart to the sides.

Memory aid: The distance created between the hands indicates the meaning.

TALL

Place the right index finger on the left flat palm and move it straight up.

Memory aid: The upward movement suggests the meaning.

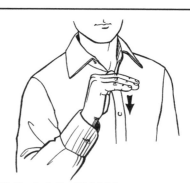

SHORT (height), SMALL

Place the right bent hand to the front and push down a few times.

Memory aid: The downward action indicates *shortness*.

RICH, WEALTHY

Put the back of the right *and* hand in the upturned palm of the left hand; then lift it up above the left hand while simultaneously forming a curved open hand with the palm facing down.

Memory aid: Symbolizes holding a bag of money.

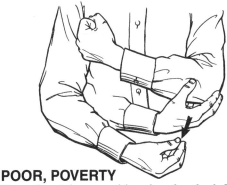

POOR, POVERTY

Place the right curved hand under the left elbow and pull the fingers and thumb down into the *and* position a few times.

Memory aid: Suggests a sleeve with a hole at the elbow.

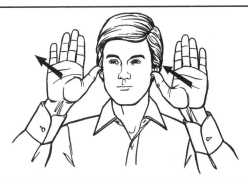

WONDERFUL, EXCELLENT, FANTASTIC, GREAT, MARVELOUS, SPLENDID

Move the flat open hands up and forward a few times with the palms facing out.

Memory aid: A gesture symbolizing an attitude of awe that is used in some forms of religious worship.

LOUSY, ROTTEN

Place the thumb of the right 3 hand on the nose, then pivot the hand sharply downward. Assume an appropriate facial expression.

Memory aid: Can suggest a person suffering from a head cold with a streaming nose.

IMPROVE

Move the little-finger edge of the right flat hand in small arcs up the left arm.

Memory aid: Suggests degrees of *improvement*.

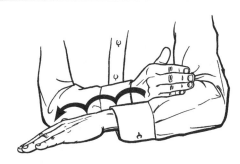

DETERIORATE, DECLINE, WORSEN

Move the little-finger edge of the right flat hand in small arcs down the back of the left forearm.

Memory aid: The downward movement suggests degrees of *deterioration*.

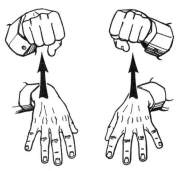

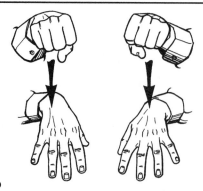

ADOPT, ASSUME, TAKE UP
With palms facing down, simultaneously lift the open hands up while closing them into *S* hands.

Memory aid: Simulates the act of grasping something.

DROP
Hold both *S* hands to the front with palms down. Drop them sharply while simultaneously changing to open hands.

Memory aid: Suggests something slipping out of the hands.

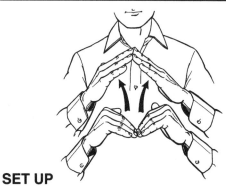

SET UP
With fingertips pointing down, touch the fingertips of both bent hands together. While maintaining contact, move the fingertips of both hands upward forming a *V* shape.

Memory aid: Resembles a tent being *set up*.

COLLAPSE, BREAKDOWN
Place the fingertips of both flat hands together in an upside-down *V* shape. Quickly bend the fingers of both hands down so that a regular *V* shape is formed.

Memory aid: Suggests a roof *collapsing*.

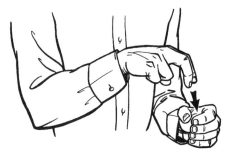

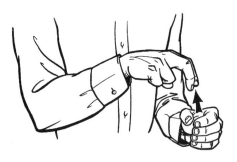

GET IN
Put the right *V* fingers into the left *O* to sign *get in*.

Memory aid: Suggests a person's legs getting into a hole.

GET OUT, GET OFF
Pull the right *V* fingers out of the left *O* hand.

Memory aid: Suggests a person's legs being pulled out of a hole.

EXCITING, EXCITE, AROUSE, THRILL, THRILLING, STIMULATE

Stroke the chest a few times, using both middle fingers alternately with a forward circular motion. Extend the other fingers.

Memory aid: Suggests the heart beating faster in *excitement.*

BORING, DULL, MONOTONOUS, TEDIOUS

Touch the side of the nose with the right index finger and twist forward slightly. Assume an appropriate facial expression.

Memory aid: Shutting off the airflow of the nose suggests there is nothing interesting to smell.

OBEY, OBEDIENCE

Hold both *A* hands close to the forehead with palms facing in. Bring them down and forward, ending in the flat-hand position with palms facing up.

Memory aid: Suggests a mind offering to cooperate.

DISOBEY, DISOBEDIENCE

Hold one or both *A* hands close to the forehead with palms facing in. Twist both hands so that the palms face forward.

Memory aid: Suggests a mind that will not cooperate.

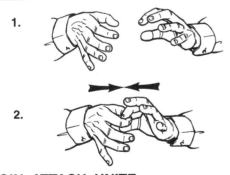

JOIN, ATTACH, UNITE

Interlock the index fingers and thumbs of both hands with all other fingers extended.

Memory aid: Suggests two links of a chain.

RESIGN, QUIT

Position the right *H* fingers in the left *C* hand and pull them out sharply.

Memory aid: Can symbolize jumping out of a hole.

BEAUTIFUL, ATTRACTIVE, LOVELY, PRETTY, HANDSOME

Place the fingertips of the right *and* hand at the chin and open the hand as it describes a counter-clockwise circle around the face. The *H* hand can be used when signing *handsome*.

Memory aid: The circular movement suggests symmetrical or balanced facial features.

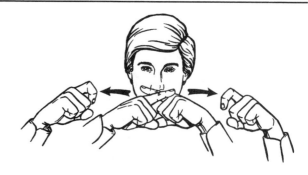

UGLY, HOMELY

Cross the index fingers just below the nose with the remaining fingers closed; then bend the index fingers as the hands are pulled apart to the sides. Sometimes only one hand is used. Assume an appropriate facial expression by frowning.

Memory aid: Suggests facial features that are distorted and pulled out of shape.

LIGHT (weight)

Hold both flat hands to the front with palms up and raise them up slightly a few times.

Memory aid: The hands appear to be bouncing a light object up and down.

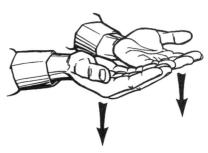

HEAVY, WEIGHTY

Hold both flat hands to the front with palms up and drop them a short distance.

Memory aid: The hands are forced down by a *weight*.

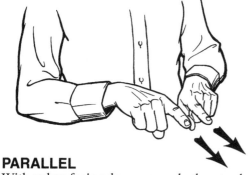

PARALLEL

With palms facing down, move both extended index fingers forward simultaneously. Fingers do not touch.

Memory aid: Two items moving in *parallel*.

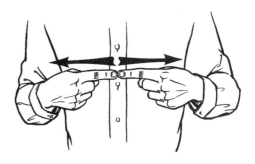

OPPOSITE, CONTRARY, CONTRAST

Point both index fingers toward each other and move them away from each other in opposite directions.

Memory aid: Suggests the idea of separation.

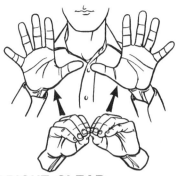

LIGHT, BRIGHT, CLEAR, LUMINOUS, OBVIOUS

Hold both *and* hands at chest level with palms down. Open the hands as they are moved up and to the sides with palms facing forward.

Memory aid: Suggests sunbeams shining over the horizon.

DARK, DIM

Cross the palms of both flat hands down in front of the face.

Memory aid: *Darkness* is created by the eyes being covered.

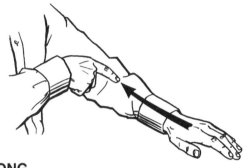

LONG

Extend the left flat hand to the front with palm facing down. Run the right index finger up the left arm, beginning at the fingertips.

Memory aid: Suggests the length of the arm.

SHORT (length or time), BRIEF, SOON

Cross the fingers of both *H* hands and rub the right *H* hand back and forth over the left index finger from fingertip to knuckle.

Memory aid: The *shortness* of the movement suggests the meaning.

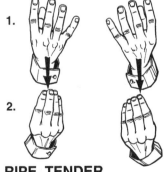

SOFT, RIPE, TENDER

Hold both curved open hands to the front with palms facing up. Move the hands slowly down while forming *and* hands. Repeat a few times.

Memory aid: Suggests squeezing something to test its *softness*.

HARD, SOLID

Strike the back of the left closed hand with the middle finger of the right curved *V* hand.

Memory aid: Suggests coming against a firm surface.

QUESTION
Use the right index finger to outline a question mark in the air. Be sure to include the period.

Memory aid: A question mark obviously indicates a *question*.

ASK, REQUEST
Bring both flat hands together with palms touching and move them in a backward arc toward the body.

Memory aid: Suggests the traditional hand position of a person engaged in prayer.

ANSWER, REPLY, RESPOND
Hold the right vertical index finger to the lips and place the left vertical index finger a short distance in front. Pivot both hands forward and down from the wrists so that the index fingers point forward.

Memory aid: Suggests an *answer* coming from the mouth.

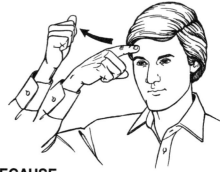

BECAUSE
Place the right index finger on the forehead. Move slightly to the right and upward while forming the A hand.

Memory aid: Touching the forehead can indicate the thought that there is a reason for everything.

HOW
Point the fingers of both bent hands down and place the hands back to back. Revolve the hands in and upward together until the palms are flat and facing up.

Memory aid: The appearance of the palms suggests the idea of showing *how*.

WHY
Touch the forehead with the fingers of the right hand; then move forward while simultaneously forming the Y hand with the palm facing in.

Memory aid: The Y hand coming from the mind suggests a question by its phonetic link to *why*.

WHERE
Hold the right index finger up with palm facing forward and shake it rapidly back and forth from left to right.

Memory aid: The right index finger seems undecided as to *where* to settle.

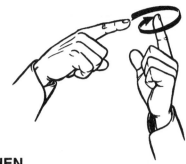

WHEN
Hold the left index finger upright with the palm facing right. Make a clockwise circle around the left index finger with the right index finger.

Memory aid: The right index finger seems to be wondering *when* it can stop circling the left index finger.

WHAT
Pass the tip of the right index finger down over the left flat hand from index to little finger.

Memory aid: The fingers of the left hand suggest alternative ideas to choose from.

WHICH, EITHER, WHETHER
With the palms facing, move the *A* hands alternately up and down in front of the chest.

Memory aid: Suggests two or more things being compared.

WILL (verb), SHALL, WOULD
Place the right flat hand opposite the right temple or cheek with the palm facing in. Move the hand straight ahead.

Memory aid: The forward movement indicates future intention.

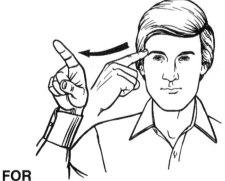

FOR
Touch the right temple with the right index finger; then dip it straight forward until the index finger is pointing forward.

Memory aid: Knowledge is directed outward *for* a particular purpose.

CONNECT THE OPPOSITES

Draw a line connecting each pair of signs that are opposite in meaning.

4.
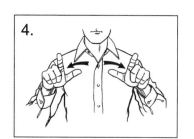

13.
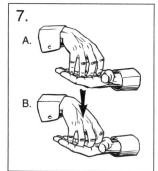

9.
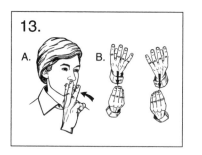

5.
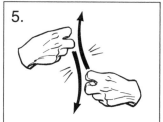

16.
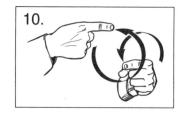

1.
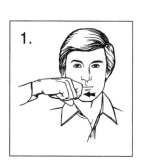

14.
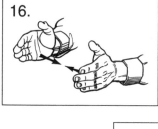

6.
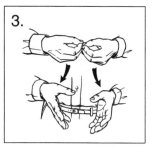

15.
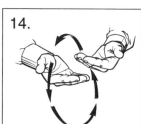

2.

3.
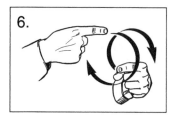

12.
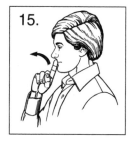

7.

11.
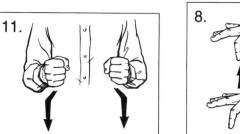

8.

10.

Answers are on page 285.

16

Technology

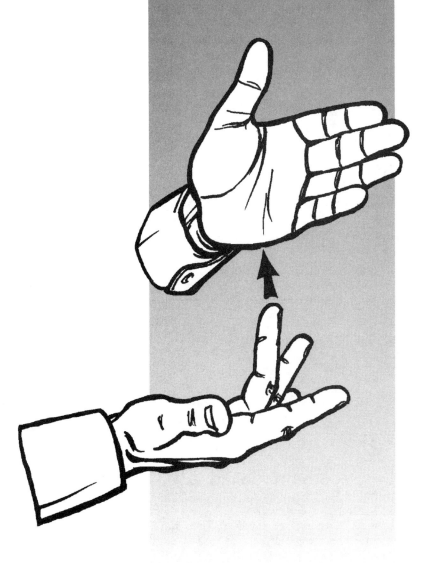

COMPUTER

Move the right *C* hand, palm left, across the forehead in two arcs from right to left. *Note: Computer* can be signed several ways. See *alternative* at right.

Memory aid: The initial indicates the word, and the location in front of the brain suggests *computers* contain knowledge.

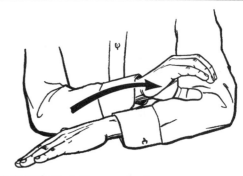

COMPUTER (alternative)

Place the thumb of the right *C* hand on the back of the horizontal left flat hand and move it up the left arm in an arc.

Memory aid: The initial indicates the word, and the movement suggests *computers* are everywhere.

PERSONAL COMPUTER, PC, DESKTOP COMPUTER

Fingerspell *P-C*. Sign each letter near the right shoulder.

Memory aid: The initials indicate the words.

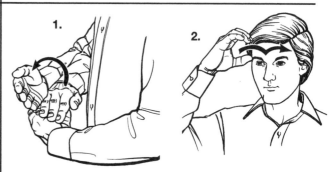

LAPTOP COMPUTER, NOTEBOOK COMPUTER

Place the right flat hand on the left flat hand, palms facing, fingers pointing in opposite directions; twist right hand up while still making contact with right little finger on left palm. Move the right *C* hand across forehead in two arcs from right to left.

Memory aid: Mimics opening a *laptop computer*.

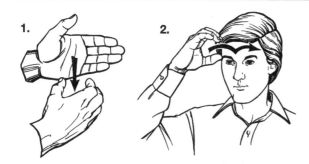

PALMTOP COMPUTER, HANDHELD COMPUTER

Move the thumb and fingertips of the right *C* hand downward across the left flat palm. Then move the right *C* hand, palm left, across the forehead in two arcs from right to left.

Memory aid: Outlining the shape of a *palm computer* in the hand.

CLONE

Hold up the left extended index finger in front of the chest. Place the modified right *C* hand fingertips on the left index and pull the right hand away to the right ending with a flattened *O* hand.

Memory aid: The initial indicates the word, and the movement suggests something *cloned*.

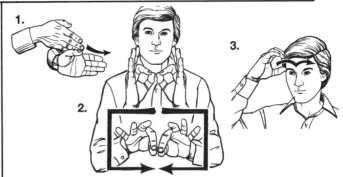

MAC (Macintosh Computer)

Fingerspell *M-A-C*. Sign each letter near the right shoulder.

Memory aid: The initials indicate the words.

MAINFRAME COMPUTER

With left fingers forward, palm right, move little-finger edge of right flat hand forward along left index. Touch upright *F* hands in front of chest with palms facing. Move hands apart simultaneously to sides, down, and together below. Move the right *C* hand across forehead in two arcs from right to left.

Memory aid: *Major, frame,* and *computer* signs.

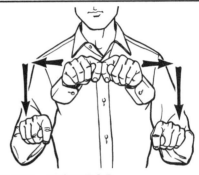

DISPLAY SCREEN, SCREEN, FLAT PANEL SCREEN, CATHODE RAY TUBE, CRT

Place both extended index fingers side by side in front of the chest, palms down and pointing forward, and draw a rectangle by moving the hands to the sides, down and in.

Memory aid: Suggesting the shape of a *screen*.

TERMINAL, MONITOR

Place both *T* hands together and side by side in front of the chest, palms forward, and move them apart horizontally to the shoulders, then down several inches.

Memory aid: The *T* hands outline the shape of a *terminal*.

MOUSE

Brush the right index finger to the left across the nose tip twice.

Memory aid: Suggests the twitching nose of a *mouse*.

KEYBOARD

Fingerspell *K-B*. Sign each letter near right shoulder. *Alternative* (not illustrated): Pretend to type with open curved hands. Outline keyboard shape in front of body with modified *G* fingertips touching and pointing down; move them apart several inches horizontally to sides; stop and close fingers.

Memory aid: The initials indicate the word.

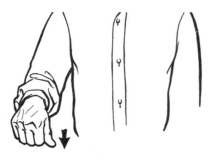

KEY, KEYSTROKE

Press the extended right *A*-hand thumb down a few inches in front of the right side of the body as if pressing a *key*. *Note:* This sign can be finger-spelled *K-E-Y*.

Memory aid: The action imitates pressing a *key*.

DISK, DISKETTE

Place the right *D* hand, palm down with index pointing forward, on the left flat hand, palm up, and circle twice.

Memory aid: The movement suggests a *disk* spinning in a computer or drive.

HARD DRIVE

Fingerspell *H-D*. Sign each letter near the right shoulder. *Alternative:* Sign *hard* and fingerspell *D-R-I-V-E*.

Memory aid: The initials indicate the words.

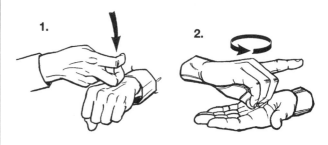

HARD DISK

Strike the back of the left closed hand with the middle finger of the right curved *V* hand. Place the right *D* hand, palm down with index pointing forward, on the left flat hand, palm up, and circle twice.

Memory aid: The signs for *hard* and *disk*.

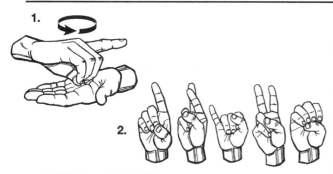

DISK DRIVE, DRIVE

Place the right *D* hand, palm down with index pointing forward, on the left flat hand, palm up, and circle twice. Fingerspell *D-R-I-V-E*. Sign each letter near the right shoulder.

Memory aid: The movement suggests a disk spinning in a computer or *drive*.

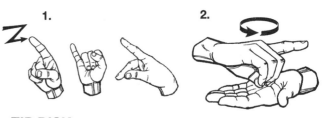

ZIP DISK

Fingerspell *Z-I-P*. Sign each letter near the right shoulder. Place the right *D* hand, palm down with index pointing forward, on the left flat hand, palm up, and circle twice.

Memory aid: The initials indicate the word, and the movement suggests a *disk* spinning in a computer or drive.

CPU (Central Processing Unit), MICRO-PROCESSOR, PROCESSOR

Fingerspell *C-P-U*. Sign each letter near the right shoulder.

Memory aid: The initials indicate the words.

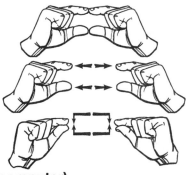

CHIP (computer)

Hold both modified *G* hands in front of the body with fingertips touching and outline the shape of a *chip* by moving the hands apart a couple of inches and closing the thumb and index finger.

Memory aid: Outlining the shape of a computer *chip*.

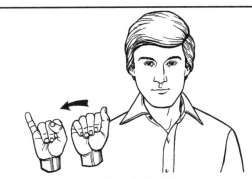

ARTIFICIAL INTELLIGENCE

Fingerspell *A-I*. Sign each letter near the right shoulder.

Memory aid: The initials indicate the words.

SYSTEM

Place both *S* hands touching in front of the chest, palms down, and move them apart together horizontally to the shoulders, then down several inches.

Memory aid: Outlining the shape of a *system* with *S* hands.

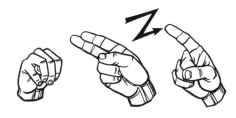

MEGAHERTZ, MHz

Fingerspell *M-H-Z*. Sign each letter near the right shoulder.

Memory aid: The initials indicate the word.

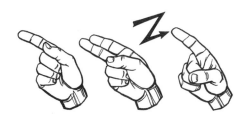

GIGAHERTZ, GHz

Fingerspell *G-H-Z*. Sign each letter near the right shoulder.

Memory aid: The initials indicate the word.

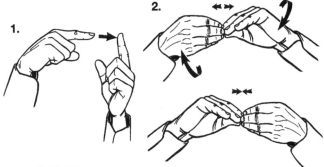

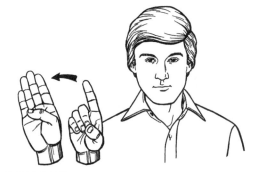

DIGITAL

Hold left index finger up and move right index finger toward it until fingertips touch. Touch fingertips of both flat *O* hands in front of chest, right palm angled in, and left palm angled forward. Pull the hands apart a little while twisting the hands in opposite directions touching the fingertips again.

Memory aid: The signs for *to* and *number*.

DATABASE

Fingerspell *D-B* near the right shoulder.

Memory aid: The initials indicate the word.

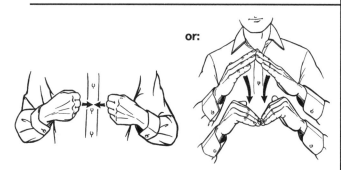

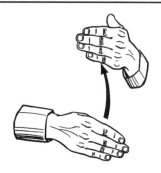

CRASH, BOMB (computer or disk)

Strike the knuckles of both clenched hands together. The sign for *accident*. Alternative: Sign *collapse* by placing the fingertips of both flat hands together in an upside-down *V* shape. Quickly bend the fingers of both hands down into a *V* shape.

Memory aid: Symbolizes a *collision*. Alternative: Suggests a roof or system *collapsing*.

BOOT (start a computer)

Sweep the index side of the right flat hand upward to strike the little-finger edge of the flat or closed left hand.

Memory aid: Symbolizes *kicking* a ball.

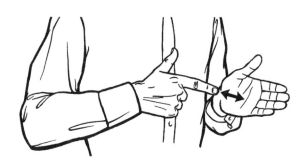

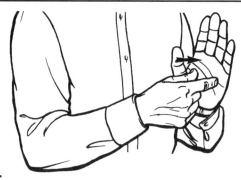

LASER, BURN

Point the right *L*-hand index finger at the left flat-hand palm and move the right *L* hand back and forth two times.

Memory aid: The *L* hand simulates a *laser* shooting a beam of light.

PORT

Point the fingers of the left flat hand up, palm right, and place the fingertips of the right modified *G* hand on the left flat palm.

Memory aid: The fingers represent something being attached to a computer *port*.

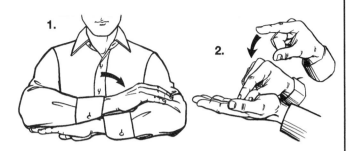

DESKTOP PUBLISHING

Place both arms to the front horizontally with the right forearm over the left. The right flat hand can pat the top of the left forearm a few times. Then move the right index finger and thumb together as though picking something up; then place them on the left flat palm.

Memory aid: The signs for *table* and *print*.

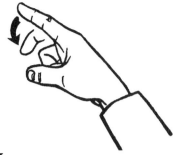

CLICK

Point the right index finger forward and bend it downward.

Memory aid: Suggests *clicking* a mouse.

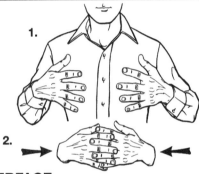

INTERFACE

Place both open hands in front of the chest and to the sides, palms in and several inches apart. Move both hands toward each other until the fingers intertwine.

Memory aid: The intertwined fingers suggest the *interface* of computer and user.

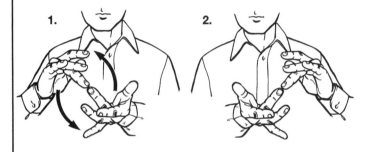

NETWORK

Hold both open hands facing with middle fingers bent and touching at the right side of the chest, the right palm angled forward and left palm facing in. Then switch positions at the left side of the chest with fingers touching again.

Memory aid: The fingers touching suggest the axis of the earth, and a *network* can cover the world.

INTERNAL

Move the closed fingers of the right *and* hand into the left *C* hand.

Memory aid: The right hand is going into the left hand indicating an *internal* device is inside a computer or other equipment.

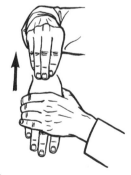

EXTERNAL

Place the downturned fingers of the open right hand in the left *C* hand with the right fingers protruding below the left *C*. Draw the right hand up and out two times.

Memory aid: Symbolizes coming out indicating a peripheral device is *external* to a computer.

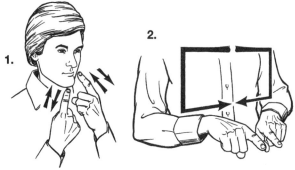

DIALOG BOX

Move both index fingers back and forth from the lips alternately. Place both extended index fingers side by side in front of the chest, palms down and pointing forward, and draw a square by moving hands to the sides, down and in.

Memory aid: The signs for *talk* and *square*.

PERIPHERAL

Place the hands in front of the body and circle the right *P* hand, palm down, around the left *B* hand fingers, which are pointing up, palm toward body.

Memory aid: The initial indicates the word, and the motion implies *peripheral* items attach to and near the computer.

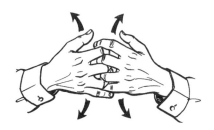

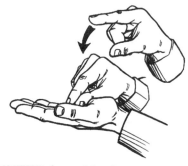

DEVICE, EQUIPMENT, HARDWARE

Intertwine the fingers of both curved open hands in front of the body and pivot at the wrists a few times. *Note: Hardware can be fingerspelled H-W.*

Memory aid: The movement suggests the meshing of gears in a *device* or in *equipment*.

PRINTER (machine)

Move the right index finger and thumb together as though picking something up; then place them on the left flat palm.

Memory aid: Symbolizes the old-fashioned method of hand-setting type.

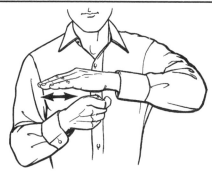

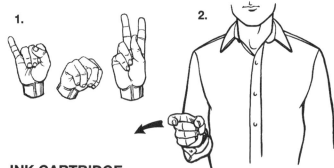

SCANNER

With palm facing left, move the right *X* hand back and forth two times under the palm-down left flat horizontal hand.

Memory aid: The movement mimics the action of a light in a *scanner*.

INK CARTRIDGE

Fingerspell *I-N-K* near the right shoulder. Move the right curved *L* fingers forward several inches in front of the chest.

Memory aid: The *L* fingers indicate the size of an *ink cartridge*.

JOYSTICK

Place the right *S* hand in the left flat palm which is facing up. Swivel the right *S* hand in several directions, such as forward, backward and side to side a few times.

Memory aid: The action imitates the movement of a *joystick*.

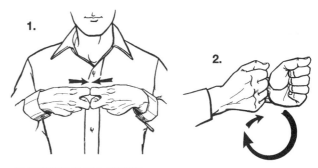

BATTERY BACKUP

Strike bent index and middle fingers of both hands (or just index fingers) together two times, other fingers are closed. With both *A* hands in front of the body and side by side and a few inches apart, move the right *A* hand in an arc down, back and forward until it touches the heel of the left hand.

Memory aid: The signs for *battery* and *backup*.

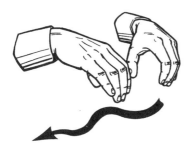

CABLE

Hold both *C* hands to the front with palms down and hands touching. Move the right hand away from the left hand to the right side in a wavy motion.

Memory aid: The movement suggests the shape of a *cable*.

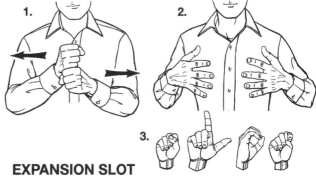

EXPANSION SLOT

Place both *S* hands in front of the chest with the right hand on the left. Move the hands to the sides as they change to open curved hands and palms facing each other. Fingerspell *S-L-O-T* at the right shoulder.

Memory aid: The signs for *expand* and *slot*.

PLUG

Move the right *V* hand forward with palm down in front of the right shoulder until the fingers straddle the left extended index finger, palm right, which is pointing up.

Memory aid: The extended fingers resemble the prongs of a *plug*.

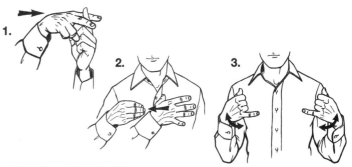

PLUG AND PLAY

Straddle the left extended index finger with the right *V* hand. Place the right open hand in front with palm facing in and fingers pointing left. Move the hand to the right while bringing the fingertips and thumb together. Hold *Y* hands in front of the chest and pivot them from the wrists a few times.

Memory aid: The three signs for *plug, and,* and *play*.

SCAN
Point the right *V* fingers at the left flat palm and move them downward twice.

Memory aid: The *V* fingers symbolize a laser *scanning* a bar code.

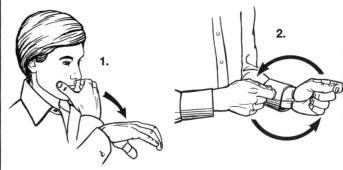

HOT SWAPPING, HOT PLUGGING
Place fingers and thumb of right *C* hand at sides of mouth; quickly pivot hand forward to the right. Hold right modified *A* hand a few inches behind left modified *A* hand. Move both hands in a backward circle, right under left hand and left over right hand, until hands have exchanged places.

Memory aid: The signs for *hot* and *exchange*.

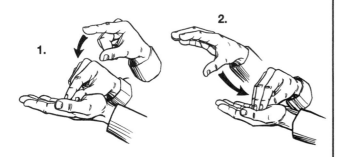

HARD COPY
Move the right index finger and thumb together as though picking something up; then place them on the left flat palm. Next, move the right open hand into the left flat palm while simultaneously closing into the *and* hand shape.

Memory aid: The signs for *print* and *copy*.

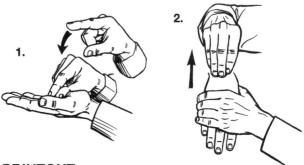

PRINTOUT
Move the right index finger and thumb together as though picking something up; then place them on the left flat palm. Place the downturned fingers of the open right hand in the left *C* hand with the right fingers protruding below the left *C*. Draw the right hand up and out.

Memory aid: The signs for *print* and *out*.

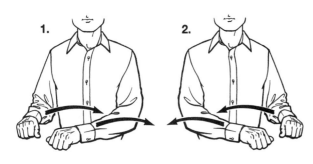

ANALOG
Place the *A* hands in front of the right side of the body, palms down, and move them simultaneously in arcs to the front of the left side of the body then back to the right side again.

Memory aid: The initial indicates the word, and the movement resembles a sound wave.

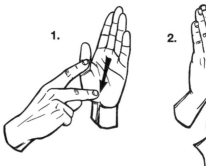

PROGRAM, APPLICATION
Move middle finger of right *P* hand down left flat palm; then twist left hand slightly and move middle finger of right *P* hand down back of left hand.

Memory aid: Suggests a piece of paper printed on both sides.

SOFTWARE

Fingerspell *S-W.* Sign each letter near the right shoulder.

Memory aid: The initials indicate the word.

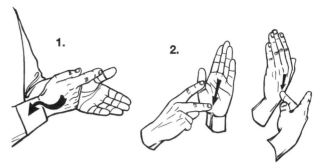

GRAPHICS PROGRAM, GRAPHICS SOFTWARE

Hold both hands in front of the chest and draw a wavy line with the little-finger side of the right *G* hand, palm in, over the left flat palm. Move the middle finger of the right *P* hand down the left flat palm and down the back of the left hand.

Memory aid: The signs for *graphics* and *program.*

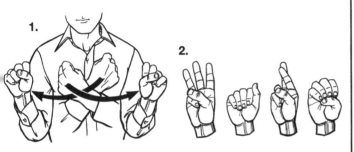

FREEWARE, SHAREWARE

Cross the closed hands on the chest with palms facing in; then rotate them to the sides with palms facing forward. (The sign for *share* can also be signed first.) Then fingerspell *W-A-R-E.* Sign each letter near the right shoulder.

Memory aid: The signs for *free* and *ware.*

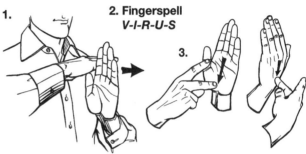

ANTI-VIRUS PROGRAM

Bring little-finger edge of right flat downturned hand against index finger of left flat vertical hand; move hands forward. Fingerspell *V-I-R-U-S.* Next, move middle finger of right *P* hand down left flat palm; then twist left hand slightly and move middle finger of right *P* hand down back of left hand.

Memory aid: Signs for *prevent, virus,* and *program.*

MICROSOFT

Fingerspell *M-S.* Sign each letter near the right shoulder.

Memory aid: The initials indicate the word.

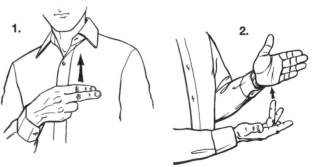

HIGH-TECH

Raise the *H* hand in front of the chest with palm facing in. Tap the tip of the bent palm-up-middle finger of the right open hand twice on the little-finger edge of the left flat hand, palm right.

Memory aid: The signs for *high* and *technology.*

GRAPHICS

Hold both hands in front of the chest and draw a wavy line with the little-finger side of the right *G* hand, palm in, over the left flat palm.

Memory aid: The right hand draws an imaginary image on the left.

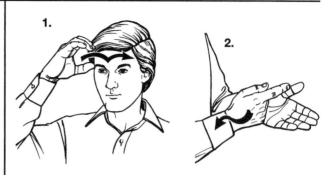

COMPUTER GRAPHICS

Move the right *C* hand, palm left, across the forehead in two arcs from right to left. Hold both hands in front of the chest and draw a wavy line with the little-finger side of the right *G* hand, palm in, over the left flat palm.

Memory aid: The signs for *computer* and *graphics*.

DATA, INFORMATION

Place the fingertips of both *and* hands on each side of the forehead, then move them in a downward forward arc to an open hand position with palms facing up. *Alternative:* Fingerspell *D-A-T-A*.

Memory aid: Suggests offering *information* from the mind.

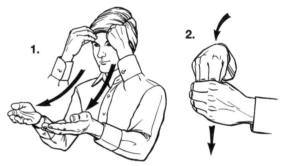

DATA ENTRY

Place the fingertips of both *and* hands on each side of the forehead, then move them in a downward forward arc to an open hand position with palms facing up. Next, push the right fingers down through the left *C* hand.

Memory aid: The signs for *data* and *enter*.

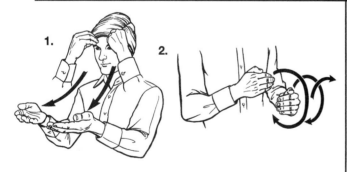

DATA PROCESSING

Place the fingertips of both *and* hands on each side of the forehead, then move them in a downward forward arc to an open hand position with palms facing up. Next, with palms facing in, roll both bent hands over each other a few times with a forward motion.

Memory aid: The signs for *data* and *process*.

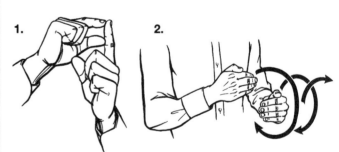

WORD PROCESSING

Hold the left index finger up with palm facing left; then place the thumb and index finger of the right *Q* hand against it. Next, with palms facing in, roll both bent hands over each other a few times with a forward motion. *Note:* Some fingerspell *W-P* for this sign.

Memory aid: The signs for *word* and *process*.

INPUT

Move the closed fingers of the right *and* hand into the left *C* hand two times.

Memory aid: The action suggests putting information in a computer.

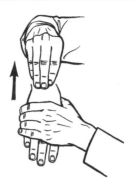

OUTPUT

Place the downturned fingers of the open right hand in the left *C* hand with the right fingers protruding below the left *C*. Draw the right hand up and out.

Memory aid: The action suggests getting information from a computer.

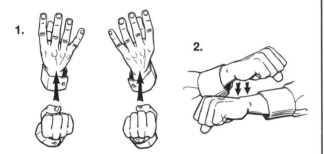

MULTITASKING

Hold both *S* hands in front with palms facing up. Flick the fingers and thumbs open several times. Strike the wrist of the right *S* hand on the downturned wrist of the left *S* hand a few times.

Memory aid: The signs for *many* and *work*.

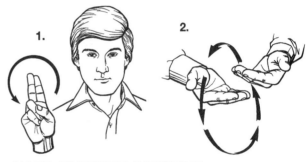

USER-FRIENDLY, INTUITIVE

With the palm facing forward, make a clockwise circle with the right *U* hand. Hold the left curved hand to the front with the palm up. Then brush the little-finger edge of the right curved hand upward over the fingertips of the left hand several times.

Memory aid: The signs for *use* and *easy*.

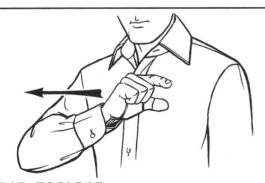

BAR, TOOLBAR

Move the right modified *G* hand in front of the chest from left to right with palm facing forward. *Note:* Some fingerspell *T-O-O-L* and sign *bar*.

Memory aid: The two fingers appear to be outlining the shape of a *toolbar* found in software programs.

PULL DOWN MENU

Place the little-finger edge of the bent right hand on the fingers of the left flat hand. Move the right hand down the left hand in several short arcs.

Memory aid: The right hand seems to be pointing out items on a *list* in the left hand.

POINT AND CLICK

Move the closed right index finger and thumb forward a few inches, other fingers closed. Point the right index finger forward and bend it downward.

Memory aid: The signs for *period* and *click*.

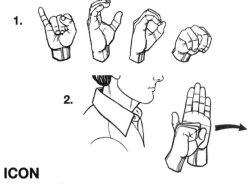

ICON

Fingerspell *I-C-O-N*. Sign each letter near the right shoulder. Sign *symbol* by placing the right *S* hand, palm forward, on the palm of the left flat hand, palm right, and move them forward a little.

Memory aid: The initials indicate the word, and the *S* hand on the left suggests an *icon symbol* on a screen.

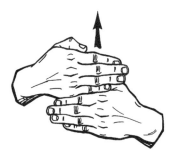

WINDOW (on computer screen), WINDOWS (software), MICROSOFT WINDOWS

Place the little-finger edge of the right flat hand on the index-finger edge of the left flat hand with palms facing in. Move right hand up a short distance. *Note:* Some move right hand up and down.

Memory aid: Suggests raising a sliding *window*.

PAGE

Move the extended thumb of the right palm-down *A* hand upward as it strikes the open palm of the left hand twice.

Memory aid: The action imitates turning *pages*.

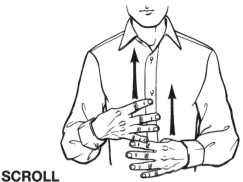

SCROLL

Place both *4* hands in front of the body, right over left, with right little finger on left index and palms in, fingers pointing in opposite directions; move both *4* hands up together a short distance two times.

Memory aid: The hands represent images *scrolling* on a computer screen.

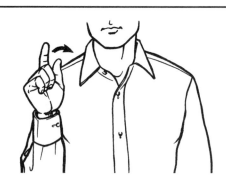

CURSOR

Hold up the modified *G* hand in front of the right shoulder, palm angled forward, and pivot the hand and arm a couple of inches to the left. *Alternative* (not illustrated): Some move the modified right *X* hand forward with a double bounce.

Memory aid: The small space between the fingers suggests the point where typed characters are inserted on the screen.

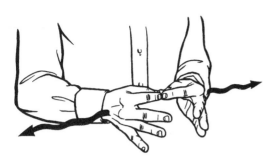

TEXT, SENTENCES
Touch the thumb and index fingers of both *F* hands in front of the chest. Pull the hands apart to the sides, either with a wavy or straight motion.

Memory aid: Suggests that words linked together stretch out to form *sentences* or *text*.

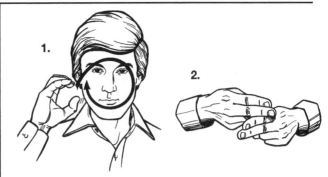

ALIAS
Make a few circular motions across the face from right to left with the right *C* hand, palm left. Then cross the middle-finger edge of the right *H* fingers over the index-finger edge of the left *H* fingers.

Memory aid: The signs for *search* and *name*.

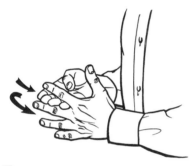

FILE
Slide the palm-up right *B* hand between the index and middle fingers then between the middle and ring fingers of the left open hand, palm in.

Memory aid: Placing the flat hand between the fingers suggests a *file* placed in its proper place.

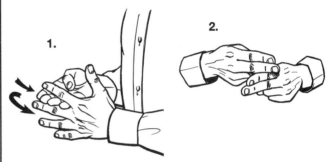

FILE NAME
Slide the palm-up right *B* hand between the index and middle fingers then between the middle and ring fingers of the left open hand, palm in. Cross the middle-finger edge of the right *H* fingers over the index-finger edge of the left *H* fingers.

Memory aid: The signs for *file* and *name*.

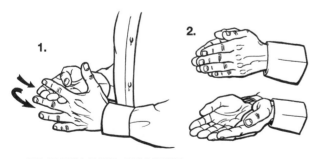

FILE FOLDER, FOLDER
Slide the palm-up right *B* hand between the index and middle fingers then between the middle and ring fingers of the left open hand, palm in. Place the hands palm to palm, fingers pointing forward; open both hands with palms up, maintaining contact with the little fingers.

Memory aid: The signs for *file* and *book*.

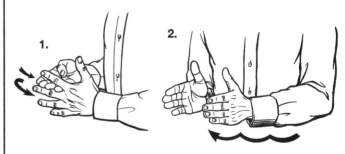

FILE MANAGER
Slide the palm-up right *B* hand between the index and middle fingers then between the middle and ring fingers of the left open hand, palm in. Place flat hands to the front left side, palms facing and fingers pointing forward. Move hands simultaneously to the right while moving them up and down slightly.

Memory aid: The signs for *file* and *plan*.

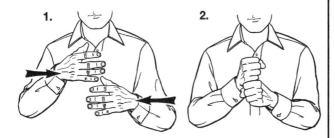

COMPRESS

Place both open curved hands in front of the chest with palms in and fingers pointing in opposite directions, the right hand above the left. Move the hands toward each other as they close to *S* hands placing the right hand on the left.

Memory aid: The action suggests the meaning.

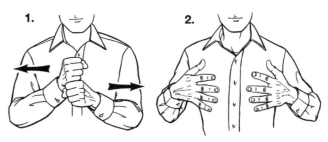

EXPAND

Place both *S* hands in front of the chest with the right hand on the left. Move the hands to the sides as they change to open curved hands with palms facing each other.

Memory aid: The action suggests the meaning.

FORMAT, INITIALIZE

Hold the right *F* hand at the right side of the chest, palm forward, and the left flat hand near it, palm right. Make a small upward circle with the right hand, and place the thumb and index finger side of the right *F* hand on the left flat palm.

Memory aid: The initial indicates the word, and motion symbolize a disk being *formatted*.

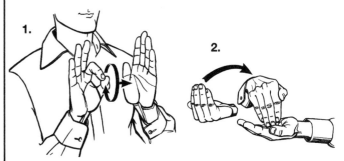

REFORMAT

Hold the right *F* hand at right side of chest, palm forward, and left flat hand near it, palm right. Make a small upward circle with right hand, and place the thumb and index finger side of right *F* hand on left flat palm. Next, turn the bent right hand up and over until the fingertips are in the left flat palm.

Memory aid: The signs for *format* and *again*.

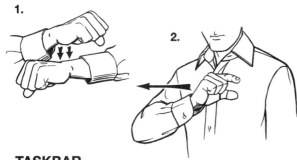

TASKBAR

Strike the wrist of the right *S* hand on the downturned wrist of the left *S* hand a few times. Move the right modified *G* hand in front of the chest from left to right with palm facing forward.

Memory aid: The signs for *work* and *bar*.

BACKUP

With both *A* hands in front of the body and side by side and a few inches apart, move the right *A* hand in an arc down, back and forward until it touches the heel of the left hand.

Memory aid: The right hand plays *backup* to the left; *backup* files often.

ARCHIVE

Place (or tap) the right *V* fingers on the back of the closed left hand with both palms facing in.

Memory aid: The *V* can symbolize the bars of a bank vault where items are kept safe, and *archiving* files or software keeps them safe for a long time.

BANDWIDTH

Fingerspell *B-A-N-D*. Sign each letter near the right shoulder. Place both flat hands to the front with palms facing and draw them apart to the sides.

Memory aid: The initials indicate the word, and the distance created between the hands indicates the meaning.

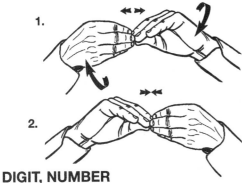

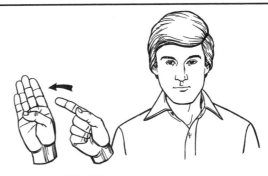

DIGIT, NUMBER

Touch the fingertips of both flat *O* hands in front of the chest, the right palm angled in and the left palm angled forward. Pull the hands apart a little while twisting the hands in opposite directions touching the fingertips again.

Memory aid: The flat *O* hands represent *digits* or *numbers*.

GIGABYTE, GB

Fingerspell *G-B*. Sign each letter near the right shoulder.

Memory aid: The initials indicate the word.

BIT

Hold the left flat hand up in front of the body, palm facing right, and place the index-finger side of the right *B* hand on the fingers of the left hand at a forward angle. Slide the right hand down the left hand from fingertips to heel keeping the right hand at the same angle.

Memory aid: Only the fingertips of the right *B* hand touch the left as a *bit* is smaller than a byte.

BYTE

Hold the left flat hand up in front of body, palm facing right, and slide the index-finger side of the right *B* hand down the right flat hand from fingertips to heel.

Memory aid: The entire side of the right *B* hand touches the left as a *byte* is larger than a bit.

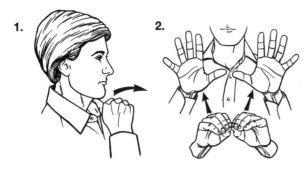

LOW RESOLUTION

Place the right *A* thumb, palm left, under the chin and move it forward and away from the chin. Hold both *and* hands at chest level with palms down. Open the hands as they are moved up and to the sides with palms facing forward.

Memory aid: The signs for *not* and *clear*.

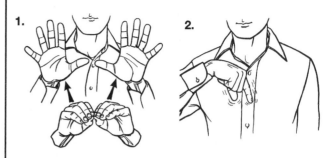

HIGH RESOLUTION

Hold both *and* hands at chest level with palms down. Open the hands as they are moved up and to the sides with palms facing forward. Shake the right *Q* hand in front of the chest with palm and fingers down.

Memory aid: The signs for *clear* and *quality*.

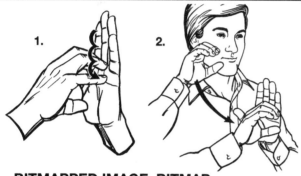

BITMAPPED IMAGE, BITMAP

Hold the left flat hand with fingers pointing up, palm right. Touch the fingertips of the right open-curved hand on the left from fingertips to the heel. Hold the right *C* hand close to the face; then move it forward until the thumb side of right *C* hand is against left flat palm, which faces right or forward.

Memory aid: The signs for *dots* and *picture*.

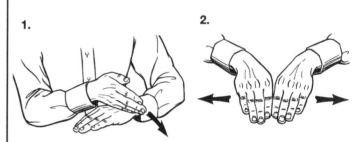

CROSS-PLATFORM

With the left flat hand facing down, move the little-finger edge of the right flat hand over the knuckles of the left hand. Place the index-finger edge of both flat hands together with palms facing down; then move both hands apart to the sides.

Memory aid: The signs for *across* and *floor*.

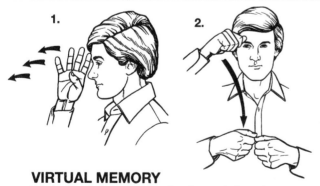

VIRTUAL MEMORY

With the right *4* hand palm facing left and touching the right side of the forehead, move the right hand forward in several short movements. Place the thumb of the right *A* hand on the forehead; then place it on top of the left *A*-hand thumb.

Memory aid: The signs for *fake* and *memory*.

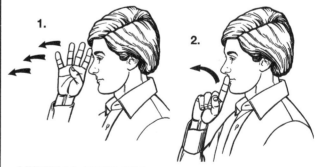

VIRTUAL REALITY

With the right *4* hand palm facing left and touching the right side of the forehead, move the right hand forward in several short movements. With palm facing left, move the right index finger in a forward arc from the lips.

Memory aid: The signs for *fake* and *real*.

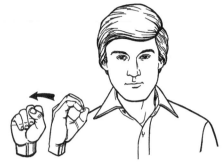

OPERATING SYSTEM, OS
Fingerspell *O-S.* Sign each letter near the right shoulder.

Memory aid: The initials indicate the words.

VERSION
Fingerspell *V-E-R.* Sign each letter near the right shoulder.

Memory aid: The initials indicate the word.

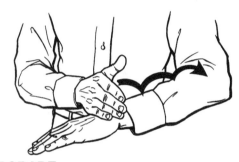

UPGRADE
Move the little-finger edge of the right flat hand in small arcs up the left arm.

Memory aid: Suggests degrees of improvement.

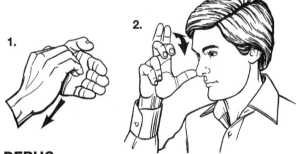

DEBUG
Move the bent fingers of the right hand downward across the left flat palm. Touch the nose with the thumb tip of the right 3 hand. Bend and unbend the index and middle fingers a few times. *Alternative:* This sign can be fingerspelled *D-B.*

Memory aid: The signs for *delete* and *bug*.

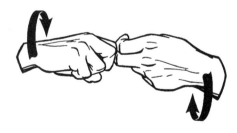

GLITCH
Touch the bent knuckles of the two *U* (or *V*) hands together and twist in opposite directions while moving downward slightly.

Memory aid: The rubbing knuckles cause friction which suggest a *glitch* or problem.

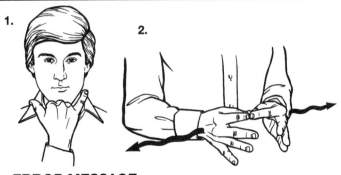

ERROR MESSAGE
Place the *Y* hand on the chin with the palm facing in. Touch the thumb and index fingers of each *F* hand in front of the chest. Pull the hands apart to the sides, either with a wavy or straight motion.

Memory aid: The signs for *wrong* and *sentence*.

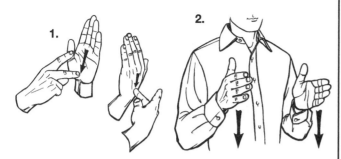

PROGRAMMER

Move middle finger of right *P* hand down left flat palm; then twist left hand slightly and move middle finger of right *P* hand down back of left hand. Hold both flat open hands to the front with palms facing; then move them down simultaneously.

Memory aid: The signs for *program* and *person* (*pesonalizing word ending*).

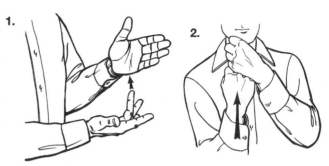

TECHNICAL SUPPORT

Tap the tip of the bent palm-up-middle finger of the right open hand twice on the little-finger edge of the left flat hand, palm right. Bring the right *S* hand up under the left *S* hand and move both hands upward together a short distance.

Memory aid: The signs for *technology* and *support.*

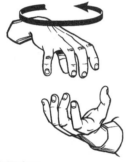

ENCRYPTION

Place the left curved open hand in front with palm facing up. Circle the right curved open hand above the left.

Memory aid: The circular action suggests the information is scrambled and therefore *encrypted.*

PASSWORD, ACCESS CODE

Place the right *A* thumb over the pursed lips a few times. Next, hold the left index finger up with palm facing right; then place the thumb and index finger of the right *Q* hand against it.

Memory aid: Suggests that the *password* is secure because one's lips are sealed. The signs for *private* and *word.*

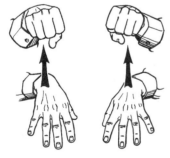

DEFAULT

Place both open hands in front of the body with palms facing down; simultaneously lift the open hands up while closing them into *S* hands.

Memory aid: To take something into one's hands and assume responsibility; a computer program assumes a *default* setting when none is chosen.

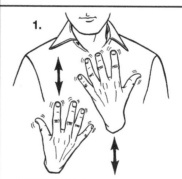
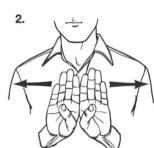

FIREWALL

With palms facing in, move both slightly curved open hands up and down alternately in front of the body while wiggling the fingers. Then place both *B* hands to front, palms out and touching at index fingers; move them apart simultaneously to the sides stopping in front of the shoulders.

Memory aid: Symbolizes an imaginary wall of leaping *flames* protecting valuable computer files.

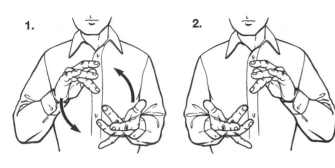

INTERNET, THE NET

Hold both open hands in front with bent middle fingers facing each other. Then twist the hands to switch positions.

Memory aid: The rotation suggests the worldwide communication available through the *internet*.

BLOG (to journal/diary on the internet)

Fingerspell *B-L-O-G*. Sign each letter near the right shoulder.

Memory aid: The initials indicate the word.

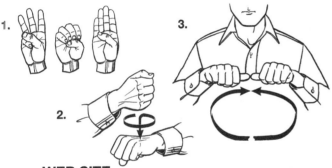

WEB SITE

1. Fingerspell *W-E-B*. 2. Make a circle with right *A* hand, palm left, above the left closed hand, palm down; place right *A* hand on left. 3. Palms down, touch the thumbs of both *A* hands together a short distance in front of the chest. Circle both hands toward self and touch thumbs again near chest.

Memory aid: *Web, establish*, and *area* signs.

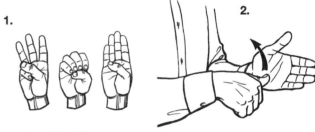

WEB PAGE

Fingerspell *W-E-B*. Sign each letter near the right shoulder. Move the extended thumb of the right *A* hand upward as it strikes the open palm of the left hand twice.

Memory aid: The signs for *web* and *page*.

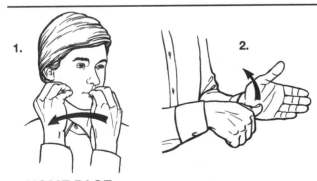

HOME PAGE

Place the fingertips of the right *and* hand first at the mouth, then at the right cheek. Sometimes the position at the cheek is made with a slightly curved hand. Move the extended thumb of the right *A* hand upward as it strikes the open palm of the left hand twice.

Memory aid: The signs for *home* and *page*.

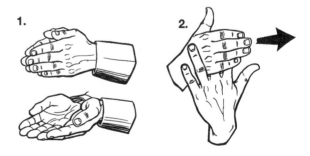

BOOKMARK, FAVORITE, PLACE MARKER

Place both hands palm to palm, fingers pointing forward; open both hands with palms up, maintaining contact with the little fingers. Push the right flat hand, palm inward, through the ring and middle fingers of the left open hand, palm right, and fingers pointing up.

Memory aid: The signs for *book* and *insert*.

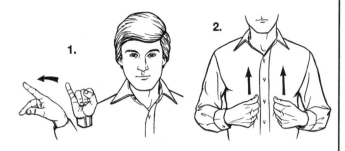

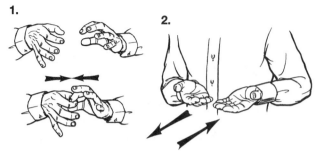

IP ADDRESS, INTERNET ADDRESS

Fingerspell *I-P* near the right shoulder. Then move the palm sides of both *A* hands up from the abdomen to the chest.

Memory aid: The signs for *internet protocol* and *address*.

ONLINE SERVICE, INTERNET SERVICE PROVIDER, ISP, NETWORK SERVICE PROVIDER, NSP, SERVICE PROVIDER

Interlock the index fingers and thumbs of both hands with all other fingers extended. Move both upturned flat hands back and forth alternately.

Memory aid: The signs for *connect* and *service*.

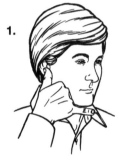

DIAL-UP ACCESS

Position the *Y* hand at the right of the face so that the thumb is near the ear and the little finger near the mouth. Push the right fingers down through the left *C* hand.

Memory aid: The signs for *telephone* and *enter*.

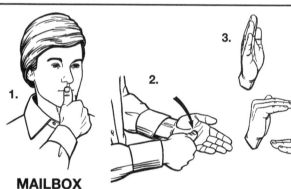

MAILBOX

Place the right *A* thumb on the mouth and then on the palm of the upturned left hand. Next, point the fingertips of both flat hands up with the palms facing each other in front of the chest. Bend both hands with the right hand positioned over the left. Can also be done with hands held horizontally.

Memory aid: The signs for *letter* and *box*.

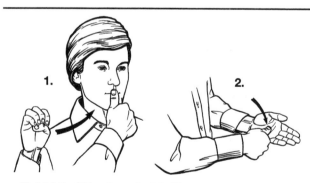

E-MAIL (Electronic Mail)

Fingerspell *E* near the right shoulder. Next, place the right *A* thumb on the mouth and then on the palm of the upturned left hand.

Memory aid: The signs for *E* and *letter*.

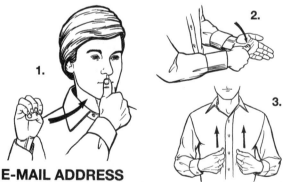

E-MAIL ADDRESS

Fingerspell *E* near the right shoulder. Next, place the right *A* thumb on the mouth and then on the palm of the upturned left hand. Then move the palm sides of both *A* hands up from the abdomen to the chest.

Memory aid: The signs for *E-mail* and *address*.

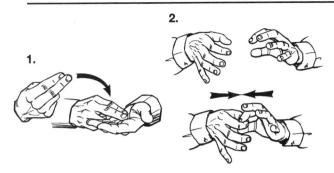

LOG ON, LOG IN, SIGN ON

Slap the right *H* fingers down onto the left upturned palm. Then interlock the index fingers and thumbs of both hands with all other fingers extended.

Memory aid: The signs for *sign* and *connect*.

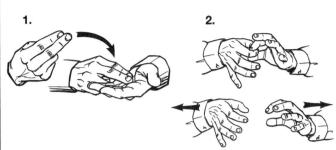

LOG OFF, LOG OUT, SIGN OFF

Slap the right *H* fingers down onto the left upturned palm. Interlock the index fingers and thumbs of both hands with all other fingers extended. Pull them apart.

Memory aid: The signs for *sign* and *disconnect*.

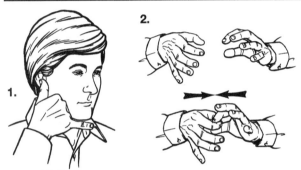

MODEM

Position the *Y* hand at the right of the face so that the thumb is near the ear and the little finger near the mouth. Then interlock the index fingers and thumbs of both hands with all other fingers extended.

Memory aid: The signs for *telephone* and *connect*.

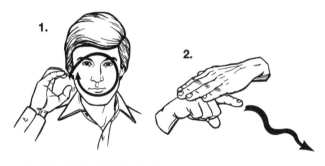

SURF, SURF THE NET

Make a few circular motions across the face from right to left with the right *C* hand, palm left. Move the extended right index finger, which points forward with palm down, in a wavy movement from under the left flat hand as the left flat palm moves up the right arm.

Memory aid: The signs for *search* and *sneak*.

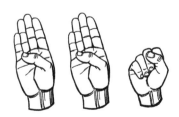

BULLETIN BOARD, BULLETIN BOARD SYSTEM, BBS

Fingerspell *B-B-S*. Sign each letter near the right shoulder.

Memory aid: The initials indicate the words.

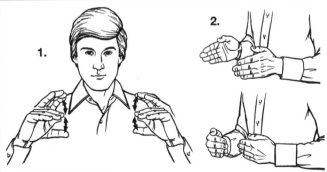

CHAT ROOM

Place both flattened *C* hands at sides of upper chest, palms facing each other, and close and open them together a couple of times. Place both flat hands (or *R* hands) in front, palms facing; move left hand near body and right hand in front, palms facing body.

Memory aid: The first action imitates people *chatting*, and the second outlines the shape of a *room*.

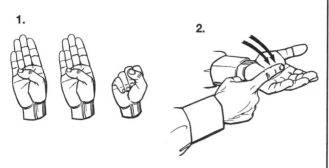

NEWSGROUP, FORUM

Fingerspell *B-B-S*. Sign each letter near the right shoulder. Srike the left palm with the right index finger several times.

Memory aid: The signs for *bulletin board* and *discuss*.

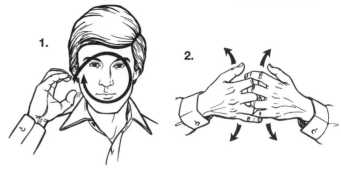

SEARCH ENGINE

Make a few circular motions across the face from right to left with the right *C* hand, palm left. Then intertwine the fingers of both curved open hands in front of the body and pivot at the wrists a few times.

Memory aid: The signs for *search* and *engine*.

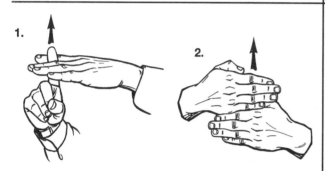

POP-UP WINDOW

With palm left, move right index finger upward between the index and middle fingers of the left flat hand, which has its palm facing down. Place the little-finger edge of the right flat hand on the index-finger edge of the left flat hand with palms facing in. Move the right hand up a short distance.

Memory aid: The signs for *appear* and *window*.

REFRESH, RELOAD

Pass the back of the slightly curved right hand across the left flat palm from fingers to heel. Continue the movement of the right hand in a slight upward direction.

Memory aid: The right hand seems to be suggesting a new direction to the left hand.

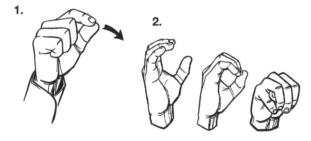

DOT-COM

With the right index finger or right index finger and thumb, which touch at the tips, other fingers are closed, draw the shape of a period in the air by pushing the hand forward a few inches. Fingerspell *C-O-M*. Sign each letter near the right shoulder.

Memory aid: The signs for *period* and *com*.

SPAM (unwanted e-mail)

Fingerspell *S-P-A-M*. Sign each letter near the right shoulder.

Memory aid: The initials indicate the words.

FILTER

With both *4*-hand palms facing in, place the left in front of the right and pull both hands apart simultaneously downward at an angle two times.

Memory aid: The hands resemble a *filter* as they are placed over each other.

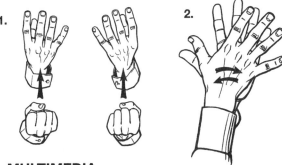

MULTIMEDIA

Hold both *S* hands in front with palms facing up. Flick the fingers and thumbs open several times. Place both flat open hands palm to palm with left palm facing somewhat forward. Slide right hand back and forth over the left hand a few times. Most of the movement is from the right wrist.

Memory aid: The signs for *many* and *movie*.

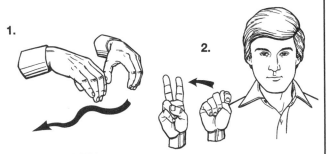

CABLE TV

Hold both C hands to the front with palms down and hands touching. Move the right hand away from the left hand to the right side in a wavy motion. Fingerspell *T-V*. Sign each letter near the right shoulder.

Memory aid: The signs for *cable* and *television*.

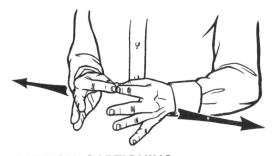

CAPTION, CAPTIONING

Position both *F* hands together in front and touching, palms facing, and pull them apart simultaneously to the sides in a straight line two times.

Memory aid: Suggests the *captioning* at the bottom of the screen.

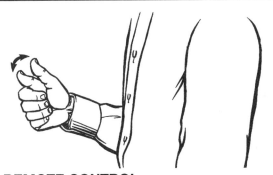

REMOTE CONTROL

Point the extended right *A* hand thumb forward, palm left, and move the thumb up and down a few times.

Memory aid: The movement mimics the action of using a *remote control*.

BUTTON

Push the right extended *A* hand thumb, palm left, forward several inches in front of the chest.

Memory aid: The movement suggests pushing a *button*.

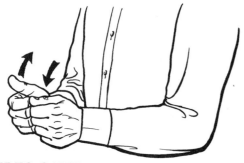

VIDEO GAME

Hold both *A* hands to the front and side by side and alternately move the thumbs up and down.

Memory aid: Mimics using a game controller to play a *video game*.

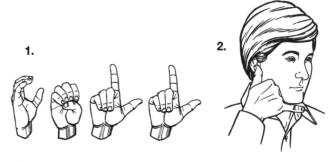

CELL PHONE

Fingerspell *C-E-L-L*. Sign each letter near the right shoulder. Then position the *Y* hand at the right of the face so that the thumb is near the ear and the little finger near the mouth.

Memory aid: The signs for *cell* and *telephone*.

CALCULATOR

Hold the right curved open hand over the left flat palm which faces up, and wiggle the bent fingers of the right hand near the left palm.

Memory aid: The fingers imitate the movements of using a *calculator*.

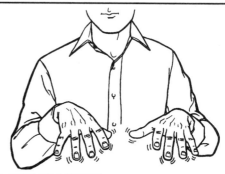

TYPE, TYPEWRITER

Place both open hands in front of the body, palms down, and alternately wiggle the fingers as if typing. To sign *typewriter*, move the hands alternately up and down a couple of times.

Memory aid: The natural action of *typing* at a keyboard or *typewriter*.

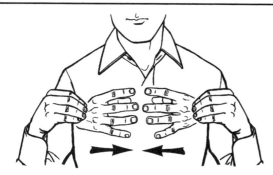

MICROWAVE

Place both flat *O* hands facing each other and to the sides of the chest. Throw the hands towards each other while changing them to curved open hands twice.

Memory aid: The movement suggests a sudden burst of *microwaves*.

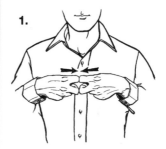

POWER SURGE

Strike the bent index and middle fingers of each hand (or just the index fingers) together a few times. The other fingers are closed. Then strike the knuckles of the right closed hand against the left upright index finger.

Memory aid: The signs for *electricity* and *hit*.

TECHNOLOGY, TECHNICAL

Tap the tip of the bent palm-up-middle finger of the right open hand twice on the little-finger edge of the left flat hand, palm right.

Memory aid: The movement suggests *technology* pushes the world upward to greater achievements.

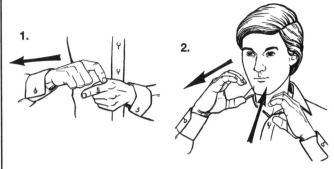

TELECOMMUNICATIONS

Point the left index forward, and move the right *X*-hand-index finger, palm down, from the base of the left index finger along its length and off the finger. Move both *C* hands back and forth from the lips alternately.

Memory aid: Suggests words and data coming and going using *telecommunications*.

SATELLITE

Circle the right *S* hand around the left *S* hand.

Memory aid: The right hand imitates a *satellite* circling the earth.

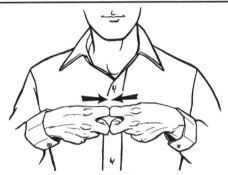

ELECTRONIC, BATTERY

Strike the bent index and middle fingers of each hand (or just the index fingers) together a few times. The other fingers are closed.

Memory aid: Suggests electrical power flowing through *electronics*.

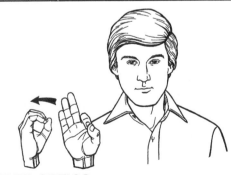

FIBER OPTICS

Fingerspell *F-O* near the right shoulder.

Memory aid: The initials indicate the words.

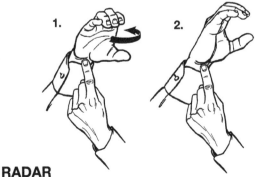

RADAR

Place the base of the right *C* hand, palm forward, on the upturned left *one* fingertip, palm in, and turn the *C* hand in towards the body.

Memory aid: The movement suggests a *radar* screen.

VIDEO

Place the thumb side of the right open hand on the left flat palm which faces right and points up, and wiggle the fingers.

Memory aid: The wiggling fingers reminds one of old time flickering movies.

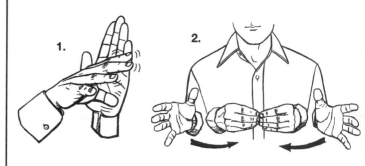

VIDEOCONFERENCING

Place the thumb side of the right open hand on the left flat palm which faces right and points up, and wiggle the fingers. Bring both open hands in from the sides while forming *and* hands, and let the fingertips touch.

Memory aid: The signs for *video* and *meeting*.

FAX (Facsimile)

Fingerspell *F-A-X*. Sign each letter near the right shoulder.

Memory aid: The initials indicate the word.

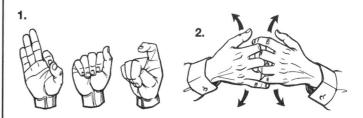

FAX MACHINE

Fingerspell *F-A-X*. Sign each letter near the right shoulder. Then, intertwine the fingers of both curved open hands in front of the body and pivot at the wrists a few times.

Memory aid: The initials indicate the word, and the movement suggests the meshing of gears in a *machine*.

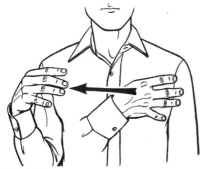

BAR CODE, UNIVERSAL PRODUCT CODE

Move the right *4* hand two times across the chest from left to the right with fingers pointing left and palm in.

Memory aid: The four separated fingers draw imaginary lines across the chest which suggest the lines of a *bar code*.

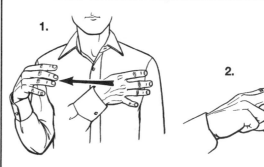

BAR CODE READER

Move the right *4* hand two times across the chest from left to the right with fingers pointing left and palm in. Point the right *V* fingers at the left flat palm, and move them downward two times.

Memory aid: The four fingers draw imaginary lines across the chest which suggest *bar code* lines. The *V* fingers symbolize a laser *reading* a *bar code*.

ROBOT

Place flat hands at each side, right hand higher than left, and move the arms up and down alternately like a *robot*. *Note:* Some move the legs and arms alternately up and down.

Memory aid: Imitating a *robot*.

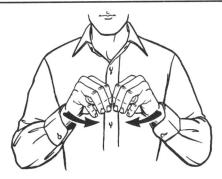

MAGNETIC, MAGNET

With palms down, place both *M* hands to the front of the chest and a few inches apart; pivot the hands towards each other until the index fingers (or fingertips) touch once or twice

Memory aid: The movement imitates the pull of *magnetism*.

COPIER, PHOTOCOPY, COPY

Move the right *X* hand, palm forward, from side to side under the palm down left flat hand.

Memory aid: The movement simulates the light from a *copier* making *photocopies*.

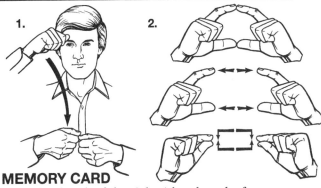

MEMORY CARD

Place the thumb of the right *A* hand on the forehead; then place it on top of the left *A*-hand thumb. Touch the fingertips of both *L* hands in front of the chest with palms forward. Pull the hands apart to the sides, stop and close the index fingers and thumbs.

Memory aid: The signs for *memory* and *card*.

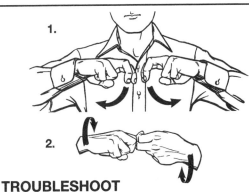

TROUBLESHOOT

Place both crooked *V* hands in front of the body with palms facing down. Pull the hands apart sideways a few times. Then touch the bent knuckles of the two *U* (or *V*) hands together and twist in opposite directions while moving downward slightly.

Memory aid: The signs for *analyze* and *problem*.

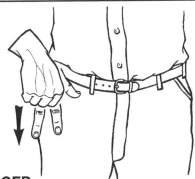

PAGER

Place the right *S* hand in front of the right side of the hip and thrust the thumb, index and middle fingers (3 hand) down simultaneously once or twice.

Memory aid: The location many people keep *pagers*.

ACRONYMS, Etc.

Many of the words associated with technology are acronyms and initialisms. Acronyms, generally, are words that are made by combining the first letters of a group of words or a phrase. An initialism combines the first letters but does not form a word in itself. Some words have no formal sign and are fingerspelled. Sign each letter near the right shoulder.

Memory aid: The initials indicate the words.

AGP (Accelerated Graphics Port)
Fingerspell *A-G-P.*

ATM (Automatic Teller Machine)
Fingerspell *A-T-M.*

CACHE (temporary data storage space)
Fingerspell *C-A-C-H-E.*

CAD (Computer Aided Design)
Fingerspell *C-A-D.*

CD-R (Compact Disc-Recordable)
Fingerspell *C-D-R.*

CD-ROM (Compact Disc-Read Only Memory)
Fingerspell *C-D-R-O-M.*

CD-RW (Compact Disc-Rewritable)
Fingerspell *C-D-R-W.*

DPI (Dots Per Inch)
Fingerspell *D-P-I.*

DSL (Digital Subscriber Line)
Fingerspell *D-S-L.*

DVD (Digital Video Disk)
Fingerspell *D-V-D.*

DVD-RW (Digital Video Disc-Rewritable)
Fingerspell *D-V-D-R-W.*

ACRONYMS, Etc.
continued

ETHERNET
Fingerspell *E-T-H-E-R-N-E-T*.

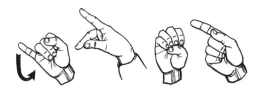

JPEG (Joint Photographic Experts Group)
Fingerspell *J-P-E-G*.

FONT (type face)
Fingerspell *F-O-N-T*.

LAN (Local-Area Network)
Fingerspell *L-A-N*.

HACKER
Fingerspell *H-A-C-K-E-R*.

LCD (Liquid Crystal Display)
Fingerspell *L-C-D*.

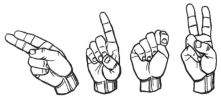

HD-TV (High Definition Television)
Fingerspell *H-D-T-V*.

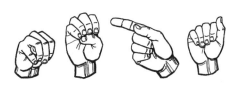

MEGA-(A prefix; approximately one million)
Fingerspell *M-E-G-A*.

HTML (HyperText Markup Language)
Fingerspell *H-T-M-L*.

MS-DOS (Microsoft Disk Operating System)
Fingerspell *M-S-D-O-S*.

IM (Instant Messaging)
Fingerspell *I-M*.

PDA (Personal Digital Assistant)
Fingerspell *P-D-A*.

ACRONYMS, Etc.
continued

PIN (Personal Identification Number)
Fingerspell *P-I-N*.

TTY (teletype)
Fingerspell *T-T-Y*.

PIXEL
Fingerspell *P-I-X-E-L*.

URL (Uniform Resource Locator)
Fingerspell *U-R-L*.

RAM (Random-Access Memory)
Fingerspell *R-A-M*.

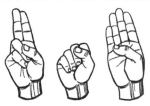

USB (Universal Serial Bus)
Fingerspell *U-S-B*.

RFID (Radio Frequency Identification Device)
Fingerspell *R-F-I-D*.

VCR (Video Cassette Recorder)
Fingerspell *V-C-R*.

TCP/IP (Transmission Control Protocol/Internet Protocol) Fingerspell *T-C-P-I-P*.

VIRUS
Fingerspell *V-I-R-U-S*.

TIFF (Tagged Image File Format)
Fingerspell *T-I-F-F*.

ZIP DRIVE
Fingerspell *Z-I-P* and *D-R-I-V-E*.

Cemetery   *See* Bury, 85
Cent, 217
Center, 132
Central   *See* Center, 132
Cents   *See* Cent, 217
Certificate   *See* License, 205
Chain, 45
Chair, 42
Chairman   *See* Boss, 186
Challenge   *See* Game, 96
Change, 82
Chapel   *See* Church, 172
Chaplain   *See* Priest, 171
Chapter, 180
Character (individual), 32
Character   *See*
   Personality, 144
Charge   *See* Cost, 218
Chase   *See* Follow, 132
Chat Room, 295
Cheap, 219
Cheat, 157
Check, 72
Check (bank), 219
Cheer   *See* Celebrate, 91
Cheese, 55
Chef, 186
Chemistry   *See* Science, 119
Chewing Gum, 61
Chicago, 198
Chicken, 111
Chief   *See* Prominent, 188
Child, 28
Children   *See* Child, 28
Chilly   *See* Cold, 260
China, 203
China   *See* Glass, 67
Chinese   *See* China, 203
Chip (computer), 277
Chipmunk   *See* Squirrel, 108
Chocolate, 59
Choke   *See* Stuck, 85
Choose, 82
Christ   *See* Lord, 162
Christen (sprinkling)   *See*
   Baptize, 168
Christian, 168
Christmas, 125
Chubby   *See* Fat, 264
Chuckle   *See* Laugh, 91
Church, 172
Cigarette, 229
Cinema   *See* Movie, 99
Circumstance   *See* Envi-
   ronment, 115
Cite   *See* Quote, 180
City, 198
Clap, 91
Class   *See* Group, 31
Clean, 259
Clear   *See* Light, 269

Clergyman   *See* Priest, 171
Clever   *See* Smart, 136
Click, 279
Climb, 100
Clippers   *See* Scissors, 44
Clock   *See* Time, 242
Clone, 274
Close, 257
Close To   *See* Near, 130
Clothes, 45
Cloud, 116
Clumsy   *See* Awkward, 157
Coat, 46
Coax   *See* Persuade, 79
Cock   *See* Rooster, 110
Coffee, 62
Coincide   *See* Agree, 141
Coins, 216
Cold, 260
Cold (sickness), 228
Collapse, 266
Collar, 48
Collect   *See* Earn, 218
College, 176
Collision   *See* Accident, 124
Colon   *See* Period, 38
Color, 49
Combine   *See* Match, 81
Come, 256
Comfort, 149
Comical   *See* Funny, 147
Comma   *See* Period, 38
Command, 192
Commandments, 166
Commence   *See* Start, 257
Commercial   *See*
   Advertise, 84
Communicate   *See* Talk, 189
Communion, 168
Community   *See* City, 198
Company   *See* Group, 31
Compare, 159
Compassion   *See* Pity, 149
Compel   *See* Force, 79
Compete   *See* Race, 97
Competent   *See* Can, 263
Competent   *See* Expert, 158
Competition   *See* Race, 97
Complain, 191
Complete, 70
Complete   *See* Finish, 70
Comprehend   *See*
   Understand, 140
Compress, 288
Computer, 183, 274
Computer (alternative), 274
Computer Graphics, 284
Concentration   *See*
   Attention, 144
Concept   *See* Idea, 137
Concern   *See* Wonder, 138

Concerning   *See* About, 131
Conclude   *See* Complete, 70
Conduct   *See* Do, 70
Conduct   *See* Guide, 72
Confer   *See* Gift, 126
Confess, 170
Confidence, 145
Confidential   *See* Secret, 141
Conflict, 143
Confuse, 142
Congratulate, 91
Congress   *See* Member, 188
Connection, 159
Conquer, 85
Conscience, 137
Consent   *See* Agree, 141
Consider   *See* Evaluate, 137
Consider   *See* Think, 136
Consider   *See* Wonder, 138
Consistent   *See* Regular, 245
Constantly   *See* Always, 259
Constitution, 204
Construct   *See* Build, 187
Consume   *See* Eat, 65
Contact   *See* Touch, 236
Content   *See* Satisfaction, 145
Contest   *See* Race, 97
Continue, 73
Contradict   *See* Disagree, 141
Contrary   *See* Opposite, 68
Contrary To   *See* Disagree, 141
Contrast   *See* Compare, 159
Contrast   *See* Opposite, 268
Contribute   *See* Gift, 126
Control, 82
Controversy   *See* Argue, 191
Conversation   *See* Talk, 189
Conviction   *See*
   Conscience, 137
Cook (verb), 65
Cook (verb)   *See* Boil, 65
Cook (noun)   *See* Chef, 186
Cookie, 58
Cool, 260
Cooperate, 159
Cop   *See* Police, 207
Copier, 301
Copy (photocopy)   *See*
   Copier, 301
Copy, 81
Cord   *See* String, 44
Corn, 54
Corner, 132
Correct   *See* Cancel, 80
Correct   *See* Right, 259
Correspond   *See* Agree, 141
Cost, 218
Costly   *See* Expensive, 219
Cough, 228
Could   *See* Can, 263
Counsel   *See* Advice, 190

Count, 215
Counterfeit   *See* False, 261
Country (national
   territory), 200
Country (rural)   *See*
   Farm, 115
Courageous   *See* Brave, 152
Course, 177
Court   *See* Judge, 206
Courteous   *See* Polite, 33
Cousin, 26
Cover, 86
Covet   *See* Want, 153
Cow, 109
CPU (Central Processing
   Unit), 277
Cracker, 55
Crash   *See* Accident, 124
Crash (computer), 278
Crave   *See* Hungry, 64
Crazy, 142
Cream, 63
Create   *See* Invent, 138
Credit Card, 219
Crime   *See* Evil, 166
Criticize   *See* Cancel, 80
Crook   *See* Thief, 32
Cross (adjective), 149
Cross (noun), 163
Cross   *See* Across, 131
Cross-Platform, 290
CRT   *See* Display Screen, 275
Crucifixion   *See* Crucify, 163
Crucify, 163
Cruel   *See* Mean
   (adjective), 154
Cry, 152
Cry Out   *See* Shout, 191
Cup, 66
Curious, 138
Current   *See* Now, 244
Curriculum, 177
Cursor, 286
Custom   *See* Habit, 144
Cut   *See* Scissors, 44
Cute, 30
Cycle   *See* Bicycle, 101

D

Dactylology   *See* Finger-
   spelling, 194
Dad   *See* Father, 24
Daily, 247
Damage   *See* Destroy, 84
Damage   *See* Tease, 88
Dance, 99
Danger, 229
Dark, 269
Data, 284
Database, 278
Data Entry, 284

Answers to Practice Pages

Chapter 1
NAME THE SIGN p. 37
Answers: 1. Mother; 2. Son; 3. Cousin; 4. Aunt; 5. Father; 6. Cute; 7. Kid; 8. Wedding; 9. Husband; 10. Famous; 11. Boy; 12. Bachelor.

Chapter 2
MATCHING SKILL p. 52
Answers: l. Clothes; 2. Shoes; 3. Orange; 4. Black; 5. Scissors; 6. Home; 7. Mirror; 8. Bed; 9. Shave; 10. Hat; 11. Rope; 12. Candle; 13. Purple; 14. Window.

Chapter 3
FIND THE FOOD SIGNS p. 68
Answers: 1. Popcorn; 2. Banana; 3. Candle; 4. Pie; 5. Apple; 6. Pizza; 7. Cat; 8. Cookie; 9. Friend; 10. Bacon; 11. Tomato; 12. Like; 13. Jelly; 14. Bread; 15. Shave; 16. Butter; 17. Corn; 18. Israel; 19. Peach.

Chapter 4
NAME THE SIGN p. 92
Answers: 1. Run; 2. Push; 3. Laugh; 4. Keep; 5. Slide; 6. Clap; 7. Help; 8. Support; 9. Wait; 10. Turn; 11. Match; 12. Hurry; 13. Abandon; 14. Steal; 15. Conquer; 16. Blame; 17. Do; 18. Walk; 19. Tease; 20. Break; 21. Send; 22. Smile; 23. Change; 24. Warn.

Chapter 5
MATCHING SKILL p. 104
Answers: 1. Baseball; 2. Fishing; 3. Jogging; 4. Drums; 5. Tennis; 6. Guitar; 7. Ball; 8. Golf; 9. Climb; 10. Paint; 11. Jump; 12. Sing; 13. Piano; 14. Tent.

Chapter 6
NAME THE SIGN p.120
Answers: 1. Giraffe; 2. Ocean; 3. Horse; 4. Earth; 5. Machine; 6. Cloud; 7. Sunshine; 8. Grass; 9. Earthquake; 10. Tree; 11. Fire; 12. Bee; 13. Science; 14. Wood; 15. Universe; 16. Star; 17. Silver; 18.Environment; 19. Sky; 20. World; 21. Fish; 22. Gold; 23. Mountain;

Chapter 7
MULTIPLE CHOICE p.134
Answers; 1C. Far; 2C. Vacation; 3A. Street; 4B. Gasoline; 5A. Gift; 6C. Above; 7B. Travel; 8A. Visit; 9C. High; 10B. Bridge; 11B. Between; 12A. Across; 13 B. In; 14C. Camera.

Chapter 8
MATCHING SKILL p. 160
Answers: 1. Happy; 2. Know; 3. Lazy; 4. I Love You; 5. Invent; 6. Stubborn; 7. Dream; 8. Wish; 9. Proof; 10. Skeptical; 11. Obedience; 12. Please; 13. Respect; 14. Love.

Chapter 9
MATCHING SKILL p. 174
Answers: 1. Jesus; 2. Resurrection; 3. Bless; 4. Faith; 5. Worship; 6. Communion; 7. God; 8. Gospel; 9. Believe; 10. Kneel; 11. Spirit; 12. Evil; 13. Tithe; 14. Angel.

Chapter 10
NAME THE SIGN p. 196
Answers: 1. School; 2. Write; 3. Opportunity; 4. Lawyer; 5. Artist; 6. Nurse; 7. Study; 8. Sell; 9. Speech; 10. Expression; 11. Sign (language); 12. Announce; 13. Complain; 14. Whisper; 15. Business; 16. Chapter; 17. Library; 18. Diploma; 19. Read; 20. Television; 21. History; 22. Book; 23. Work; 24. Teach.

Chapter 11
NAME THE SIGN p. 208
Answers: 1. City; 2. Hawaii; 3. Authority; 4. Stamp; 5. Vote; 6. America; 7. Africa; 8. Prison; 9. Flag; 10. Chicago; 11. License; 12. Mexico; 13. Seal; 14. New York; 15. Arizona; 16. Kingdom; 17. Duty; 18. Foreign; 19. International; 20. Law; 21. Israel; 22. Canada; 23. Nation; 24. Boston.

Chapter 12
MULTIPLE CHOICE p. 226
Answers: 1C. 100; 2A. Expensive; 3B. Coins; 4B. None; 5C. Profit; 6B. Multiply; 7A. Money; 8C. Spend; 9B. Empty; 10C. Lend; 11A. Exact; 12C. Enough; 13A. Weigh; 14C. Some.

Chapter 13
MULTIPLE CHOICE p. 240
Answers: 1C. Medicine; 2B. Birth; 3B. Smell; 4A. Pill; 5C. Shower; 6A. Lips; 7C. Hospital; 8B. Healthy; 9A. Sick; 10A. Dizzy; 11C. Tongue; 12B. Pneumonia; 13C. Operation; 14B. Bones.

Chapter 14
NAME THE SIGN p. 254
Answers: 1. Night; 2. Monday; 3. Ice; 4. Last; 5. Noon; 6. Friday; 7. Thunder; 8. Spring; 9. Are; 10. Time; 11. Year; 12. Now; 13. Day; 14. Until; 15. Week; 16. Minute; 17. Future; 18. Forever; 19. Were; 20. Snow; 21. Wind; 22. Saturday; 23. Sunrise; 24. Yesterday.

Chapter 15
CONNECT THE OPPOSITES p. 272
Answers: 1 Dry; 13 Wet; 4 Big; 16 Small; 15 True; 9 False; 14 Easy; 5 Difficult; 10 Come; 6 Go; 8 Find; 3 Lose; 11 Strong; 7 Weak; 2 Good; 12 Bad.

The Most Comprehensive Library of Signing Books Available!

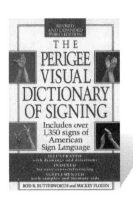
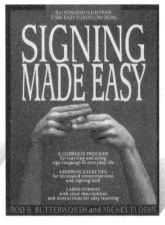
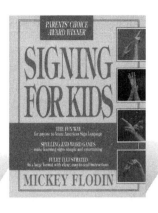
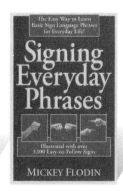

These books are available at your bookstore or wherever books are sold, or, for your convenience, we'll send them directly to you. Call 1-800-631-8571 (press 1 for inquiries and orders) or fill out the coupon below and send it to:

The Berkley Publishing Group
390 Murray Hill Parkway, Department B
East Rutherford, NJ 07073

Signing Illustrated   by Mickey Flodin
ISBN 0-399-53041-X   U.S. $16.95   Can $25.00

The Perigee Visual Dictionary of Signing,
revised edition
A comprehensive signing dictionary containing over 1,250 signs of American Sign Language.
by Rod R. Butterworth and Mickey Flodin
ISBN 0-399-51695-6   U.S. $13.00   Can $19.00

The Pocket Dictionary of Signing,
revised edition
The first pocket guide to American Sign Language, containing over 600 signing entries with accompanying directions and illustrations.
by Rod R. Butterworth and Mickey Flodin
ISBN 0-399-51347-7   U.S. $6.95   Can $9.99

Signing for Kids
An easy-to-follow large-format categorized book, including games, photos, and topics related to kids.
by Mickey Flodin
ISBN 0-399-51672-7   U.S. $11.00   Can $16.00

Signing Everyday Phrases
An easy-to-follow small-format categorized book, for teaching sign language in sentence format for everyday life. by Mickey Flodin
ISBN 0-399-52236-0   U.S. $13.95   Can $19.95

Signing Is Fun   by Mickey Flodin
ISBN 0-399-52173-9   U.S. $9.00   Can $13.00

Signing Made Easy
A text-and-workbook-in-one, teaching sign language in sentence format for everyday life.
by Rod R. Butterworth and Mickey Flodin
ISBN 0-399-51490-2   U.S. $10.95   Can $15.99

Order Today. ------

Subtotal $_____

Postage & handling* $_____

Sales tax (CA,NY,NJ,PA) $_____

Total amount due $_____

Payable in U.S. funds (no cash orders accepted). $15.00 minimum for credit card orders.
* Postage & handling: $2.50 for 1 book, 75¢ each additional book up to a maximum of $6.25.

Enclosed is my   ☐ check   ☐ money order
Please charge my   ☐ Visa ☐ Mastercard
                        ☐ American Express

Card #_____

Expiration date_____

Signature as on charge card

_____

Name_____

Address_____

_____

City_____

State_____ Zip_____

Please allow six weeks for delivery. Prices subject to change without notice. You can copy this form to order books.

Source Key # 69